JOURNALS OF A METHODIST FARMER

1871-1875

LOT 3.

A Valuable

FREEHOLD FARM

KNOWN AS

THE BINBROOK HALL FARM

AND CONTAINS

523 a. **3** r. **16** p.

OF WHICH

10 a. **3** r. **1** p. **are PLANTATIONS**

This Farm lies practically in a Ring Fence, as will be seen on the Plan. It is divided into Arable and Pasture Land Enclosures of convenient size. The Arable is good Wold Land, well adapted for Sheep Farming and Barley growing. The pasture is healthy, and good for Breeding and Rearing purposes. Subsoil, Chalk.

THE FARM COMPRISES:

A NEWLY AND SUBSTANTIALLY ERECTED

Residence

Built of brick and slated. Great care was exercised in the building, and the result is a capacious and comfortable house. It contains: DINING ROOM, DRAWING ROOM, BREAKFAST ROOM, LARGE ENTRANCE HALL, Kitchen (with modern Cookery Appliances), Sculleries (with Water supply), good Landing, Six Bedrooms, Bathroom (hot and cold), W.C., etc.

It is surrounded by LAWNS, KITCHEN GARDENS, ORNAMENTAL SHRUBBERIES and TREES, and commands an Extensive View of this beautiful Wold Country.

THE FARM BUILDINCS

are ample for the Holding, there being Cart and Nag Horse Stabling, Barns, Granaries, Crew Yards, Wagon and Implement Sheds, and, generally, the complete accommodation of a well-equipped Farmery.

COTTAGES

There are Two Double and One Single Labourers' Cottages, nearly new.

Source: Lincoln Archives Office.

JOURNALS OF A METHODIST FARMER 1871-1875

Edited by Jean Stovin

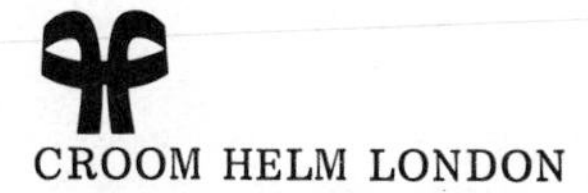

CROOM HELM LONDON

Croom Helm Ltd, Provident House, Burrell Row,
Beckenham, Kent BR3 1AT
Reprinted 1983

British Library Cataloguing in Publication Data

Stovin, Cornelius
Journals of a Methodist farmer 1871-1875.
1. Farm life – England – Binbrook
2. Binbrook (Lincolnshire) – Social life and customs
I. Title. II. Stovin, Jean
942.5'32 DA670.L7

ISBN 0-7099-2324-4

Printed and bound in Great Britain by
Biddles Ltd, Guildford and King's Lynn

Contents

'The more labour man puts into his work the more proportionate energy does God impart. Man receives aid from Heaven in proportion to his own exertions... In looking round my farm I am gazing upon a part of God's dominions.'

Cornelius Stovin

Foreword

The journals which are the body of this book are those kept by Cornelius Stovin. Cornelius Stovin was a tenant farmer occupying a large farm set high on the Lincolnshire wolds in the middle of the last century. He was also a Methodist lay preacher. It is the relationship and tension between these two aspects of his life, recorded in the journals, that create their fascination for me, and contribute one element in my understanding of that period in history. It gave me great pleasure, therefore, to accept the publisher's invitation to write this Foreword; it gives me an opportunity to share my reading of the journals with other readers and to invite them to read them within a national and theoretical as well as within their apparently local context.

I first read the journals nearly thirty years ago when Jean Stovin, Cornelius's granddaughter, and I were teaching together at Bath Technical College. And I was fortunate enough to do so when it was still possible to talk about them to his son Walter Stovin, a retired Lincolnshire tenant farmer himself and a man, it seemed to me, made in much the same mould as Cornelius. Through long conversations with Walter Stovin, stimulated by a shared familiarity with his father's journals, I lived for a moment in and around their farmhouse, Binbrook Hall, in the 1860s and 1870s. Looking back on that experience I think it was my earliest sustained attempt to live inside the head of a man with whom I was not in natural sympathy, in another age; my first serious 'verstehen' experience as an historian. Reading them again after a lapse of years I found them even more enlightening. After my first reading of the journals I mentioned them to Dr Joan Thirsk and she, too, found them a rare and valuable source for her work on agrarian history.[1] Since then other historians have also become familiar with the journals and Cornelius's hope that the journals, begun as a help and guide to himself, might also 'assume importance in other eyes' has been partially realised. But now, through the work of Jean Stovin, under the supervision of Alan Rogers at the Centre for Local History in the University of Nottingham, the journals should come into their own and assume fully the importance that is properly theirs.

Jean Stovin's careful and detailed annotations amplify the text of the journals and her lucid, comprehensive and sympathetic assessment of Cornelius sets them in their broader context. Her contributions are substitutes for the sort of conversations I had with Walter Stovin. Yet these are but marginal aids to answering minor queries about places and people, whereas the journals, written simply from the heart by a man who, in some respects, knew himself better than most of us know ourselves, speak directly to the reader, frequently telling him more than Cornelius intended. And that whether the reader be a student of religion, agriculture, labour relations, culture or the family, a local historian, or a general reader more interested in sensing the ambience of rural life in a remote corner of England a century ago than in seeking evidence for particular themes or aspects of nineteenth-century history.

Certainly there is much in the journals for students specialising in all those fragments of history listed above. They are especially rich for students of agricultural and economic history, and for those working in the area of capital/labour relations, ideology and the development of consciousness. However, I will be brief in writing of their significance for me.

Cornelius was the tenant of a very large farm. It was some 600 acres in extent and devoted to mixed farming. Although Cornelius kept no systematic financial accounts in the journals he did make periodic entries of income and expenditure which may be used as guides to the magnitude of his operation, especially in 1872. In that year he recorded sales of the following amounts: wheat, £489; barley, £149; oats, £53; sheep, £870; wool, £680, heifers, £8. Cornelius also carried 42 crew cattle worth about £24 each which he would not sell because the price was not right; he occasionally sold a horse and slaughtered pigs. It seems, therefore, that his receipts were in the region of £2,300. His recorded expenses were almost as high: rent, £754, taxes, £600; wages for regular employees (7 men in summer, 6 in winter, assisted by two lads and three boys) I estimate at £250. These items alone total £1,604. In addition he paid 2s.6d. per day for unspecified amounts of casual labour, kept 8 cart horses, and bought cattle and sheep as well as seed; in 1872 he bought 20 steers for £500, 130 lambs for £330 and 8 pigs for £8. Therefore, his statement that his net money income was in the region of £300 was probably not far off the mark.

It was the last of the good years, 1872. But, even in that year, yields at harvest were not as good as they had appeared in prospect early in the year. In the spring, of 309 ewes promising lambs, barely 250 were dropped. The ensuing summer was very wet and, according to Cornelius, unbearably hot - having dispensed with both blanket and sheet he lay in bed at night with his feet quite bare! But while he luxuriated the golden-winged fly and the wire worm devoured his turnips! Although his wheat was cut, raked and finished without harm his unthatched stacks were damaged by rain and his spring corn was 'so heavy and laid and curled and twisted' that it had to be cut by scythe. And one consequence of this was that he had to pay his casual labourers 20s. per week.

This bare outline of Cornelius's economic situation reveals the essence of his position as a capitalist tenant farmer; he was obliged by that position to adopt an instrumental approach to the world about him, renting land, buying labour, and buying and selling corn and stock and selling wool as the market dictated and the weather permitted. The need to adopt a rigorous, rational and calculating approach in order to survive in a competitive situation had, perhaps, been greater for him than for many other tenant farmers. For twenty years he had worked to bring the farm from a rubbishy and barren state to the healthy condition it was in in 1872 and he was then paying rent of about 25s. per acre. However, one consequence of the boom years in agriculture in the mid-nineteenth century was that landowners sought to increase their share of the value of the land they owned and Cornelius reported apprehensively on the fact of neighbours' rents being forced up to £2 to £2 2s. per acre. This prompted him to record that a farmer could not live on the wold hills at that rate. And throughout the journals there is a sense of his frustration that he was not a landowner and not directly a tenant of God. Fearing increased economic pressure from his new landlord, and experiencing the vagaries of climate and competition and demands for higher wages from newly formed agricultural unions, Cornelius's life was a struggle to ward off the falling rate of profit. One consequence was that he welcomed all the labour-saving innovations he could find. In 1872 he embraced the use of the double plough declaring:

> We shall not be locked up with ploughing work as we were last spring. We then hailed the double plough, for it opens our way for the summer work. We looked upon it as a Providential gift. The reaper, the steam engine, and thrashing apparatus, the double plough, are Divine gifts to the agriculture of the nineteenth century. What a marvellous economy of labour, and at the same time a beneficent enlargement of our rick yards by their development of the resources of the soil. Farming has become a scientific as well as an industrial occupation.

Yet he was also aware of the worst economic and social effects of this marvellous economy of labour and would like to have done something about it. Of course, that something would have excluded all socialist solutions such as those 'scores of experiments [which] have been tried upon the vast and open fields of America by communistic communities and failure was inscribed upon their attempts. There has scarcely existed a solitary case of success.' Far better, he thought, to set free men like himself who laboured and encouraged others to labour. And in this respect he deplored the breakdown of what he regarded as proper, because traditional, relationships between masters and servants, oblivious of the fact that his life's activity as a capitalist farmer contributed to the destruction of those relationships. In short, he welcomed the advantages gained from a system based on private property, even though he regretted his own merely intermediate position as a tenant farmer. It is true that he deplored the worst economic and social effects of that system but, as is always the case with advocates of economic systems based on absolute property and absolute self-interest, he placed the blame for the loss of a truly human community on moral failure, particularly on the moral failure of those with only their labour to sell. He wrote:

> The acknowledged immoral condition of the servants and the broken and disorganised relationships existing between them and masters and mistresses. Authority, human and Divine, appears to be clear set at nought. Obedience, whether to God or man, is well nigh repudidated. Both morality and religion are trampled under foot. No kind or degree of good treatment produces corresponding industry or decent behaviour. Shrinking from work except for self is fast becoming the order of servant life...Better wages and better living and more kind treatment does not in the least change their moral dispositions. The intensity of moral corruption only luxuriates and fattens and becomes more gross in proportion to the increase of material prosperity. Luxuries are only a richer soil for sin and iniquity to grow in unless the carnal nature is destroyed by supernatural power... Oh! for a larger measure of this seasoning power! I would want and plead for it. Glory to God it may be obtained in overflowing abundance.

Cornelius, who sometimes appears in his journals as a self-taught Adam Smith without Smith's objection to religious 'enthusiasm', was of course no such person. Rather, his ideas were the product of the hegemony of the prevailing ethos of his epoch which he absorbed through experience and the books he read. They matched perfectly his objective economic position, or nearly so.

The date of the first of the journals and the beginning of the internal debate Cornelius conducted with himself, juxtaposing facts about his farming life with thoughts about morality, religion and the human predicament, suggest to me that as he grew older and more successful by the late 1860s and early 1870s he began to reflect more and to pose to himself the question of the true direction his life should take. Then, as the world market for agricultural products became more competitive, forcing him to act even more instrumentally as a capitalist farmer (by 1876 he was in debt to the amount of £1,635), he was faced with a crisis of decision. This crisis seemed to arise from tension between his objective position in the production process and its associated instrumental ideology, and his own morally preferred position. Even in 1872 he wrote:

> If man were a purely physical being and was subject only to material laws then a science of his history might be possible; but man is a moral agent and his actions cannot be calculated according to the laws of self-interest. Even the science of political economy takes the law of self-interest as its axiomatic foundation. There is a higher moral law than this which, as a fact inscribed upon the page of history, thousands have

> obeyed - viz. the law of right... This overflowing wellspring of living moral energy which exists in man's nature forbids the power of calculation. This is the source of historical surprises... Perhaps, too, the evolution itself may come into collision and subvert for the time being the law of self-interest so that even the very axioms of some of our sciences may be swept from beneath them that they may be replaced by firmer foundations. Man's moral nature bears contingent fruit... This is a fund of dormant moral and intellectual energy which has been buried in the depths of man's nature for a wise and fatherly purpose. This marvellous evolution is going on today.

Springing from this perception of a moral law superior to that of self-interest were the plans and purposes he prepared for himself. These included the winning of a clear knowledge of literature, agriculture and manufacturing industry supplemented by 'a clear understanding of poor law and its administration, and to be able to solve the problem of pauperism and promote all remedial measures in relation thereto'. All this was to be done without neglecting to administer the laws of nature and of God in relation to his wife, family and farm, 'that they may all be kept prospering in every kind of growth and accumulation'. 'I should like', he wrote, 'to farm on a profitable principle.' According to these objectives Cornelius divided his non-working and non-family life between two areas of public service. He gave much of this time and some of his resources to the cause of the United Methodist Free Church, formed in 1857 after the secession of 100,000 members from the Wesleyan Societies. And there is much in Cornelius's journals for the local as well as the national history of this movement. When he was not involved in chapel business, he served on the Parish Council as Overseer of the Poor, on the Louth Board of Guardians and on the sanitary authority for the local rural district. In all of these capacities he was brought into even closer contact with the worst social consequences of the law of self-interest and with the men charged with mitigating some of them. His astringent comment upon the Louth Board of Guardians points to the implausibility of the idea that the system could have been expected to palliate let alone solve its social problems by piecemeal social engineering even if most men in positions of power had shared Cornelius's own reforming objectives. His comment on the Board of Guardians in 1876 is worth quoting in full:

> You will perhaps be a little surprised to learn that the leading positions occupied by the members of our Louth Board of Guardians are most inefficiently filled. The chairman is too infirm and is unwise to cling to the office. Mr Wilson has confused and muddled his brain by drink and snuff. Dr Bell's abilities are of a very attenuated order. Rev. Smith of Stewton fumbles over the medical allowances papers in a crude and blundering fashion. Colonal Smyth is a retiring, quiet, good natured gentleman without any gift of speech. Considerable

> hesitancy marks his oral performances. His brother rarely attempts to speak. Rev. Vyner seldom comes and when present he requires posting up by information and explanation. Rev. Prettyman has the clearest judgment and most forcible utterance. Mr Smith and Hewson of Louth manifest some degree of business tact but little debating power or insight into law. There is not a single mind of commanding power to cut through the many difficulties which obstruct the course of business, hence very few persons can remain to the close in consequence of the lateness of the hour. The town of Louth seems almost barren of public men.

Perhaps it was this sort of experience coupled with his sense of isolation from the majority of his fellow tenant farmers, who seemed interested only in 'shooting, hunting, horses, game, landlords...racing', that determined the predominantly religious direction of his public life; only thus could he live at peace with himself and achieve some sense of communion with his fellow men, including those who in other circumstances were his labourers.

But Cornelius's religious commitment posed problems for his family life. Consequently his journals provide as much material for the historian of culture, the family and the position of women as they do for agricultural and economic historians. As Jean Stovin points out in her introduction, Cornelius did not marry until he was 31; he seems the very model of Malthusian prudence and patience. Yet, his established pattern of religious life and belief, which contributed much to the tension producing the journals in the years after 1868, show that for all his plainly instrumental approach to life, Cornelius lacked that self-regarding prudence his wife Elizabeth thought proper. And his account of their life together and his letters to her, which on occasion serve the same purpose as the journals, although not as significant as Munby's diary of his relationship with his servant wife Hannah, throw much light on those deeper personal relationships which generally elude the social historian. Elizabeth nevertheless remains a shadowy yet tragic figure whose life, taken out of its nineteenth-century context and out of the context of Cornelius's life as I have interpreted it so far, might be used against him and the male world Cornelius may be said to represent.

As Jean Stovin points out in her introduction, Elizabeth and Cornelius never did agree about the main direction of their life together. 'You believe in business, tact and energy carried to the goal of success in life', he wrote to her, 'I look to my property in relation to God's Kingdom!' And in that acute self-analysis and sharp echo of John Locke lies the key to understanding Cornelius as a whole man and the reason he is a subject worthy of study by students of the nineteenth century. Cornelius did strive to act out his life as a tenant of God. Although, as I have said, his actual position as a capitalist tenant farmer forced him to adopt an instrumental approach to the world about him, the same set of religious beliefs that fuelled his life as a capitalist also obliged him to temper that approach with benevolent consideration. Because of his religiously derived perception of himself as working and living in harmony with God, with nature and with his fellow men, he would not lay waste God's Kingdom - at least, not entirely. Accordingly, Cornelius's journals sparkle with the tension his position and his self-perception created for him.

Because his predicament, greatly intensified, is also shared by us today, his journals can still speak to us directly and seem to invite us to respond with understanding and humility. Indeed, my own response to Cornelius's attempt to solve his dilemma, the journals written as his help and guide which are now before you, is touched with sadness, because that was how it was and because it largely remains so today, and because moral men like Cornelius never did understand what had happened to them. And neither do his successors today. What is our own approach to God's Kingdom and what of our prospects of a life lived in harmony with nature and with our fellow men?

And so I could go on telling the reader what to look for, what he should find and even what he should think about it when I have already said that the journals can speak for themselves. Perhaps what I really mean is that just as from my particular standpoint the journals speak to me of the human condition, other readers, sharing some of my interests and from similar standpoints, may also share my appreciation of Cornelius Stovin. They, too, may live for a moment in Binbrook Hall in the 1860s and 1870s, and share with Cornelius the joys and fears which filled his life and the lives of those around him. Between them, Cornelius and his granddaughter Jean have given us a rare insight into a moment of the past that will be forever a delight. The mood set by the journals will remain with you long after the details have been forgotten.

R. S. Neale
Professor of Economic History
University of New England, N.S.W.

NOTE

1 Joan Thirsk, 'English Peasant Farming', London (1957), pp. 323-33.

Acknowledgements

My grandfather's journals were handed down to me by his youngest son, Walter Stovin (my father), and his youngest daughter, Ruth Hatfield. In the late 1950s, while my father was still alive, I showed them to R. S. Neale, now Professor of Economic History at New England University, N.S.W., and he was enthusiastic about their interest and value to a wider readership than the Stovin family.

It was not until my retirement from a career in Further Education that I was able to spend time on selecting and editing them for publication, and I am greatly indebted to Professor Neale for his encouragement and advice throughout the project, and for writing a foreword to this edition. My thanks are due also to G. E. Mingay, Professor of Agrarian History, University of Kent, for his preliminary help. I could not have undertaken the work, however, had it not been for the supervision and encouragement, generously given, of Alan Rogers at the Centre for Local History in the University of Nottingham, before he became Director of the Institute of Continuing Education, University of Ulster.

Many other people have helped me in a variety of ways. I am particularly grateful to Michael M. Sleight, the present owner of Binbrook Hall, whose family have owned it almost since the Stovin family left it when it was sold in 1907. He has kindly allowed me to visit the farm and farmhouse on several occasions, and has given me valuable information about its earlier history. Among advisors on specific aspects of local history, I must single out Rex Russell, Department of Adult Education, University of Hull; William Leary, Lincolnshire Methodist History Society, who is now Connectional Archivist, Methodist Church Archives and History Committee; R. J. Olney, now at the Royal Commission on Historical Manuscripts; and David Robinson, Department of Adult Education, Nottingham University. The late W. E. R. Hallgarth of Scartho', Grimsby, and H. W. Smith of Louth also kindly provided material from their collections of photographs and reminiscences of past events and people from the north Lincolnshire wolds. My thanks are due, too, to Catherine Wilson, Keeper of Lincolnshire History, Museum of Lincolnshire Life, and to the staff of the Lincoln Archives Office, who have been most helpful in allowing me the use of documents in their possession during my research.

I must also thank the many friends and relatives who have given me information, encouragement and practical help on my way. Muriel Collier has not only assisted me with research but has encouraged and stimulated me throughout. I am indebted to Peter

Stovin for details of the Stovin genealogical table and also for research into the growth of spas and hydropathic treatment during the nineteenth century. The Stovin family at Claythorpe Manor, Alford, have enlightened me on the farming background in north Lindsey, and have provided the notes for the glossary. Mary Stovin, Shirley and John Hanson, Winifred Riggall and Peggy Sharpley have helped me to trace references to the Stovin, Riggall and Sharpley families, and Christina Hay to the early connections of the Stovin family with Methodism.

I am most grateful to Elsie Towle, Mary Baffoni, my sister, Ruth Stovin, and Kathleen Britton for their invaluable assistance with the compilation of material and correction of the typescript and to Philip Painter for compiling the index. Finally, I acknowledge with gratitude the assistance of the Marc Fitch Fund and the J. R. Walkes Trust towards the publication of the journals.

Jean Stovin

Introduction

Cornelius Stovin was born in 1830 at Binbrook Hall, a farmstead situated in a remote area of the north Lincolnshire wolds, three miles from the village of Binbrook, and some ten miles north-west of the market town of Louth. He lived there for over 60 years, two-thirds of his long life, and he has left the imprint of his lively and unusual personality in a series of journals, most of which he wrote at the Binbrook farm.

He came from a long-established Lincolnshire farming and Methodist background, and although he himself had little formal education, he had the family encouragement and personal initiative to extend his knowledge and experience through extensive reading and a variety of contacts both within and outside his remote rural area. He became a lay preacher when he was a young man, and notebooks still exist which show that from 1851 he carefully thought out and edited the material for his sermons. It was not until he was nearly 40 years old, however, that he began a series of journals.

The impetus seems to have come from a journey which he made to Ireland with two farming companions in 1868. This tour of farms and estates in Galway, ending with a visit to Dublin, excited and impressed him so greatly that he started jotting down notes about each stage of his travels in pencil in a small black notebook, transferring these immediate impressions in more elaborate form to a substantial ledger when he had the time and opportunity. This first journal set the pattern for records of the more unusual and important events in his life, and in the same ledger he later interspersed sermon notes with accounts of short visits in 1869 to an Arts Exhibition in Leeds and to Matlock Spa, where his wife was receiving hydropathic treatment.

In 1870 he visited Oxford, again with a farming neighbour, with the prime purpose of going to the Royal Agricultural Show, but the journal he kept in a Principal Teacher's Log Book[1] showed a much greater concern and interest with the University and the religious life of Oxford - both of which aroused his admiration and criticism in almost equal proportions. When he returned home, he edited his account in lecture form, completing it in March 1871.

In the following August, on the next page in the same log book, he began to 'unfold in a literary drama' his 'private, personal, domestic, social and public life'. His journal entries cover three periods during the 1870s: August 1871 to December 1872, September 1874 to June 1875, and May 1876 to January 1877. It is the first two of these records which have been selected for publication.

He gave no explanation of the lack of entries from 1873 to the summer of 1874, and perhaps one of his notebooks has been lost. A later gap between 1875 and 1876 would have been caused by the dislocation of family life when the Binbrook farmhouse was being substantially rebuilt. At other times, when he allowed a few weeks to elapse without writing in his journal, he accused himself of 'literary lethargy' or the sin of having 'a rusty pen'. The concluding entry on January 1st, 1877 was a stark statement of a crushingly heavy bank overdraft.[2] He did not resume his personal writing for some 13 years, and these later journals, except for a farm and family record of some weeks during the year 1891 and brief accounts of important personal and national events, concentrate more on moral and religious issues.

He was very conscious of his small part in the history of his age, and his journals not only tell his own story, but provide his personal commentary on events, changes and controversies which particularly concerned or excited him. In 1872 he wrote: 'A quarter of a century of my own life of thought and action is woven into the very warp of modern history. The threads may not be visibly identified, but still they are there.'[3] Some twenty years later, as he looked back over his life, he reiterated: 'There is something that makes my life and character and history of vast importance. The fact of having lived through six decades of the world's most progressive career.'[4]

The few years which the earlier volumes cover bridge the period of general prosperity and confidence which had developed from the middle of the nineteenth century and the beginning of the depression which gradually cast its shadow over the countryside. The period was a critical one in several ways in the writer's own life, a time when his natural optimism and buoyancy of character, reinforced by a compelling and unswerving religious faith, was being tested by problems and difficulties on the farm, within his family, and also in the branch of the Methodist church to which he belonged. The year 1871 to 1872 was still a year of progress and hope, but from 1875, like many other farmers, he suffered from rising costs and lower prices as competition from abroad began to affect the agricultural community. Although, as his later journals showed, he and his family survived the harsh years in the late 1870s and 1880s at Binbrook Hall, it was in much straitened circumstances. Cornelius, however, retained throughout his life a capacity to free his mind from the physical effects of bad times. A pessimistic thought or a sad mishap was quickly overtaken by new enthusiasms, hopes and interests, and these were eagerly recorded in his journals.

He wrote with care and concentration, in a uniformly legible and flowing hand, and a hundred years after they were written they can be read with comparative ease. As he was largely self-taught, his spelling and punctuation are at times curious and inconsistent,[5] but his vocabulary is impressively extensive, the result of much reading. The journals, too, are written in a variety of styles according to the purpose and use of the entry: prices of farm stock and crops, wage bills and other short business jottings are juxtaposed with sensitive and delicate descriptions of the countryside, succinct and humorous comment on the peculiarities of neighbours and friends, and, not least, himself, and a florid exuberance of exhortation and homily. When he was using his journals as drafts for sermons or addresses, his consciousness of his future audience is often amusingly demonstrated. He harangued his Methodist 'brothers' at length and with passion in a splendidly figurative style, as he sat alone in his farmhouse dining room. He took every opportunity to add new entries, sometimes jotting down events or thoughts as they occurred, two or three times a day, and exactly recording the hour and the place each time. When he was in Ireland visiting a large estate, his host was considerably upset when he found his English guest quietly setting down his observations in his small notebook. Often he wrote in the Louth Mechanics Institute Reading Room before the weekly market, and, when travelling by train to Methodist conferences or agricultural shows, he used the 'travelling carriage', the hotel bedroom, or the dim light of the lamp on the station platform.

Cornelius was a descendant of a well-known Lincolnshire family, and his ancestors were owners of an estate at Tetley, near Crowle.[6] The Stovin family spread fairly widely over south Yorkshire, Nottinghamshire, and Lincolnshire, and branches of the family emigrated to Canada in the nineteenth century. The writer's grandfather, George Stovin, became tenant of Binbrook Hall Farm in 1810, one year before he died. Cornelius's father carried on the tenancy until increasing ill-health made it necessary for his two sons, George and Cornelius, to take over the management of the farm. Cornelius junior was then only 18 years old and after his elder brother George's marriage in 1854, he was left with the full responsibility for the farm and his father's parish and business commitments. His mother and elder sister died in 1855, and after his two younger sisters married he lived alone at the farmhouse until his own marriage in 1861. His wife was Elizabeth, the eldest daughter of Francis and Elizabeth Riggall of Dexthorpe Farm, near Spilsby, some 20 miles south of Binbrook. They had a family of seven, four sons and three daughters, born between 1864 and 1883.

In 1892, when Cornelius was 62 years old, his eldest son took over the Binbrook tenancy, and he and his wife, and those of the family who were still living with them, moved to a much smaller farm on the marsh at Hogthorpe, and it was here that he wrote the last journals of 1893 and 1894. It was the first of a number of moves to financially unviable rented farms within the next 20 years, and he retired in some poverty in 1918 at the age of 88, living at Louth until his death three years later in 1921. He remained a leading figure in the Free Methodist Church to the end of his life, and died only three weeks before he had been asked to take the chair at the Louth chapel anniversary, retaining to the last, as the minister who gave the memorial address testified, his intellectual freshness, spiritual alertness, and 'jubilant and fervent manner'.[7]

He was one of a strong minority of Methodist farmers in north Lincolnshire, and his commitment to Methodism was within a family tradition. It is reported that a 'Mr. Stovin' helped to save John Wesley from a rioting mob in Crowle.[8] Other Methodist and local records refer to members of the family from the early days of Methodism, and Stovins intermarried with other Methodist families from that time.[9] Both his mother's family, the Sharpleys, and his wife's family, the Riggalls, were well-known and respected Methodists in their own districts. His mother's cousin, J. B. Sharpley, a Louth businessman and three times mayor of the town, was one of the leaders of the Wesleyan Reformers, who seceded from the Wesleyan connection in the 1840s and were later named the 'Free' Methodists. The Louth revolt was one of many throughout England by Wesleyans who felt frustrated by the trend towards increasing authority of the ministers, and, in his journals, Cornelius referred on a number of occasions to the reasons for the separation of the branches of Methodism during the earlier part of the nineteenth century.

He was 21 years old when the first repercussions affected Binbrook Wesleyans, in 1851. Membership dropped by over 80 in that year, and continued to decrease in the years immediately following,[10] and the Binbrook Stovin family would certainly have seceded at this time. He was a founder member of the Binbrook Free Methodist chapel, built in 1855, but meetings were held before this in the village Temperance Hall, and most probably also in the houses of individual members - which would certainly have included Binbrook Hall Farm. His strong and specific religious convictions were undoubtedly nurtured by his family, and he was particularly influenced by his mother and her cousin, to both of whom he paid tribute in his journals. He became one of the most passionate advocates of the Free Methodist faith and doctrine, which emphasised the more fervent emotional evangelism characteristic of earlier Methodists, and the provision of a freer and more democratic organisation within each chapel: 'We regard every society as a church who have obtained faith in our crucified Lord. The government is carried on by representation. No one class of men can form themselves into a hierarchy.'[11]

He was against any form of human authority which intervened between God and man, or which separated any one section of men from the gifts of creation or the benefits of civilisation, which he felt should be granted to all. There was never any division in his mind between his faith and his farming (other than the problem of too much to do in too short a time); the one irradiated and gave purpose to the other. Work and worship, sacred and secular, formed a natural unity, and he felt as surely a tenant of God on his farm as the agent of God in the pulpit. Although he paid his rent to his absentee landlord, he farmed his 600 acres as 'part of God's Dominions': 'Everything living and inanimate, the stock on the farm, the implements of husbandry, the home panoply and home life are sacred and consecrated.... Each harvest is a monument to earthly and heavenly co-operation.'[12]

He always regretted his lack of formal schooling and lack of culture while he was young, but his family environment must have been one in which self-development was encouraged, and visiting preachers and leading laymen of the Methodist church who preached in the circuit, and sometimes stayed at the farm, may well have stimulated his eager pursuit of knowledge. While books became his constant and beloved companions, his explorations into the world of architecture and art were more limited by his circumstances. His excitement, on the few occasions when he visited towns and cities where he was able for a short time to enjoy the visual arts, is conveyed in his journal entries with infectious enthusiasm. He studied the paintings at the Leeds Arts Exhibition until his 'eyeballs burned', marvelled at the beauty of the college buildings in Oxford, the frescoes in the Rochdale Town Hall. Nearer home, he welcomed the then fairly new practice of hanging engravings and 'chromos'[13] on the walls of farmhouse living rooms, and one of his first purchases for the newly renovated Binbrook Hall, in 1875, was 'an old painting... I have to give £3 for it, but it is to be cleaned and the frame regilded.'[14] Art had a moral as well as an aesthetic purpose for him, and in narrative paintings he saw 'tangible witness and illustration to the facts of history'. But although his opportunities to see the works of great artists were few, colour and form in the natural world surrounded him every day, and his verbal expression of the beauty of the changing seasons is visually perceptive and exact in his journal entries:

> The dying processes of Autumn... the gentle and unabrupt mingling of all possible shades of rainbow hues. The sunshine is not glaring but flows through the valleys and clothes the hills with a mild and mellow radiance.[15]

> How brightly the wheatfields glow and gleam, all golden in the warm sunshine. There is the bloom of health in the ripening. When the green becomes grey, there is ghastly mildew...[16]

> Last night as I commenced my journey home, the wind gently sighed through the trees which looked like globes of black shadows darkening the space they fill.[17]

If the farm and district around him were his ever-present picture gallery, they were also his library. Whether sitting in the farmhouse, riding to market or meeting, or walking in the fields, he always had books and pamphlets with him, 'tumbled in confusion in every room and case' in the house, or stuffing his pockets when he was out and about. In his choice of books, his Methodism propelled him towards sermon literature and moral philosophy, but his delight in and curiosity about the natural world led him to read all he could find concerning the physical sciences. He was fascinated, too, by the history of civilisation from the early days which archaeologists were bringing to light within his own lifetime.

He was equally enthusiastic about developments in his own age, and kept up to date with social and political events and foreign affairs by reading 'The Standard' and 'The Daily News', which were delivered from the Binbrook Post Office by mail cart, and a fairly wide range of periodicals, some of which were delivered by post and some which he regularly looked at in the Louth Mechanics Institute Reading Room. It gave him great pleasure to purchase books when he could: 'If it please God to prosper me in business, I shall be delighted to obtain more space and convenience for the new editions I may wish to make to my book stores.'[18]

When he could not buy, he borrowed and exchanged with friends. He seemed to read novels rarely - the only two he mentioned by name in the journals were two of Disraeli's that had a particular significance for him, although he discussed 'novels and their authors' with his friends, and would have at least glanced at those serialised in 'The Cornhill' and 'Macmillan's' magazines, two of the periodicals that he seemed to look at fairly regularly. The works that he accumulated during his life, and those which he mentioned reading with interest and enjoyment, were those of the more serious authors of his day, Macaulay, Carlyle, Froude, Emerson, May's 'Constitutional History', among many others: one of the extravagant purchases that he indulged in was an edition of Milton's 'Paradise Lost' with Doré's illustrations.

His reading at times impinged on other aspects of a very active life. In a revealing passage in one of the journals he identified particular fields on his farm with favourite authors whose books he had studied while leaning against a tree sheltering from the rain, or in the intervals of 'tenting' crows, gun in one hand, book in the other. Unfortunately at such times his thoughts were deflected from the farm work, and he often took himself to task for mishaps that were partly or wholly due to his divided mind. The Methodist minister who gave a warmly appreciative memorial address at the service after his death commented that 'he was a farmer by accident of birth, a preacher by personal choice. He was a manual worker by necessity but a student by preference.' There is obvious truth in this, but it is an easy simplification about a man who entered enthusiastically into a number of roles, one crowding in upon another. What he lacked was the discipline and training to follow up idea with action in one sphere before involving himself heartily and happily in another. In his journals, for a short time, he tried to separate in two notebooks his 'religious and literary jottings' from his 'farm and household diary', but his thoughts flowed freely from one to another, an entry recording the death of a bullock, or the inroads of the turnip fly, provoking an idea for next Sunday's sermon. He soon gave up a vain attempt to divide his life and his journals into compartments; but his wife found the curious logic of his thought connections provoking rather than endearing, and the practical consequences often unfortunate.

He did not marry until he was 31 years old, and by then the pattern of his life, and his priorities within it, were firmly established. After his marriage, although he welcomed the warmth of family life, and the comforts and refinements which his wife brought to his home, he never compromised in his belief that his resources, however slender, should be shared between his home and family, and his work for God. His wife had been brought up in a more affluent Wesleyan Methodist household, one in which success in business did not seem to conflict with strongly held religious principles, and she never reconciled herself to the views of her less worldly husband. He continued to give loans to village chapels and to pay off circuit debts when his family was increasing and difficulties on the farm were becoming more serious in years of lower prices and increasing costs. 'Lizzie' became more and more frustrated as she found the 'respectable establishment' which she looked forward to for herself and her family receding from view, and her husband's optimistic (but largely unrealised) faith that the guiding hand of Divine Providence, amongst other blessings, would relieve them from debt became a source of great irritation. Cornelius loved and respected his Lizzie, and could analyse their differences of outlook clearly: 'You believe in business, tact and energy carried to the goal of success in life... I look at my property in relation to God's kingdom.'[19]

He seemed, however, to have only occasional perception about her real problems, or of his own contribution towards them - those of an active and intelligent woman shut up for most of her married life in an isolated and uncomfortable farm house, sick and weary with miscarriages and child-bearing and the worry of cheap and untrained young servants whom she had not the strength to cope with. They were dependent on the village three miles away for their two basic necessities, bread and drinking water, as their own corn was ground a sack at a time at the mill, and their drinking water was brought from the village pump by water cart. When snow made the roads impassable, stocks would run low, and social contact would be minimal. Even the few outings Lizzie made in the basket phaeton with the groom boy and her children would cease in the winter. Cornelius spent much of his time away from the house, but the view that he held of a wife and mother's role did not allow for her equal need for change and company, and he was perplexed at the length of the periodic visits she made to the house of her parents and brothers, as he showed in the long letters, carefully copied into his journals, which he wrote to her while she was away:

Nov. 7th. 1876, Tues eve. 6.15.
My dearest wife,
You must not forget that your absence detracts from the sweetness and joy of life. Of course, I can cheerfully submit to the sacrifice when convinced that the little ones and yourself are increasing in health and vigour...

But he added, more emphatically, two days later, when there was still no sign of her return: 'While you remain twenty miles away it is self-sacrifice for me to live in the midst of so terrible a vacancy. It has been comfortless for me through the night by reason of the cold.'

He depended on her a good deal, and not only to warm his cold bed. She gave him much needed practical support and advice in matters of detail on the farm - the spreading of manure on the fields at the right time, more severe treatment of his foreman who was proving lazy and inefficient. In his letters, he kept her in touch with day-to-day work, the progress of those of the family whom she had not taken with her, and the long-drawn-out problems connected with the rebuilding of the farm house, which, under her pressure, he had negotiated with the landlord - and which is a major theme of the Second Journal, written between 1874 and 1875.

Their affection for their children was their strongest bond, although their ambitions and concerns were inevitably somewhat different. Cornelius enjoyed his children's company and by inclination and necessity involved himself in their care, their play and their education. He commented that he wished 'to arouse their memory and imagination early to receive while tender a larger and more ineraceable seal than I ever had the priviledge to experience'.[20] 'Books, society and business', he wrote, 'have composed the main instruments of my education.' He was determined to enliven and broaden his children's education, and eagerly watched their development. He passed on to them his enthusiastic delight in simple natural processes, and understood the importance of play. He bought them picture books, and after pointing out details in a picture to his small son, Frank, he commented: 'I have paid some attention to picture lessons, and the more I study them myself my conviction deepens regarding the aid they render the youthful mind in realising history truth'.[21] He tried to involve his wife in a project based on a book he saw advertised called 'Mary's Garden':

> with your permission I will secure the book and we can study the contents together these winter evenings... and with God's blessing in the opening of Spring, fill up the brown barren waste with a new series of beauties while we fill up many vacant hours in the dear children's minds which might otherwise be void and irksome.[22]

He took them farming with him, 'I on Charlie and Denison on Topsy and Mabel on the donkey', and when the two elder children were only eight and seven years old encouraged them to travel on their own to their grandparents' farm, some 20 miles away, to the consternation of his wife and mother-in-law. Although she firmly prevented their return alone, he commented with satisfaction that the outward journey was 'an adventure highly beneficial in teaching observation, self-reliance and courage'. After the birth of the third and fourth child, a nursemaid was added to the previous domestic staff of cook and housemaid, and the two elder children had a succession of cheap untrained governesses - three in two years.[23] He did his best to supplement the dull instruction given by these young women by his involvement in the children's other activities, and also by visits to 'the school room'. All his efforts were aimed at stimulating their desire to learn. In consequence, when his eldest son went to Louth Grammar School, he was disillusioned with the school and the education it provided:

> It is entitled King Edward's Grammar School. Then educational forces of a royal character ought to centre here, as elsewhere... As soon as I entered their room a gloomy feeling of disappointment suddenly came over me. I deeply felt the defective character of the boys' surroundings.[24]

He found the studies dull, irrelevant and narrow, with Latin and Greek every day and English Grammar only once a week; the buildings and schoolrooms were dark and prison-like, the walls without pictures, 'bare as when the plaisterer laid down his trowel'. The interest which he had in the educational developments of his age led him to the further comment: 'It is a most astonishing fact that with the growing wealth of our country and even the endowments of our existing schools, we are so weak and poverty-stricken in educational machinery.'[25] He was not so expressly critical of the small private school to which he sent his eldest daughter, Mabel, and the subjects that she studied at least included three that he valued, 'Geography, Modern History and Poetry'. He wanted for all his children an education to foster their own particular talents:

> in active business or more retired meditative life, whether the bent of their talents leads them into a profession or a farm into the arts and sciences and scholarship, that they may find the congenial sphere where they can best serve God and their own age.[26]

With a realism that was not always evident about his own prospects he remarked that he was not likely to leave his children material wealth but that his chief desire was to 'place their fortune in their heads and characters as well as, or rather than, the pocket'.[27] In fact, it has been his grandchildren and their descendants who have had the academic and cultural opportunities which he so desperately wanted himself as well as for his children. What they inherited from him was the 'ineraceable seal' of his own eager questing mind, and his radiant and sensitive response to life in all its manifestations.

The farm at Binbrook of which Cornelius was tenant was on the outskirts of the village which was itself isolated from the nearest market towns of Market Rasen and Louth by hilly and twisting roads, and the recently built railways which skirted the wolds were some miles distant.[28] The village itself lay in a hollow, watered by the source of a rivulet which flowed east to the sea near Tetney. In the mid-nineteenth century Binbrook was a large 'open village' of some thirteen hundred inhabitants. At least half of the population worked on the farms in the neighbourhood, while many of the others were craftsmen who provided services to the farmers, and tradesmen who provided basic necessities such as shoes and clothes for the villagers. A number of small farmers were owner-occupiers of land around the centre of the parish, but a few larger farms, situated on the chalk uplands which rise steeply from the village to heights of 300 or 400 feet, had been brought into cultivation only after the village Enclosure Award of 1740, and they were owned by non-resident landlords only one of whom had any previous connection with the district.

Binbrook Hall was one of four farms acquired by the Denison family in 1820.[29] It consisted of nearly 600 acres of arable and pasture land, and included some ten acres of plantations - largely used by the landlord and his friends as a preserve for game. The thin chalk and flint soil made cultivation difficult and expensive, even with the use of manure from the cattle and sheep raised or fattened for sale on the farm. Cornelius had inherited from his ailing father a badly run-down farm, but, with the help and advice of his first landlord, had brought it out of its 'rubbishy condition' by the time that he wrote his first journal in 1871. But although it was then producing adequate crops of cereals, turnips and seeds, he had missed the advantage gained by many other farmers in the prosperous middle years of the nineteenth century.

In 1872 he commented with satisfaction that he had 'balanced income with expenditure', but he had no reserve with which to meet the coming years of recession and, year by year, hindered also by the unusually wet seasons between 1871 and 1880,[30] and disease in his flocks and herds, his financial position became more and more precarious. A more single-minded farmer who had concentrated all his energy and resources on the farm might have fared better, but the prospect was becoming increasingly serious for all farmers. 'Is this non-success to be ascribed to the farmer or the farm,' he asked in one of his letters to his wife. 'I believe, without self-flattery you ascribe it mainly to the farm.'[31] His particular strength as a farmer was in his intelligent appreciation of the help to be gained from new inventions in farm machinery which saved labour, his use of the new fertilisers coming on the market to enrich the light soil, and his readiness to experiment in new techniques and methods, whether for salving sheep, altering the traditional time for threshing, or devising a new enlarged corn drill. He took notice of suggestions and practices of his experienced workers, and of neighbouring farmers. Admiring the 'perfection of cultivation' of his cousin Isaac's farm, he added drily that on any other subject but farming his cousin was 'as ignorant as a Hottentot'.

Like other farmers with a large acreage, he delegated the main supervision of the farm work to his foreman - unwisely during the

1870s, as he found to his cost. He spent a good part of his own time at the numerous markets and fairs in the district, assessing prices and comparing yields, if not buying or selling himself. His own work on the farm was peripheral in his middle life, although he had obviously played a much more active role as a young man. During the years of his journal-writing he still enjoyed helping out with the threshing, harvesting, turnip-dragging and the like, as the need arose. The journals gradually build up a detailed picture of his life on the farm, the slow rhythm of work through the changing seasons, the interaction of the members of that remote rural community, and, more unusually, the interaction which the writer took so much for granted between natural and supernatural, as part of his experiential faith. A fine harvest, a luxuriant crop of turnips, a good lambing season, were accepted with gratitude as a sign of the working of Divine Providence. When the mysterious ways of God seemed to thwart his immediate aims - when rain ruined the crops, when disease decimated his sheep and cattle, when his horses went lame at a critical time - he was equally ready with his justification that the anxieties of men must be aroused to quicken their inventive powers and awaken them to self-reliance and industry: 'Natural disasters in this sense may become the clearest proof of Divine beneficence, the brightest manifestation of His goodness as disciplinary and educational instead of discordantly conflicting with that golden aspect of His character.'[32] He suggested, some 80 years before its actual invention, that a 'drying apparatus' might be the answer to wet corn rather than an appeal to the Almighty to change his mind about the weather.

During the writer's lifetime, changes were gradually taking place in rural society which were loosening the traditional bonds between landlord, tenant farmer and labourers. In the second half of the century, movement from the land that had tied them together was a real possibility, whether to the new industrial centres or overseas. Although the 'miniature aristocracy' of the wolds, as Cornelius later described it, was still firmly structured in the 1870s, he came up against changes in the attitude of his landlord and his labourers towards himself and his farm which caused him increasing concern. His liberal nonconformist views had not affected his relationship with his first landlord, Mr. Edmund Beckett Denison (knighted in 1871 and thereafter mentioned as 'Sir Edmund Beckett').[33] This landlord had a genuine interest in his estates and his tenants, although an absentee landlord. He had known Cornelius all his life and his annual supervisory visits when the writer was a young man were warmly appreciated, as a letter written to him on August 16th, 1871 showed:

> I have long had a desire to express my gratitude to you for the many favours conferred upon me.
>
> In counting them up, my mind has been thrown back many years even almost as far as reccollections of business extends. I am indebted to you for being pushed out into business so

> early in life. Instead of kicking us out for bad management, you came over and gave us a fatherly impetus in the direction of agricultural progress. We responded to your excessive kindness and today the farm is transformed. It is with real pleasure and satisfaction that I can revert to these days of landlord visitation and converse with unmingled satisfaction and delight. I could almost question whether such free and happy conversation ever took place between landlord and tenant.

But when his son, the second Sir Edmund, inherited the family estates, differences in attitudes and interests between owner and tenant became matters of greater concern. His second landlord's ambitions were centred on business and political advancement (he was created Baron Grimthorpe in 1886), and he left the management of his estates largely to his agent, 'Mr. Vesey'. Cornelius felt strongly about the disregard he showed of his tenant's interests, in particular the preservation of plantations and hedgerows as coverts for game in spite of repeated complaints that they shaded and spoilt the crops, and the landlord ignored requests for cottages to house his tenant's labourers.[34] He was sensitive, too, to the landlord's chill and arrogant manner to him on the few occasions when they met in connection with the rebuilding of the farmhouse - although he reluctantly recognised his business acumen and practical sense. His experience of this new landlord strengthened his view of the iniquity of a system by which 'grasping landlords' held a stranglehold over the productive use of the land.

His attitude to his labourers was more complex than to his landlord. As a lay preacher and official of the Free Methodist church, his congregation and class meetings were composed largely of craftsmen and labourers, including some of his own farm workers. In the chapel he believed in equality in the sight of God, and democratic participation in the conduct of affairs. The repentance of every sinner, no matter what his rank, was a matter for rejoicing in the saving of another soul. But on the farm his labourers were still his 'hands'. The co-operation he expected from them was on his terms - gratitude and loyalty and hard work in return for generous treatment - and he was proud of paying above the average rate of wage for his district in 1872. He was genuinely concerned about them when they were sick (as well as when they sinned), but in common with other farmers, he was 'maister', and they were 'his' men. If they were 'confined' men, hired annually, they had some security, and additions to their wage in 'kind'. If they were day labourers their wage was fixed for the particular work they were required to do, and they were paid only for days worked. Although he gave his regular, local day workers odd jobs to do in the winter months when he could, the system meant that they had least work when they needed their wage the most.

As a member of the Louth Union Board of Guardians, he was faced directly with the problem of pauperism, and was concerned by its consequences for individual men and their families, but he did not express, in his journals at least, equal concern that farmers like himself were contributing to the problem by their hiring and dismissing of men at their convenience and according to the seasonal nature of farm work. When the farm workers in Lincolnshire joined the new agricultural workers' union in the district in 1871 and 1872, and combined to agitate for an improved standardised wage, Cornelius felt 'grief and consternation' that some of his own men were involved.

In spite of his own desire for more consideration by his landlord, and more independence from him, he was not yet ready to accept that a similar spirit was arising among his labourers towards him, now that they were gaining strength through a new solidarity with their fellows. The intervention of outside interests in the dispute, the new overt separation of interests between himself and men whom he had known for years, both distressed and confused him. It led him first to indecisive action when two of his labourers confronted him in his farmyard to ask for higher pay, and he first refused and then gave way to their demands.[35] But in 1874, he associated with other farmers in a confrontation with their workers in which they answered strike action with a lockout which embittered relationships over a long period.[36] He was trapped within a hierarchical structure which he could not approve in his heart, but from which he felt he could not extricate himself, and in his journals he criticised all classes - landlords, tenant farmers and labourers - for their increasing desire to further their own interests rather than co-operate in a common creative enterprise. It was not until he moved from the wolds to the marsh village of Hogsthorpe in 1892 that he found a community of small farmers, village craftsmen and labourers where there was less distinction of rank, and which was less at variance with the beliefs and practices of his chapel fraternity:

> I descended the hills and tracked the flat marsh. I felt a great difference between the wold and marsh people. There is not so much distinction between classes. They run together in a kind of social blend. We hear more at Binbrook about class and mass.[37]

As Binbrook had no resident squire and the absentee landlords took little part in the parish, the leading inhabitants were the tenants of the larger farms and a small professional group led by the parson, the Rev. John Thomas Huntley, a county magistrate, who himself owned an estate of nearly 350 acres, and included two doctors and a solicitor. The neighbourhood was a Tory stronghold[38] and the other tenant farmers and local gentry differed from Cornelius in their interests as in their politics, and he had few social contacts with them. He found the half-yearly rent dinners given by his landlord's agent for the four tenants on the Dennison estate a trying experience, and he was obviously considered the odd man out. The conversation was chiefly concerned with 'shooting, hunting, horses, game, landlords...racing, and other incidental topics'. He felt 'reserved', was seldom invited to give his opinion, and resignedly commented, 'I suppose politics are designedly excluded, and arguments of a controvertial character'.[39] Because in some ways he was, and felt, an outsider among his own class he was perhaps the more honoured to be elected as a member of the Louth Union Board of Guardians in 1871, and wrote to his landlord with some pride:

> I am appointed guardian in his [Mr. Iles - a retired farmer who had left the district] place, so that you will perceive I am not without honour in my own country. I hope to be humbly thankful for the confidence of my neighbours.[40]

He had been Overseer of the Poor within Binbrook parish for many years[41] but his new position was proof of wider acceptability and respect in spite of his nonconformist views. He took his responsibilities seriously, although at first he found the board business 'singularly distasteful to me for some time, and singularly novel'. He wondered whether he would have health and vigour enough of mind and memory to occupy a position of general influence in the board, the power to comprehend 'the details of law and apply them with justness to each case as it arises'.[42] After a year's experience, he became highly critical of the membership and the way business was conducted on the board. He seems to have confined his own activities to following up cases in his district, some of which he detailed in the journals. His experience on the board, however, led him to think seriously about the problem of pauperism, and he contemplated writing a paper on it. Unfortunately, if he did it no longer exists. It would have been interesting to read his more connected thoughts on the problem.[43]

Except for his membership of the Board of Guardians and of the parish vestry, his time away from the farm was largely spent in furthering the cause of Free Methodism both locally and nationally. Occasionally, as circuit representative, he went on journeys by 'steam coach' to conferences at Manchester, Rochdale or London. Most of his year, however, was spent in fulfilling a crowded programme of services and missions, anniversary teas, the opening of new village chapels, circuit meetings in Louth, Grimsby and Market Rasen - all of which involved him in a continual round of visits on foot or horseback, or in his dog cart or gig. He enjoyed the slow pace of his local travels and, when he was not reading as he walked or rode, looked around him with his usual enthusiastic response both to the beauty of the landscape and the promise of the farming seasons. He played a leading role in the evangelistic work of the circuits, always welcoming the 'absence of clericals' from platform and pulpit. He entered fully into social occasions for the converted, and described them in detail and with relish in his journals. Mission services had a more serious purpose, and genial tea-party pleasantries were exchanged for strongly worded exhortations to repentance: 'I had a powerful time at night.

There were three unconverted sinners much affected, but would not yield. The congregation was very thin, but the Divine glory was manifest.'[44]

His wife was less than enthusiastic at the fervency of his outpouring when 'filled with the Spirit', and on occasion wounded him 'with the cold knife of criticism', when he was particularly demonstrative.[45] In emotional appeal his sermons were no doubt similar to many given by his fellow preachers, as was his emphasis on conveying strict 'gospel truth' to his listeners. One of his strongest criticisms of the 'Church of Rome' was that the priests interpreted rather than revealed the word of God. The use he made of his extensive reading to illustrate his texts set him apart from other local preachers, and also from some of the circuit ministers, of whose sermons he was often genially critical. Excursions into the history of Dissent, the contribution of the great Puritan Divines, the theological doctrine of rewards and punishments, the advance of the new ritualism within the Church which was so abhorrent to him - these may at times have baffled his rural congregations; but his sermons could rarely have been considered 'dull and pedestrian', a criticism he levelled at one local minister.

Although his primary allegiance was to the Free Methodist church, he was proud of being within a wider tradition of Dissent, with its insistence on the complete separation of religion from state control and civil legislation. There had been some alleviation of the disabilities from which nonconformists still suffered, during his lifetime. When he was 24 years old, matriculation was freed from religious tests at Oxford University; when he was 41 years old, religious tests for university teachers and officials were abolished. But when he visited Oxford in 1870 and 1871 and discussed with his friend, Mr. Bond, the Methodist minister in Oxford, the reception of nonconformists in the university, he found it 'chilly and unwelcome'. A number of comments in the journals show how deeply he deplored the use of national resources for a state-endowed church which represented barely half of the population of the country, and he strongly resented the fact that 'the splendid patronage of Royalty' was lavished on one sect.[46] After initially welcoming the Education Act of 1870, his reactions to it gradually became more hostile as he realised its implications in placing 'a new seal upon church and state', and 'throwing the youth of the counties into the hands of the clergy'.[47] To counteract the influence of the teaching of the Church of England doctrine in the National School at Binbrook, he helped to found and manage a Free Methodist Day School, although this was short-lived.[48]

In the last decade of the century, a bitter personal experience convinced him that the passing of legislation to remedy specific disabilities was having little effect on attitudes within the clergy. The Burial Act of 1880 allowed the burial of nonconformists within churchyards by their own ministers, but, in 1893, at the funeral of Francis Riggall of Dexthorpe (Cornelius's loved and respected father-in-law), the local clergyman refused the invitation to attend the burial service, and when the family party passed the church door they heard the door close and 'the click of the key in the lock'.[49] Cornelius's real admiration for the scholarship and eloquence displayed by the higher clergy, whose sermons he heard and read 'with intense pleasure and rich profit never to be erased from the memory', was always checked by their refusal to admit the 'gigantic accomplishments of Nonconformity'. He maintained: 'they are guilty of throwing stones who live in glass houses. They claim a right to discuss political questions which they charge upon us as a crime!'[50]

His concern with social and political affairs went beyond that of many of his Methodist friends, and he found the periodicals published and supported by the Congregational Church - 'The Congregationalist', 'The Independent' and 'The Expositor' - more to his taste than the more narrowly religious 'Methodist Recorder'.[51] He was critical of ministerial or lay colleagues who felt that religion should not concern itself with politics and wider issues, and believed that all Christians should be democratically involved in fighting injustice in all its forms. But his recognition that democracy needed men with the will to use 'intelligence, ecclesiastical industry, wisdom and self-control' always brought him back to the belief that was central to his life and thought, 'God's universal law of co-operation, human divine... Man receives in proportion to his own exertions.' In politics, as in agriculture, man must utilise the dormant moral and intellectual energy which had been buried in the depths of man's nature for 'a Fatherly purpose'.

This interpretation of a Divine will which encouraged man's creativity and made possible his 'moral evolution'[52] allowed him to approve wholeheartedly of those scientists whose discoveries helped to unravel the mysteries of the natural world, and of those archaeologists who were uncovering the history of early civilisations. He criticised Oxford University for its backwardness in the sciences,[53] and considered the education of his children incomplete without knowledge of them. He was enthusiastic about developments in the applied sciences which contributed to the improvements in agriculture and progress in industry during his lifetime. But, like so many of his contemporaries, he was unable to follow 'these men of science' when their questioning began to involve not only the earth and the heavens, but the origin of man himself. Darwin's theories could not be reconciled with the Bible truth as he conceived and experienced it.

The aim of the new science was to 'bow God out of His Universe' and enthrone 'a blank and black law' in His place.[54] The belief that Cornelius had in God as a person was unqualified. He was a physical presence who walked the fields with him, ordered the sun and the rain, and guided him in every aspect of his daily life. His interpretation of God's design in uncovering the secrets of the universe through man might perhaps have led him to settle for the evolution of man from earlier forms of creation had it not been for the story of Genesis, which remained for him scriptural truth of a personal act by a personal God. His conflict of mind over the whole question is plainly revealed in his journals written in the 1870s, when the heat of the controversy over Darwin's work, and Huxley's clarification of the conclusions to be drawn from it, was at its height:

> These men of science are taking leave of their rational powers when applying them to questions of theology. Are mechanical instruments available for theological investigation? Are Divine truths to be tested by observation and experiment? Is it in the minds and purposes of men of science to bow God out of His Universe. Shall He be deprived of his personality...[55]

In a later journal, written in 1893, when the furor had died down, Cornelius came to honour the 'sublime discovery of Charles Darwin', putting him on a level with Newton, Harvey and Galileo.[56] By then, he would most probably have read 'The Origin of the Species' itself, rather than relying on press reports and the denunciations of Bishop Samuel Wilberforce. It had even been given as a prize by Alford Grammar School to his third son, Frank, in 1888. It is quite clear from other journal entries in 1891, that the story of Adam and Eve was not one of those 'dark sayings' in the Bible which he felt allowed for personal interpretation. He did not elaborate in these late writings on how far he was then prepared to go along with the 'new science', which had shaken but not broken the firm shell of his doctrine. As a largely self-educated man living in a remote part of north Lincolnshire, with limitations imposed on his intellectual development by his particular social and religious background, it is perhaps remarkable that he went to such lengths to explore some of the most difficult philosophical and scientific problems of his day, with the help only of books and articles that came to hand, and chance conversations with the few men he met who had similar interests and concerns.

As he stood in Oxford in 1870 and looked up at the college buildings, he wondered what he could have made of that University's 'unexampled facilities', had he been 'an industrious and persevering student'.[57] Instead, he lived his life as a 'wildly eccentric agriculturist' - and his farming friends and neighbours would have agreed with the self-description. His plans and purposes, he commented, were often more 'dazling' than their fulfilment. But the engaging personal view he has left of himself, his life and his time is a valuable gift to posterity and, a century later, surely fulfils the aim that he tentatively expressed in the early pages of his journals, that his record might not only be of use to him but also might 'assume importance in other eyes'.

Jean Stovin

NOTES

1 He was a manager of Binbrook Free Methodist Day School for the few years that it existed during the 1870s.
2 See Postscript concerning the journals written after 1875, p. 228.
3 First Journal, February 1872.
4 Last Journals, January 3rd, 1893.
5 His own spelling has been left in the text and on occasion the more usual spelling inserted in brackets after the word altered. Punctuation has only been altered where this adds to the clarity of the meaning.
6 See Appendix III.
7 Memorial Address by the Rev. J. Mitchell, January 3rd, 1921.
8 'His visits to his native county were frequent. All classes were impressed by his ministry. Two of his staunchest adherents, Mr. Stovin and Mr. Brackenbury, who saved him from the mob at Crowle and Horncastle, were Justices of the Peace' (Charles Bears, 'Lincolnshire in the 17th and 18th centuries', 1940).
9 Information from Miss Christina Hay, Cleethorpes.
10 Wesleyan Methodist Records, Lincoln Archives Office.
11 First Journal, February 29th, 1872.
12 Second Journal, February 20th, 1875.
13 First Journal, see note 166.
14 Second Journal, p. 165.
15 First Journal, November 3rd, 1871.
16 First Journal, August 8th, 1872.
17 First Journal, August 12th, 1872.
18 Second Journal, December 17th, 1874.
19 Second Journal, November 14th, 1874.
20 First Journal, November 7th, 1872.
21 Second Journal, February 17th, 1875.
22 First Journal, November 16th, 1872.
23 See his description of one of them, First Journal, November 8th, 1872.
24 Second Journal, March 12th, 1875.
25 Second Journal, September 7th, 1874.
26 Second Journal, January 12th, 1875.
27 Second Journal, February 11th, 1875.
28 See Appendix VI.
29 See Appendix IV.
30 J. M. Stratton, 'Agricultural Records', Appendix VII, John Baker (1969).
31 Second Journal, November 27th, 1874.
32 First Journal, September 7th, 1871, and Second Journal, January 23rd, 1875.
33 See Appendix IV.
34 Second Journal, September 9th, 1874.
35 First Journal, February 14th, 1872.
36 Rex Russell, 'The Revolt of the Field in Lincolnshire', 1957, p. 54.

37 Last Journals, May 6th, 1893.
38 R. J. Olney, 'Binbrook in the mid-nineteenth century', Occasional papers in Lincolnshire History and Archaeology.
39 Second Journal, January 6th, 1875.
40 Letter to landlord, August 16th, 1871.
41 Binbrook Vestry Minutes, Lincoln Archives Office.
42 First Journal, February 8th, 1872.
43 First Journal, November 2nd, 1871.
44 Second Journal, November 16th, 1874.
45 'He will long be remembered as a preacher and an evangelist. His apt and quaint remarks kept his audiences alive as he proceeded from end to end of the puplit in exuberant enthusiasm' (Memorial Address).
46 First Journal, March 2nd, 1872.
47 First Journal, December 22nd, 1871.
48 Second Journal, December 6th, 1874.
49 Last Journals, August 25th, 1893.
50 First Journal, November 30th, 1871.
51 First Journal, November 8th, 1872.
52 First Journal, February 28th, 1872.
53 Oxford Journal, 1870.
54 First Journal, November 8th, 1872.
55 First Journal, November 8th, 1872.
56 Last Journals, May 6th, 1893.
57 Oxford Journal, August 6th, 1870.

FIRST JOURNAL

BINBROOK HALL FARM

August 7th, 1871 to December 19th, 1872

THURSDAY, AUGUST 17TH, 1871

Last night and this morning we have had much lightening and many loud peals of thunder with teeming showers. Upon the whole my farm looks remarkably well. The wheat straw a little rusty, the barley and oats appear to be doing fairly. The turnips are richly promising. On Tuesday last I rode the mare I bought of Frank.[1] She was purchased by Frenchmen for Paris. I think it was not a very empty day's work. Rose before four o'clock, rode the mare to Horncastle and back with my brother to Sotby[2] for tea, then walked home. In the meantime read Punchion's lecture on Bunyan.[3] My mind must have been variously exercised. My richest sentiments were deeply stirred by the variously undulated and tinted landscapes ever opening out before me as the day dawned and brightened and the teeming suggestions arising from the life of Bunyan.

FRIDAY, AUGUST 18TH, 1871

We had thought of commencing harvest today but I fancy these thunderstorms will throw us off this week. The other day I bought of Mr. Barton of Louth 50 qr. of oats at 26/- 12st. per sack. This is somewhat of an eventful year in my farming career. The year 1871 marks the era of the double plough on the farm.[4] In availing myself of it I have been able to dispense with the third waggoner, also with two draught horses. The waggoner looks after six and the second four. The keep of two horses will make a considerable difference to my oatsack. I have been able so far to keep the work well in advance. Between forty and fifty acres are already ploughed for wheat. We have put down Hornsby's old horse works at the barn door to turn the chaff-cutter and mill. There is a continual modification of our implements of husbandry taking place and if we do not keep a vigilant eye towards all real developments and improvements we shall not be able to keep up with the times. We must look out for every aid which these skillful [skilful] and enterprising times present to us. Hornsby is said to have a plough now in construction whose execution is to astonish the world. Who can count the untold wealth the plough has turned up. A large amount of inventive faculty is being brought to bear upon it and grand and important results are already accruing.

However imperfect my farm may be, and it has many imperfections, it has one remarkably good quality. It is a good turnip farm.

It produces an abundance of winter feed. Perhaps there is scarcely another wold farm of larger production for twenty years past. When I look back for twenty years it leads me to think of the transformation the farm has undergone in my hands, the result with God's blessing of modern appliances skillfully used.

Charles Smith, who has succeeded Gilbert in the foremanship, appears to be a man of singular honesty and activity, cheerful, well-behaved, industrious, intelligent, uniformly well-constructed both physically and morally. As a servant he is well rounded in his physical, moral and spiritual qualities. He will not only work himself but has the courage to look after and remonstrate with others. He has attained large experience by the lapse of time and change of place and circumstance. He has exercised keen observation and wide induction amid the constant moving panorama of his business life; hence he has become master of his situation. I look upon him with gratitude as a gift of the good Providence of God. Their coming here is the result of much prayer and I have not the least doubt heaven's blessing will come to the farm through them. In addition to his own strong stalwart Christian principles there is his wife all ablaze with holy jealousy for her Divine master's cause. I believe them to be truly converted under my brother-in-law J. B. Atkinson of Grainthorpe Hall.[5] In strolling as a pedestrian from Sotby last Tuesday night I saw a light in the window of one of our tenements. I concluded it was Coney waiting, but on approaching discovered that it was Smith who with his wife were bowed at their family altar, and she was very loudly and earnestly praying and he responding. The clock had struck eleven when these delightful voices of devotion greeted my ear. I am deeply impressed with the guidance of God. I have seldom passed such a day of contrast in my own individual experience. The day has a heavenly winding up though at the Fair[6] I was brought in close contact with what was earthly, sensual and devilish. A larger amount of annoyance and distraction from without during the day than usual, while in the early morning and later eve my soul never seemed more high toned by flowing thoughts of Divine spirituality. My soul has great strength of wing for lofty contemplation.

I have sold eighty drape[7] ewes which went away on the 5th of August. This is quite exceptional on the farm. We have generally fed them until Christmas or Candlemas. The price was 50/- each. I have sometimes sold them fat for considerably less money.

I have today had abundant leisure for reading and writing. Disraeli's 'Lothair'[8] is now absorbing a good deal of interest. It is one of the few novels I have attempted to read for a lifetime. He has constructed Lothair's character like a reed shaken by the wind. We could scarcely conceive of a man of weaker calibre or of more aimless life. One vision, plan or purpose seemed to melt by the least conflicting influence. There is a large amount of material for deep reflection. The novel is a mirror in which we may read some ominous aspects of the times in which we live. The author has been unfair to Protestantism by presenting it in so weak and ignorant a light. He has unveiled the enchantment of Rome. What a masterpiece of ingenuity, talent, sense and prudence, deep subtlety, sagacious perseverance is this great system of iniquity named Roman Catholicism. It reveals the vacillating attitude of the English aristocracy towards the church of Rome. What a wily deep Jesuitically clever Romanist is the Cardinal. How he could gild over a lie with brilliant plausibility. How he could robe in rich splendour the dark and repulsive, and impart to it every variety of charm and bewitchment. How he could clothe her wrinkled and decayed form until her huge deformities were hid. He could exhaust every store of art's treasures with which to weight and adorn her. Why should Romanism have talent so lavished upon her while Protestantism continues so barren of ability?

SATURDAY, AUGUST 19TH, 1871

Mr. Elliot has been up this morning from the village and settled with me for marling[9] and new netts. He has taken £3 of me. I believe him to be a sound punctual tradesman. In taking a comprehensive view of my own farm it never looked better. With the exception of the Cadeby lane wheat, the 12 and 15 acre, which has its back to the sun, the crops look promising. The clovers young and old have flourished more this summer than ever I have known them. How cheerful and gay they have looked with blossom. The cereals are richly exuberant. I am afraid our gardens are struck with the potato blight. We have had a moderate crop of gooseberries and currants but the orchards show signs of a very meagre plucking season. Apples and plums, owing to a cold and backward spring, are few and small. Ours has never distinguished itself in fruit-bearing.

The stock-dove has built its nest in the leafy shades of the brown beach, undisturbed by our merry little family group. It is not fluttered by the sound of croquet mallet rising from the lawn or from noisy conflicts and contentions or exclamations of triumph or whining disappointment in failure and defeat. These vocal ebullitions of pleasure and regret though rather loud and confused do not ruffle one feather in that peaceful brood. The dove clings to its nest in spite of the gardener's footstep or rake or hedge-slasher or peering eyes of the children. It is little conscious of Denison's[10] destructive designs when he multiplies his persuasions to be allowed to reach Papa his gun and cartridge. I only bought or exchanged my oldfashioned muzzle-loaders for a breechloader this year. Dodson professed to charge £7-10s. and take off 50/- for the old one so I had to part with a five pound note. I have refrained shooting the feathered notable as it creates a topic for juvenile dialogue. There is a little poetic interest mingled with our family life.

TUESDAY, AUGUST 22ND, 1871

This has been a fine harvest day. My oat crop is cutting up magnificently. It waves all golden in the breeze and falls prostrate before the march of the reaper. The ring and rattle and bustle of the reaper is a joy to the husbandman. When it makes a great bustle there is an abundant crop. Yesterday it cut its way through the old 9 acre now 12 acre running up to the Skallows plantation and bounded on the further side by the Swinope brat's lane. Today a large opening is made in the 30 acre oats. It seems fortunate that these fields being previously seeds for grazing are oats instead of late sown wheat as the wheat crop is not likely at present to yield largely. Oats are not an average crop on the strong land. We have had a sharp shower rather suddenly this evening about dusk. Where can we find a more beautiful display of Divine power and wisdom than a field of ripening corn; its germination, growth and maturity has formed part of the vast dominions of Jehovah. What marvelous adjustments of the miriad atoms of which a cornfield is composed. Where is there a more manifest embodiment of the design argument which modern science after turning away from it has again come back and repeated its acknowledgements of its truth and force. Every cornfield is pregnant with Divine plan, purpose and governmental power. How easy and natural is the inference we draw from finite power and wisdom to infinite. The government of the varied activities of a landscape is practically infinite. They are beyond the calculation of human thought or appreciation.

My reading has today been confined to Punchion's Bunyan and the 'Daily News'.[11]

WEDNESDAY, AUGUST 23RD, 1871

This is a fine breezy morn though the sky is cloudy and dull and somewhat threatening for rain. It is about a quarter after 5 o' clock and in looking into the back yard the waggoners are on the preparatory stir in gearing their horses for harvest operations. What a pleasure to behold them so earnestly absorbed in cutting and binding and rearing them up in little pyramids. Is it not a picturesque scene for the painter or the poet? When does nature appear so golden as when our harvestfields glisten in the yellow and warm sunshine and wave after wave all lustrous follow each other in rapid succession. All nature partakes the character of Autumnal mellowness. There is a sweet mellowness in the air and sunshine which regales the senses and delights the poetic sensibilities. The excitements and impressions of a God-loving spirit are truly Paradisaical. The sublimity and beauty becomes so excessive as to awake the most sublime feelings of reverant wonder and astonishment.

This is the third season we have used Hornsby's reaper. It is not nearly so cumbrous as Burgess and Keys. Hornsby's is more simple in construction and easily managed. It requires 3 horses to work it effectually. It will cut about 20 acres on good long days.

Development is the order of the day amongst my implements of husbandry. Grant has considerably enlarged my corndrill this summer. It is now about 8½ feet in width. He has also repaired the turnip cutter. Though this year may be one of considerable expense in the total, it is one of retrenchment in horses and labour. I have just paid George Smith for a new drag, £10 and 10/- off discount. It has four bulls after the pattern devised by Mr. Croft Sharpley of Acthorpe[12] who has lately gone to his long home.

The morning had brightened about breakfast time but has quickly overcast with a drizling shower. The turnips are revelling luxuriantly in the balmy season of sunshine and shower. We have three acres grubbed in the Binbrook field but fortunately early enough to be planted with cabbage. They are pricking up very nicely.

I have made large use of the two-horse scarifier this year. Most of the turnips have been cleaned twice over with it. The ploughing and other work has been much facilitated by it. The sainfoin stacks are finished thatching and the lane hedges trimmed through the south and west side of the farm.

Today I have met with a most brilliant article in the 'Standard'[13] upon the formation of an Italian Association for the purpose of excavation. The King and government of Italy have taken complete possession of Rome as its capital. The spirit of historical enterprize has taken hold upon the people in consequence of this fact. Many obstructions have been broken down and many facilities created for the disentombment of the Romes of past ages. The stately palaces and splendid villas of the days of Constantine have sunk beneath the dust and rubble of centuries.

THURSDAY, AUGUST 24TH, 1871

I felt strongly tempted to cut out the article referred to last evening. It suggests so much in relation to the entrance of freedom into Rome. The clouds of Romish legend is necessitated to give place to the pure light of historical fact. Three thousand years of buried history is destined to be dragged to light. Vast masses of monumental evidence now hid beneath the city and in the bed of the Roman river are about to be uncovered. The enthusiasm of the historical student is already rekindling in the unfolding of the plan of search. It would be impossible for the most vivid imagination to paint the gigantic results which will accrue from the investigation. When the Tiber has disgorged her treasures a perfect museum of Roman antiquities will be presented to the nations of the earth. It is a work worthy of the world's loftiest genius. Some of the best mechanical skills should be concentred here. It will mould and brighten and render more legible the page of history. Poor old moth-eaten Rome (for what are Jesuit priests but moths created by the grub of superstition?) is already receiving the washing of political regeneration. Rome is now being infused with national life. And who shall be branded with enthusiast for predicting that Rome under the quickening influence of Bible truth will before half a century has elapsed undergo an architectural renovation? Past generations will be made to live again. Personality will assume a bolder shape. Where do the rays of historical light converge? It is a sublime arrangement of Divine Providence that history shall form part of the world's education.

SATURDAY, AUGUST 26TH, 1871

Yesterday I went by train to Alford for Dexthorpe[14] and Partney Fair. Beast and sheep made extravigant prices. Will was over from Birstall to buy a fresh horse. Mealey turned lame. Trade is very good with them at present. He is fast repairing his losses though he is scarcely so well off as when he commenced. Ma[15] is talking of taking them a house and forming them an establishment of about £200 per annum. It appears that John and he [Will][16] are not very comfortable at present. This morning I wandered through the corn. I feel more jealous of my wheat crop. I am afraid there are a great many thin and blasted ears. The reaper has been tolerably successful this week considering one very wet day.

On Thursday it poured with rain while myself and family were on the journey to Grainthorpe. We had a very comfortable day. Young Henry[17] is very bookish and appears rather ambitious to become a preacher but he has too much impediment in his speech which he must strive to correct before he can excel in that department of labour.

MONDAY, AUGUST 28TH, 1871

Last Wednesday I sold my locks at 16/6 per stone to Mr. Pinning of Louth. I have a four years stock. It must be a very good speculation on a small scale. The last two years wool has been extremely low. This morning the reaper is considerably in advance of the tyers. God is very good in sending us such seasonable weather. Yesterday was a very peaceful happy day. Mrs. Skelton came to class[18] in the morning and expressed herself as very full of selfupbraidings for her long absence and for her departure from God in the meantime. Oh! what a difficult matter it seems to keep the soul alive. Mr. G. Taylor preached afternoon and evening. In the evening the text was 'Oh that I had wings like a dove then would I fly away and be at rest'. He spoke of David wishing to fly away from the worry of life and from the sufferings of life. But he said it was not right to wish to fly away from the storm cloud. All sunshine was not good for our fields neither was it good for men nor society.

My wife's health[19] is still very unsatisfactory. Her physical frame is much out of order. Her nervous system is made up of jarring elements. What a life of unbroken suffering scarcely passing a day free from pain. Very few murmurs escape her lips.

Such weakness and loving meekness is rarely combined. Elasticity and nobleness of spirit in consequence of her being linked with the Eternal raises her to moral eminence astonishing to behold. What discriminating guardian care she exercises over her family and household. Her anxiety becomes excessive in case the children are afflicted. Her penetrating insight into character is most marvellous. Her skill in the management of domestic affairs and of servants is exquisite. She can combine economy and comfort to an almost unparalelled degree. She mingles firmness with wisdom and love in the government of her children. Her love of tydiness and order is a strongly marked feature in her character. Her strength of resolution in carrying out a scheme once formed is equally manifest. 'Never fail' is inscribed upon her banner. Her adherence to truth and right is most unswerving and unhesitating. There is not to be found the slightest particle of vacillation in her conduct. Her reverence for God and things sacred is unbounded. Her love of the beautiful is refined and deep. Her domestic affections are tender and luxuriant. In society she professes all the elements of a true lady. Amongst the poor no haughtiness is shown but kindness and generosity. Amongst her friends unlimited hospitality. In the church no bitter prejudices or bigoted exclusiveness. The happiness of her home, neighbourhood and world at large is the main object of her life. She lives to bless mankind and she diffuses blessings wherever she goes. Where shall we find the elements of a true christian character if not here.

TUESDAY, AUGUST 29TH, 1871

Today Mr. and Mrs. Riggall on their return from Hackthorne[20] dined with us. Yesterday they attended the funeral of Frank's second baby, 10 weeks' old. The weather is glorious. The fields are all white for the harvest and all-inviting to the reaper. D.V. we intend running two tomorrow. We have about 100 acres left uncut and we hope to have it all down before the week expires. The ladies have been very busy unpacking the London groceries. Mrs. Riggall has taken about three pounds worth. I have enjoyed a great luxury in reading Macauley as portrayed in Mr. Punshion's Lectures. He sets before the reader Macauley's feats of genius in a powerful and striking light.

WEDNESDAY, AUGUST 30TH, 1871

Left bed this morning about 4 o'clock and with breach-loader under arm walked round the farm. I beheld the first stirrings of industry, the first glowings of the eastern sky. Which ever way the eye turned horizontally or perpendicularly there was enough to kindle the devoutest inspiration. The surroundings were one complete display of Divine goodness. An intelligent and loving survey was enough to enlarge and strengthen one's religious convictions. It seemed to rush into my soul like the blast into the furnace. My sensations, reflections, sentiments, were blended and transformed into rapturous praise. My wife has entered the room rather excited concerning the state of her health. The flesh under the lower eyelid of her right eye has assumed a puffy appearance. It is evidently a source of considerable anxiety. It is attended with a sense of numbness which proceeds down the cheek. Her enquiry is curiously directed to know what is really the matter. What can it be the harbinger of? Is any physical significance to be attached? Is it the precurser of any malignant form of disease?

MONDAY, SEPTEMBER 4TH, 1871

Yesterday Mr. G. Taylor supplied for Mr. Crombie,[21] he being away for his holidays. The sermons were not at all equal to the productions he gave us last Sabbath. He does not appear to possess a very extensive mine of material. When he has pumped for one Sabbath the well is dry. On Saturday last we commenced carrying wheat. One stack rose in the yard in splendid condition. This morning harvest work is at a stand on account of wet. Yesterday I read a paper in 'Good Words' on our Lord's Temptation, by the Editor, Norman Maclead, and another on the religious aspects of the late war.[22] They both set forth in a strong light God's hand in history. They unfold in a most interesting manner the Divine mind in relation to human history. Oh that the world would apply their inductive philosophy to things sacred and Divine! Look at the development of historical testimony. Is it not a development of the Divine purposes? Think of the historical researches of the present century and of the historical library which has been created. What is the press of today but a vast historical mirror? Our daily, weekly, monthly and quarterly periodicals each reflect the times. They form one vast chronicle. Has the world's history ever had so much literary labour bestowed upon it? As education advances, historical jottings multiply. Under all our variations in party interpretations of the events of history there lies the substratum of facts. There are thousands of pens engaged in recording our national history. Our broad sheets contain a complete National diary of the thoughts, feelings, opinions and doings of all our most eminent men in every department of science, art, literature, industry, and of every class of men with their multitudiness institutions and organisations, civil, military and religious. It is the diary of nature. Biographies and autobiographies of our eminent artists, statesmen, etc. are they not written in the chronicles of the Kings of England? In the government of God has there been no growth in Divine designs in relation to the press? What is the press of the world teeming with today? Brethren,[23] it is historical evidence and that evidence is an increasing witness to Divine revelation. You have here at Louth a little temple of literature[24] fairly respectable in its appearence when compared with its facings and the street generally, but the beauty and brilliancy of mental and imaginative arts renders it one of the most fascinating luxuries of the town and its suburbs.

Devout minds have always looked upon the art of printing as a special Providence. That may be legitimately called a special Providence which has so specially manifested the beneficence of Jehovah.

Last Wednesday my Lizzie bought a number of tracts[25] and yesterday they were distributed through the household. Some tiny books with paper covers were drawn from the packet and read to Mabel and Denison. This morning Lizzie and Denison have gone to the village on an errand of charity.

TUESDAY, SEPTEMBER 5TH, 1871

Last night we had a pouring rain but this morning the contrast is truly resplendant! The flowing grandeur is dazzling in the extreme. Glory be to God who above worketh such marvels. We were only permitted to lead yesterday for a few hours on account of wet. Read a beautiful article in the 'Daily News' commemorating the fall of the Napoleanic dynasty. The 2nd of September, 1870 forms the greatest epoch in contemporaneous history. The historical event of that day towers conspicuously over the vast plane of history. This was the climax of the great European war. It marks the transfer of European control into other hands. The great military firebrand of Europe was extinguished on that ever memorable day. One of the most pestilential despotisms was smitten with death on that day. The previous victories were only preparatory, and opened the way for this. It is the heaviest blow given to European despotism since Waterloo. The martial spirit may be contrary to the spirit of the Gospel (and the rekindling of that spirit in this nation may be one of the evils attendant upon the late war). Still, it is a paralell with the evils of oppression. It does not appear that the world can be delivered from oppressions and thraldoms except by a baptism of blood. The thunder and lightening of artillery seem necessary to startle the world out of its slumbers that its chains of tyranny may be snapped asunder. Have not the liberties of the nations been secured by the sword and the spear and the cannon? Has not Protestantism the world's sceptre in her benignant and powerful hands? Has she not revived the nationalities of the earth?

WEDNESDAY, SEPTEMBER 6TH, 1871

In opening the broad sheet for Monday last, I was very pleasingly surprised to see a speech by our distinguished Premier, Mr. Gladstone. He is the first statesman to break the silence of our Autumnal recess. It is a manly and noble oration in vindication of the multiplied labour of the passed session. He very truthfully defends it against barrenness. Any one of the leading measures passed is enough to confer honour upon it. What a spirit of classic refinement and geniality runs through the speech. What mildness of centure [censure] is pronounced upon his antagonists. What manly courage to dare the ire of the wealthy classes or club classes or any of local interests. He fixes his eye upon the broader interest of the nation at large. Then again how pregnant are his admonitions respecting what he has coined a word to express, viz. alarmisned. His strength of judgment and firmness of resolution are well matched and happily blended. He is the modern Ajax[26] as pictured in 'Punch' a short time past. The distinction he has drawn between the criticism of the metropolitan and the provincial press and the explanation of it is most interesting and instructive. How tactfully he has sheltered himself and his government under the wing of the Parliamentary majority and shielded the Parliamentary majority by the majority of the nation whose chosen representatives they are.

THURSDAY, SEPTEMBER 7TH, 1871

Hands are so scarce[27] that we have made very slow progress with harvest operations. I have still sixty acres of barley down unbound. It is in a very critical condition. The early part of yesterday was very bright and breezy and by noon they had finished binding the wheat. By the time the barley was fairly dry the clouds had gathered and the rain began to fall. I am afraid a second drenching such as continued through the night will spoil the sample. The prospect is a very anxious and dark one. The extreme luxuriance of the clover may possibly prove fatal to the corn. We need a drying apparatus this morning to save our barley crop from deterioration if not destruction. Perhaps the Almighty may send us one. He has abundance in His stores. He can change the winds and disperse the clouds and dry up the moisture as well as send it. How delightfully welcome the streaks of blue sky which I beheld this morning in looking out from my bedroom window. The barley was no sooner dry than it became saturated a second time. Would it be presumption if I urge my case before the Lord? May I spread out my fields with their exposed treasures before Him who has all natural forces at His command? Some objectors might say it is presumption inasmuch as God's purpose is clearly indicated. The anxieties of men must be aroused to quicken their inventive powers and awaken them to self-reliance and industry. God throws men's treasures into elemental jeopardy, and fills them with consternation and alarm to add momentum to the spirit of progress and discovery. Dangers and insecurities have a thousand times over broken men's indolent slumbers and saved them from stagnation. There may in the course of the world's history be a bunch of keys found to unlock what are now regarded as the profoundest mysteries of the Divine government. As man's conquests extend over the wide domains of nature, floods and droughts may become to man's mind the clearest proofs of the Divine beneficence, the brightest manifestation of His goodness as disciplinary and educational instead of discordantly conflicting with that golden aspect of His character.

SATURDAY, SEPTEMBER 9TH, 1871

Rose this morning about 5 o'clock. I thought I heard the pattering of the rain upon my garden groves. In drawing aside the blind to my utter dismay the water was standing in a pool on the carriage drive, which indicated a heavy fall of rain for several hours. This is the third drenching for my barley. It is a mercy that it had become tolerably dry yesterday, for under the hedgerows it has already begun to sprout. This is a morning of disappointment to us farmers. Yesterday we were vigorously retrieving matters, carrying in the morning and tying in the afternoon, and the foreman and I were planning for managing most of the binding today. But all our schemes are upset by Divine Providence for some wise end. Perhaps to drive us to prayer to more humble dependence upon His Almighty power and wisdom and love. He makes us behold His severity as well as goodness. How dark and gloomy the prospect! How thick and hazy the air! How leaden the skies! Yesterday I was pulling ketlocks out of the turnips, also neadles, redrobbin and scarlet poppies. It is a proverb that weeds grow apace. Experience brings home the truth. There is not a weed now growing in my turnip fields but will come to maturity and yield its thousandfold increase many months before the turnip itself. It forms part of the curse still lingering in the ground. What a tenacious hold they have upon our soil. If we cease our vigilance they soon became predominant. A skillful and persevering hand is required to maintain empire over this department of natural laws and forces. The vegetation most valuable to us is the moist and delicate barley in its growth, while that which is most injurious is defiant in its hardiness and rampant in its march to maturity. Neither flood nor drought can jeopardise its produce. Even though torn up by the roots and cast out a thousand times over, phenix-like it obtains a resurrection from its own ashes. What a tyranny has been exercised over man by the thistle as the representative of the weed world, and how gloriously has the tyranny been broken by skillful industry. It has been expelled from the soil of England and Scotland and perhaps to a larger extent than any other country in the world, though our own agriculture is anything but complete in weed expulsion. The great contest which constitutes one portion of the battle of the farmer's life is with the organised and vital rubbish.

Though the morning is dark and the corn soaking and swelling to the very verge of germination, the turnip, cabbage and pastures are receiving an almost unprecedented impetus in expansion of leaves and enlargement of bulbs. Though the children cannot go out they have enlivened the dwelling with there precious gambols. Though my dear wife is confined to her bed she experiences somewhat of alleviation of her past sufferings, and enjoys the comforts of domestic kindness to sooth and cheer. We must be eclectic in our contemplation of human life. We must not magnify the evils until we are blinded to the mercies and favours.

MONDAY, SEPTEMBER 10TH, 1871

Rose soon after the clock struck 4 and satisfied my curiosity about the state of the weather and the corn. The morning appears fine and though the smoke from the shepherd's cottage fell to the ground, the swallows were soaring a great height above the buildings and trees.[28] They appear unusually lofty in their aspirations. I hear the rumbling and rapping sounds of waggons off to the fields. It is very cheering to find what God has done on the Sabbath for our corn shocks. Last night I preached from Psalm 76 v. 3. 'There break he the bow etc.' The great battles which Christ fought and won. The wilderness was one field of battle. Calvary another. The tomb another. The sinner's heart another.

During last week the weather has been very unsettled and harvest work considerably interrupted. There are thousands of acres of corn still uncut in the country. Yesterday there was a famous drying wind the whole day. The wheat crop is pronounced deficient in yield, the barley splendid, the oats good. Many hundreds of acres must have shaken through scarcity of hands had it not been for machinery. What an incalculable blessing has the reaper proved this season. What an economy of labour and time. The hands have generally migrated from south to north as the corn ripened,[29] but this year the corn has suddenly and uniformly whitened for the sycle [sickle]. The winter held an exceptionally large portion of the year in his tenacious grasp, thus retarding the earlier counties, and when summer burst upon us it quickened the later counties and caused a simultaneous ripening throughout the country. After the extreme wet and cold there succeeded a series of sunny days of glowing heat charged with maturing power. Hence our dismay in witnessing such scarcity of hands and the present broken character of the weather. Thus the seasons, though fruitful, are a source of deep anxiety. Thank God for the bright morn and for the help which during the last day or two has turned up. I hope during this week to behold a general clearance of our fields. The farmer ought to be well up in meteorology. He is often counting up and balancing the weather signs.

TUESDAY, SEPTEMBER 11TH, 1871

Rose this morning about six o'clock, took an early breakfast and drove Augur to Louth for Miss Allcock, dressmaker. She is very defective in utterence and almost deaf. It is only very recently my wife became acquainted with [her] and by a singular coincidence in Bowman's shop. She is a very fine respectable-looking person of agreeable manners.

The barley tying has made rapid progress these two days. God sent us hands at the right time and for the most part favourable weather to enable us to nearly complete the work and also to carry home the last stook of wheat. One stack of oats is being topped up tonight. I have spent several quiet hours amongst my turnips. They still look very promising, though the Parsonage 20 acres is very filthy with neadles and redrobbin. My wife is but weak and poorly this week. She is contemplating paying a visit to London to see Mrs. Gray Lister. Annie[30] is staying there sometime. This reminds me of the pleasant visit Mr. and Mrs. Gray paid us last shooting season. Mrs. Gray is a fine noble-spirited woman, all intelligence and animation. What energy and force of character! What loving amiability! What conversational powers! She has both personal and social attractions. How cheery in her general deportment and quick and graceful in her manners. Her ample and pleasing activities are firmly held in conformity to Christian principles. Whatever kind of new impressions will our little Denison receive from the grand novelties of London?

This morning I spent about half-an-hour in the Louth newsroom and read an article in the 'Illustrated Times' upon hedgerows, the interesting and picturesque effect they impart to our landscapes, and the large amount of waste land they incur. I also hastily glanced at an article in the 'Cornhill' magazine[31] on the advantages of exhibitions in infusing the vying spirit or the spirit of competition among the nations of the earth. It appears that our position relatively to other countries is not so exalted at the more recent exhibitions as in that of 1851. There we stood conspicuous for our superior workmanship, but since that period the rate of improvement has been more rapid in other lands.

THURSDAY, SEPTEMBER 13TH, 1871

This has proved a really satisfactory harvest day. We commenced carrying barley from black pond field. The sheaves seemed almost to fly from the ground to the waggon and from the waggon to the stack. The air was cool, breezy and refreshing for the workmen. It is an interesting and even picturesque scene to witness the stacks rise with such rapidity. The amount of physical energy and activity played out has been very gratifying. The field was cleared by about 6 o'clock this evening and only began at 9 a.m. Our agricultural prospect has been gradually brightening the last day or two. The wet weather had locked us up and threatened to destroy the barley crop. Today it is finished binding, and two good sized stacks are built. Charles Smith is a respectable harvest architect. I am afraid it is considerably stained.

Mr. and Mrs. Riggall paid us a visit today. They always add to our store of information. Their companionship is both intelligent and affectionate, pleasurable and profitable. It would be impossible to find a more genial-spirited man in all Christendom than he. He thought I had made a good bargain in the beast I bought this morning, eight cost £11 each and the drape cow £16. He judged the cow to be worth at least £1 for buying, and he valued 4 of the others at £13 each. The cow is from George Rusby's and the others from Charles Fletcher's. They have come from the village this morning and are now in the pleasure ground. Yesterday and today I have read my new number of the 'Preacher's Lantern',[32] No. 4 of our 'Minister's breakfast'. It consists of a number of conversations or dialogues upon a variety of topics. The place of convocation is beautifully described. The growth of affection for nature and natural scenery. Does it not form a part of the true progress of society and of the Christian church?

Yesterday Denison and Mabel[33] accompanied me to Louth market. It dated the commencement of his business career in the town. I placed 4/6 in his hand for the purpose of shopping, which he accomplished remarkably well. He found by experience the practical use of the little arithmetic he had gained at school. He and his sister were launched off into trade for the first time without their parents at their heels. They manifested no trepidation or misgiving at the idea of becoming orphans for the time-being but were quite reconciled to the practice of self government. I think it strengthens the moral character of children to impose confidence in them.

SATURDAY, SEPTEMBER 15TH, 1871

Yesterday I bought 4 heifers of Gillot of Louth, one heifer and a bull of Fowler and 12 Dutch bullocks of Smedley. The heifers were £22 each, the bull £12-15s., the Dutch £14 each and 20/- for luck,[34] the little steer of Fletcher £10-10s. Bill Drew rode with me to the Fair and left me to get home as I could. Of course I walked a portion of the way and was picked up by a young lawyer from Louth and rode to Cotesgrange, whence I crossed over the fields by Mr. Odling's barn.

The weather is glorious for harvest. The greater part of the top 18 acre was cleared yesterday, and this morning the oat rakings are coming in until the heavy dew evaporates.

I have felt much pleasure in reading the 'Lantern' for the month. It delineates so beautifully the growth which has taken place in the attachment of the present age to nature and natural objects. A century ago there existed scarcely any indication of this in any of the pulpits of the land. The spirit of that age was powerfully reflected in John Wesley. A great spring of pleasure has been opened to the mind of the present generation by the enlargement of our natural theology. If our love of nature is only blended by the Old Testament spirit and our scientific researches, chastened and purified from the idolatrous, then the highest earthly felicity may be permanently secured by the contemplation. It has been remarked that far more regard for the loveliness of creation is manifested and expressed by the Old Testament writers than the New. Exception perhaps may be taken to the parables of our Lord. Does progress in the tasteful propensities of modern society constitute a part of real advancement in an ethical point of view? May it not become a mere sensual indulgence instead of a lofty, pure and moral joy? Under certain circumstances eating and drinking may be sinful. But because men sin in writing, is literature to be abandoned and destroyed? If such a principle were practically applied, then man with his vast range of sinful powers must be obliterated. Man is guilty of abusing himself and all his propensions [propensities].

TUESDAY, OCTOBER 17TH, 1871

More than a month has elapsed since any note or record has been written upon my own personal doings. Great changes have taken place in nature and in business. Farming business has been considerably retarded by heavy falls of rain, especially thatching. We are busy wheat-sowing and, the weather permitting, shall finish on Friday next. The potato crop is a miserable affair. The blight is almost as severe as when it first visited the island. The Partney beasts have been folded in the yard now for more than a week. They devour the oat straw and rakings and are thriving well upon it without cake. Seven Dutch are tied up and the other five are eating grass, and all are allowed one cake per day each, half cotton and half linseed. I can scarcely tell which mend most or improve the most rapidly, the stall or the grass fed. The lambs were folded on the turnips yesterday. It is a good crop. They suffer from a very severe cough. I have now 63 head of cattle, 727 sheep. I have sold old Captain for £5 and Beauty for £8 and put the Skirbeck 3 year-old, Augur, in the waggoner's stable. Poor Brittain has been twice collicked in rather rapid succession. Last week Mr. Roberts paid me for 60 quarters oats at 18/6 and 15 quarters wheat at 56/-. I have bought 10 quarters of rye for my horses at 34/-.

BINBROOK, NOVEMBER 2ND, 1871

Yesterday and today I have been taking advantage of my wife's absence in writing rather diffusely upon pauperism,[35] and broaching what some might consider rather Utopian schemes in relation thereto (at least as some high and dry people might regard it). However it is a scheme of amelioration if applied and carried out would in course of time annihilate an evil which is becoming of gigantic proportions and annually assuming a more threatening attitude. The very nation itself is quaking before the increasing magnitude. It is already a canker worm at the vitals of our civilisation.

Yesterday I received the money of Mr. Roberts for 90 qrs. barley at 35/6.

Mormonism[36] has received its death blow. The leading men are taken prisoners!

I visited Benniworth last Monday evening and stood on the platform with my brother in the chair, Mr. Crowe on my right and Mr. Hirst on the left, two ministers who have come into the Louth circuit since last Assembly. David Bennett also, the coal carter from Louth, formed one of our platform group. Mr. Crowe spoke upon the potency of little things for good. The drop of water in the cup of the acorn refreshed the nightingale and the nightingale made the foliage ring so sweetly in the ear of some exhausted author that he was enabled to finish his book. He might have enlarged almost ad infinitum in this line of thought. The splendid pasturage of this summer was only an accumulation of tiny blades of grass. When I rose, I followed on a similar course of suggestion. There is only one Niagara. I hope to see it some day. I have seen two or three good word-paintings of it, also photographic representations of it. It excites our imaginations as the great king of waterfalls, all royal in its monopoly of sublimity and splendour. Its force suggests Omnipotence. It shows how the Almighty can handle the waters He has created. He can raise them up in mountain billows or dash them down over the gigantic precipices into helpless spray. What an isolated thing it looks on God's great globe!

FRIDAY, NOVEMBER 3RD, 1871

Last evening rode the little seven years old pony (bought last Lincoln April Fair for my son) to Louth, and heard Mr. Maclaran preach in the Wesleyan chapel from Math. 10 ch. first clause of 5 verse.

November opens brightly. Its fogs have not yet shrouded us in gloom. The Autumnal glory has not yet faded from the landscape. Some trees still tenaciously hold remnants of their summer robes, but their change of dye indicates their approaching fall, the revolutions in colouring produced by the dyeing processes of Autumn, the infinitely various light and shade, the gentle and unabrupt mingling of all possible shades of rainbow hues. The sunshine is not so glaring but flows through the valleys and clothes the hills with a mild and mellow radiance. There are no sharp contrasts of dark green and brown. It is the multitudinous character of the tints that create such a charm to the eye and imagination.

SATURDAY, NOVEMBER 4TH, 1871

Yesterday I had a rare feast of literary work. In the morning I endeavered to reproduce in my own language Mr. Maclaran's striking sermon. He made the fact of Christ's Resurrection assume a more deeply significant aspect than I had before perceived. He place[d] the Apostolic office in its true light. He showed that Apostolical succession was the mere phantom of an ecclesiastical brain. He rolled off from the Apostolic office the traditional lumber and presented it to his congregation in its true substantial and peculiar elements.

In the afternoon I had an Autumn farm stroll with two or three broadsheets in my pockets. They become so stuffed by the accumulation of lectures, pamphlets and newspaper paragraphs that the necessity arises of periodical clearances to make room for a new stock. So one pamphlet pushes aside another, and so of books. There is a constant moving panorama of literature. I have been thinking of assisting my treacherous memory by commencing an orderly succession of books. That is to say constantly have a history on hand and a work on ethical science, on the physical sciences, or natural theology, on the great compass of Christian evidence, on logical science, on rhetoric, on poetry, on the arts.

This would naturally reduce the great chaos of thought into encyclopoedic order.

In order to clothe the whole with adornment, the imagination might be regaled with an occasional work of fiction, say one or two representative or typical works of our standard writers on fiction or travel. Nothing that is mentally gained should be finally lost to reccollection.

Last evening I mounted my little steed and pursued my way to Northgate baptist chapel[37] to hear Mr. Hanson lecture on Cromwell, the greatest hero of the 17th century.

FRIDAY, NOVEMBER 17TH, 1871

Mr. Sharpe has laboured last week and this among us with a small degree of success. The church appears to be quickened. My two little gems are still at Dexthorpe, having taken the measles. Of course Lizzie was detained there in consequence. Annie was kind enough to keep house for me from Saturday, November 4th to a week on the Tuesday following, when Frank met her at Rasen.

To our great surprise Lizzie returned home on Saturday last with a very pressing letter from Wheatley.[38] The children being so much improved, she yielded to the kind pressure and left home last Tuesday. I intend D.V. to start off by the first train tomorrow morning to see her. I hope the change will invigorate her, though the weather has assumed a very wild and winterly aspect. She will not be able to get out much unless it is milder and finer in the neighbourhood of Oxford. Yesterday was clear and dry enough to admit our thrashing wheat which comes out in much better condition than is usual for November. Today has been stormy and a white mantle has once more fallen over the landscape. We have only been able to finish the wheat stack and shift the machine between two other barley stacks, ready for the morning. The wheat yields badly. It takes a far more bulky stack for 50 quarters than last year. 52 quarters came from the one just thrashed and last year about 70 quarters would have been the yield. Last Saturday we commenced boiling linseed for the crew cattle. We boil one furnace per day with 2½ pecks of linseed and 7 stones of crushed barley, distributed amongst the three crews of 42 head of cattle. I have now 12 Dutch bullocks and three cows tied up to feed, and one bull. They are still eating sainfoin, turnips, one cake, half linseed and half cotton, and it is truly gratifying to behold them assuming so beefy an appearance. A cloud of uncertainty seemed for some time to hang over them. There is however now no longer any doubt respecting their feedable propensities. The butchers are warning me not to sell them out as they weigh so much more than they can fairly be estimated.

The lambs are still eating their own way, as we have not yet turned out the cutters. Some people think I might make some first class hoggets of them if I would do so.

There are some truly beautiful things in the 'Preacher's Lantern' for the month. I have ordered the 'Christian World Pulpit',[39] the first number of which appeared a week last Wednesday. I have read 'Emmanuel Church',[40] a most charming book. What a creation of attractive and repulsive characters! What moral fragrance and moral odiousness respectively!

THURSDAY, NOVEMBER 30TH, 1871

In the order of God's good Providence, I have been permitted to pay another joyful visit to Oxford. I arrived a week last Saturday at noon, visited the Bodleyan [Bodleian] and Radcliffe library, then called and had tea with Mr. Bond and his young friend, an undergraduate. After tea my time of departure for Wheatley had arrived, which destination I reached about halfpast seven, where I pleasurably greeted my wife and we were hospitably entertained. What a break upon the monotony of pastoral life!

Being anxious to spend Sunday at Oxford, next morning I walked over the 6 miles of space lying between Wheatley and the city of education, the Dr. and his son accompanying me a short distance. It was a morning of aesthetic and religious joy. My soul had a rare experience of illumination which lighted up my senses and rendered them intensely open to the beauties spread over sky and landscape. The Oxford Autumn had not advanced so far towards winter as the Lincoln. Some of the foliage was only just assuming the fading tinge, and few of the trees were so skeleton-like as our own. We were on the highway from Oxford to London lined with evidencial [evidential] posts and wires[41] indicating its transformation into a highway of communication as well as transit. The civilisation of today is the most elaborate the world has yet known, when the lightening is harnessed for the transit of thought. When my companions turned back and I had filled my eye with photographs of external nature, the 'Preacher's Lantern' was my companion the remaining part of the journey, the Song of Solomon the theme, looked at in the light of a delineation of the marriage relation. I felt to be walking through two conservatories both of one Divine authorship, the one placed in the midst of God's Book, the other domed by the Oxford sky. What a beautiful cluster of associations will ever hang around this holy Sabbath. One delicious treat followed upon the heels of another in rapid succession. I was roused from my pedestrian reverie by the stamp of my own foot upon the street pavement, and soon found myself under the roof of the grandest church in the grandest of cities, listening with open and eager ear to the closing portion of the Bishop of Derry's University sermon. I soon felt to be listening to a master and regretted being late. The sermon closed and the University congregation of professors, scholars, undergraduates dismissed.

The seats were no sooner vacant than it became apparent that another service was about to commence. I waited for confirmation of this surmise and a congregation of citizens soon occupied the pews. The ordinary routine of Anglican worship was conducted, and Dr. Burgon mounted the pulpit; but instead of delivering a sermon from God's word, he simply gave a platform address upon the relation of the State to education, strongly advocating denominational education. He made a loud boast of what he himself had done in the cause and also what the Anglican church had on so large a scale accomplished. It was only a squeaking trumpet. The full volume of the blast of candid truthful controversy was absent as he entirely ignored the gigantic accomplishments of Nonconformity in deeper and more moulding fashions of education. Anglicans brand us as political dissenters. They are guilty of throwing stones who live in glass houses. They claim a right to discuss political questions which they charge upon us as a crime.

FRIDAY, DECEMBER 1ST, 1871

Having dined with Mr. Bond, he accompanied me in my return to the University church to hear the Bishop deliver his second discourse. I marched with stealthy and silent step along the side aisle and obtained a good side view of the preacher, who had commenced his sermon. My attention was rivetted at once. A threefold eloquence of manner, matter and style enchained and entranced me. It was an hour of intense pleasure and rich profit never to be erased from the memory. His scarlet robe peering out through the sacerdotal indicated his degree of scholarship; his dignity and florid eloquence gleaming from a pulpit wreathed with honours of learning and scholarship of more than Demosthenic eloquence, of profound disquisition, of acute acumen, of breadth of thought more than Platonic, all blended with a poetry Miltonic in its sublimity. This wreath is the work of centuries of the loftiest art. Was it not an exciting scene to gaze upon a bishop set in the golden framework of such accumulated honours, and himself adding another pleasing ray or another posy to the surrounding beauties?

Alas for us, for England and the world that a pulpit so honoured, so rosy in the aesthetic, so brilliant in the intellectual, so high-toned in the moral, should be so thorny and braky in the religious. Here the great lack manifests itself. What is peculiar to the teaching of the Gospel is ignored. The Sword of the Spirit which is the word of God is turned wrong side up, the broad blunt back instead of the sharp edge. Hence the ineffectiveness. How is the carnal mind to be destroyed when it is to a large extent ignored?

After the service Mr. Bond and I had a stroll through the city. Two or three times we met Professor Liddell of Christ Church, joint author with Scott of the great Greek and English dictionary. He is tall, gentlemanly-looking [with] none of the sacerdotal expression in his countenance. In the evening we worshipped together in his chapel, he leading the devotions and preaching in his usually practical and hortatory style. At the close of the prayer meeting, we surveyed the chapel. I mounted the rostrum and gazed round with pleasing surprise at its neat and respectable appearence. It has the type of Methodist dissent. The building augurs well for free Methodism in Oxford.

We were no sooner out of the chapel than our arms were linked and in the crowd of street pedestrians wending our way towards Wheatley. A very short space of time found the city at our backs. The air was clear and frosty. The road was crusted into a clean pavement. The moon shone through the trees and banished sombre thoughts and prosaic sentiments. Our step became elastic with the friction. A line of cheery conversation was commenced which ran without pause or break until the time of separation. When we had reached a considerable distance beyond the bar, Mr. Bond returned bidding me a kindly farewell. It was anything but a dusty or miry wearisome road in the moon's silvery ray but a truly suburban promenade which my joyful feet traversed on that memorable night. Pleasant reviews and ruminations of the day rushed in upon my spirit, filling my whole nature with heavenly satisfactions.

It was some little after ten when I greeted my wife at the supper table. I hastily partook my simple meal of bread and milk and ascended the region of retirement, leaving Fred to ruminate over his cigar in his back little study.

SATURDAY, DECEMBER 2ND, 1871

They were exceedingly hospitable and kind. My sister[42] has numerous domestic talents. She is largely endowed as a housewife, a creator of home comforts. Neatness, order, cleanliness, added to the virtues and affections of family life characterise the dwelling. Authority and obedience meet in harmonious government. Their energies and motives are all concentered here. This is [a] circle within which all the wheels of parental thought and activity revolve. Family progress in education, in discipline, in classics, in arts, in manners, in professional aptitudes, in household arrangements, constitute the fundamental routine of Wheatley house. Can a man become an intellectual or so spiritual an athlete within so small a spherical range? Can the arm be tested in its strength or developed in muscular power by lifting a pound weight? Could the Divine purpose be fulfilled concerning the human race were man's moral and intellectual nature and corresponding energies to be cooped up, imprisoned within the narrow sphere of domestic life? The Doctor is domestically kind but domestically godless. There is no formal recognition of the great Father of all. He contributes all his energies to the family treasury. He builds up domestic life and government while parochial, civil, and national are left to take care of themselves. Still, we cannot withhold our admiration and acknowledgement of the Dr. and sister's parental thought, ingenuity and love. It forms a fragrant atmosphere of sweeter incense than exales from garden or oliveyard. It is an infusion of roses, pleasant to the moral taste.

One evening I spent quarter of an hour with him in his little study smoking room. Here he spends the closing hours of the day running over the broad sheet, etc. He gave me a sketch of the studies in which his son was engaged. He showed me his school books with specimens of his writing from dictation, of compound sums, etc., with his general progress not only in elementary English but also in the classics. He was very proud of the progress he has made and in the interest he takes in Greek which he has recently commenced. He remarked that if my son were as far advanced by he was twelve and a half I might be well satisfied. He thinks there are few boys so advanced at his age. He pays great attention to his education. He engages both a school master and tutor, and personally superintends and supervises with his own eye. He brings to bear a large measure of personal influence and stimulus to quicken the boy and impel him forward in elementary learning. His ambition evidently is early to bring him out as a first class scholar. Is there no danger in his health succumbing beneath the pressure of mental exertion overstrained?

FRIDAY, DECEMBER 8TH, 1871

Last Wednesday Mr. Roberts paid me for 80 quarters of barley at 34/-. Yesterday Mr. Riggall of Dexthorpe looked round my Dutch beasts. They are thriving well. We are giving the crew beasts creed linseed and barley meal, and neither turnips nor cake. 7 stones meal and about 2 pecks linseed for 42 beast, allowing a little for the horses. I have bought a new saddle of Osborne, £3.10.0., also sent the little pony harness to him to sell. Parker has made me two tumbrells in his own shop out of the material and also two others in our yard out of my larch and deal. The deals I bought at the Louth market auction sale. Britton horse died last autumn. He had often been colicked during his life. We have only 8 cart horses. Augur is in those stables at present, making 9 for the land. We only commenced cutting for the sheep about a week ago. Drew and T. Smith are performing the work. Shepherd drags and prepares the artificial food. Skelton and the Foreman's boy assist in topping and tailing.

WEDNESDAY, DECEMBER 13TH, 1871

On Monday morning last, Mr. Crombie and I rose at 3 o'clock and the groom drove us to his house at Market Rasen where we arrived at 5 o'clock. The morning was fine though snow was on the ground and the air a little frosty. The roads were coated with ice which rendered caution necessary in driving, a characteristic which belongs to Scotchmen, though it was not very vividly displayed in Mr. Crombie when he spread out his limbs on the flags before his own door and cast his specktales [spectacles] away in the fray! Of course he had not their assistance in his endeavour to find the lost. When we recovered our catastrophe a bright fire greeted us in Mr. C's drawing room, where a second breakfast was spread over the table. A few minutes after six and we found ourselves seated in the railway carriage, Antony having joined us.[43] He and myself booked for Rochdale,[44] Mr. C. and his party for Godley Junction, where he changed for Liverpool.

To return to Mr. Crombie's breakfast which was singularly interesting.

THURSDAY, DECEMBER 14TH, 1871

We were soon gathered around the breakfast table. Mrs. Crombie, her Aunt, nephew, myself and Mr. C. The Aunt complained of being rather dizzy and no wonder considering her years, 78 years of age and turning out of bed so early. She has been staying some months at Rasen. Before the breakfast was over she began to relate her earlier Methodistic struggles. I was not aware at the commencement of her story that she was reverting so far back as the struggles of 1835, it appeared to resemble so much the times of 1849.[45] Her manner of speech, tone of voice, expression of countenance clearly indicated a strong feeling of injury and injustice. I was reminded of the power of conscience in quickening and refreshing memory. Her heart was evidently the seat of a strong feeling of justice. Her sense of right recoiled against the priestly arrogance of irresponsible power trampling down the liberties of Christ's church. An organised priesthood, whether for doctrinal or disciplinary purposes in Protestantism or Popery, has been at the bottom of all the disturbances, quarrels, divisions, recorded in ecclesiastical history.

When we arrived at Manchester we found ourselves miserably encompassed by a dense drizling fog, such an one we have never witnessed in Lincolnshire. We were soon under the shadow of the Peel and Wellington monuments. The great hive of industry was lost to our view in consequence of thick haze. The black mud below and the thick envelope of gloom above attended us along our stroll in search of Mr. Barton's residence and searched us through with a chill. Then imagine the climatic disappointment when we beheld the brass plate vanished from his door and an advertisement pronouncing it empty and inviting a new tenancy. Our utter disgust of the city's illtemper pushed us off with all the haste which a cab and steam would allow to a bright home in Rochdale. Antony had no need to send in his card for Mr. Petrie[46] was at the door to greet us with a most gentlemanly and cordial welcome to a house, home and furniture indicating an outlay of about £1500 per annum. We spent a very pleasant evening of chat, and alternate reading. Preachers of our own and other denominations, books and events of the day formed our stock of conversation.

Before tea Mr. Petrie showed us his gardens and conservatories where chrysanthemums were blooming. These crystal houses are necessary here the year round as the climate is too humid and chilly to admit of flowers under the open sky. In fact hardier shrubs and trees are tardy of growth and the eye is not gratified by the rich luxuriance of vegetation. Its dwarfish character was the topic of conversation at the lunch. Mr. Petrie remarked that his garden was planted with trees and shrubs 12 years ago. I suppose this will somewhere about date the completion of the residence. It is a substantial, double-story, spacious house with four well-furnished rooms, a drawing, dining, breakfast room, and library. The walls are covered with engravings.

Next morning we visited the Town[47] Hall with its gilded pinnacles and spire. The heavy clouds hung over it like thick drapery so there were no bright sunbeams for its golden exterior to reflect. It is not only unique as a public building in Rochdale, but in the British Empire. I have visited several great specimens of splendid architecture, ancient and modern, sacred and secular, but none so elaborately beautiful. Nature is here reproduced in art. In passing from one room to another my surprise continued to increase. It was a series of splendid surprises. From floor to roof and ridge it is frescoed with novel designs. One anteroom has its walls lined round with representative designs, historically portraying in succession the stages of modern invention and development in machinery. The game, poultry, fruits and other animals painted on the walls of the dining room indicate the necessities of the table.

Here is the most charming hieroglyphical wording immortalising the great facts of English history without any admixture of myths and legends or ecclesiastical impostures of a superstitious character. This artistic setting of the great facts of English history is the most pleasing feature of our Isle. I am only astonished the Rochdalites have managed to rear a structure so elaborately beautiful for the comparatively small sum of £100,000. It is a marvel of cheapness. The banks of the Roach has never been adorned with such artistic nobleness since its crystal stream commenced winding through the meadows. The expenditure named includes the laying out of the surrounding ground as well as a portion of the park.

WEDNESDAY, JANUARY 3RD, 1872

We held our Watch night[48] at Binbrook in the schoolroom. Brothers Hodson, G. Smith, Blanchard and Shadlock spoke, then two or three females gave their experience. The last five minutes were spent in silent prayer. It was a Pentecostal season. G. Smith spoke of the necessity of closet prayer. So few of us close the door. We allow the world to enter in with us. He complimented Brother Fridlington upon the sermon he preached in the afternoon. Blanchard referred to the progress that has been made during the past year in legislation. The reasons of non-aggression of the church upon the world were stated. It is our great church problem which with a firm determination we must face. Church life is the centre from which all other life proceeds. It imparts stimulus and permanence to every other kind of growth.

The weather during the last few weeks has presented to us farmers a fine opportunity to advance our field work. The early frosts we had broke up without injuring young vegetation such as grasses, clovers, wheats. The turnips are rich in nutritious juices. In passing through the cutter they fly into irregular fragments, being too brittle to cut into uniform squares. My Dutch beasts continue to accumulate in flesh and fat. We have nearly finished fallowing as only a part of the old 9 acres remain unploughed. When it is completed the double ploughs become available for the turnip-land ploughing.

The crew beasts have had no cake this season. It is the second year of creeing linseed. 2 pecks of it and 7 stones of barley meal for 42 beasts allowed, and a few days ago commenced giving a few turnips, also today ordered the largest beasts in for crew 2lb of cotton and 2lb of linseed in addition to other allowances to freshen them up for sale at Spring. Last evening we killed 2 little pigs, one stuck with a beast's horn, the other an affection of the lungs. Tomorrow all being well we shall bottle our whole flock of sheep with tobacco water[49] and soft soap. I have never had them so lousy before, they pluck as if scabbed. The plucking has fearfully increased since Christmas.

We have very much enjoyed our Christmas at Dexthorpe, until a deep gloom was thrown over the house by the severe attack of hysteria which appeared to bring her [Annie] Almost to death's door. We had to leave on Wednesday in consequence and this intensified Mrs. Riggall's grief for she had very much wished us to remain through the week. (My Lizzie was quite upset on her return home). It was with tears almost of anguish that she allowed us to leave. It was a very touching scene to witness her sorrowful reluctance. It seemed more severe than amputation. It caused a painfully violent vibration of heartstrings such as seldom happens in the history of domestic institutions. Poor Annie! She lives to droop before her moral and physical beauty is fullblown! May heaven's joys bear them up amid life's sorrows and afflictions. Mabel is on a visit to Hackthorne for the first time.

Yesterday I walked down with Mr. Wadmough to visit Davison whose wife has just been confined. They have four children and receive 9/- per week. He appears to be consumptive. The woman was up on the stir though she looked sallow and thin and complained of cold. The house did not feel very wholesome. It was close, ilventilated [ill-ventilated], and the effluvia offensive and noxious. Health and happiness cannot dwell in such regions. Physical purity is closely connected with moral. The one may flourish without the other but not vice versa. Moral purity cannot flourish in the midst of filth and miasma. The laws of bodily health are closely intertwined with the laws of moral and spiritual health.

SATURDAY, JANUARY 6TH, 1872

Yesterday and today, we are tobaccoing our sheep. They are cleaner than I expected. From the shepherd's report I supposed they would be very lousy and faggy. We are mixing one gallon of tobacco water to three of water with about 8lb. soft soap to the hundred. A large proportion of wet is falling just now, though generally during the night. We shall not be locked up with ploughing work as we were last Spring. We then hailed the double plough, for it opens our way for the summer work. We looked upon it as a Providential gift. The reaper, the steam engine, and thrashing [threshing] apparatus, the double plough, are Divine gifts to the agriculture of the nineteenth century. What a marvellous economy of labour, and at the same time a beneficent enlargement of our rickyards by their development of the resources of the soil. Farming has become a scientific as well as an industrial occupation. Science digs down into the earth, travels along the surface, and all kinds of material riches spring up around her. Our material civilisation is but the embodiment of science.

At present the wheat looks gay and promising. On the way to Lincoln yesterday to meet Mabel Stovin. I believe it was in Market Rasen Station Mr. Fieldsend of Kermond remarked we had not had a good crop of wheat since 1862 across our wolds. It was a very strong complaint to make against our cold hills. The winters destroy our plant and nothing has yet been discovered to preserve the root against the severe frosts.

Saturday Evening
Today we have finished fallowing. Denison has made himself really useful in filling bottles. Bratley, Welsh and Skelton have been three days bottling 381 hoggetts. My own health has been anything but satisfactory during the last 2 months. I took a violent cold which I carried with me to Wheatley. It appeared to be of a more complicated character than is generally the case with colds, being attended with great irritation of the kidneys and a frequent desire to visit the water closet or a urinal of some kind. Dr. Stovin observed this frequency, and sometimes burst forth in exclamations as we travelled together through London. I attempted to describe some painful sensations somewhere in the neighbourhood of my neck gland and which afterwards extended through my shoulders and chest.

THURSDAY, JANUARY 11TH, 1872

Yesterday I sold the little pony Denison has ridden since last Lincoln Fair. The price is £14. The purchaser is Mr. Kirk's father-in-law, his name I cannot call to mind just now. He lives at Little Grimsby. It is rising eight.

I received a letter yesterday morning from Mr. R. Riggall Jun. of Ulceby inquiring about Mr. Hobbes's farm of Stainton-le-Vale. Having heard a report that Mr. Hobbes was under a discharge, he was anxious to know whether it was fairly at liberty. I met with him in the exchange after having had an interview with Mr. C. Fieldsend who kindly told me all particulars. As far as memory served I echoed the whole affair to Mr. R. I gave him a few particulars about the landlord.[50] His character is very low at Wheating. His tenantry in Norfolk hold him in scorn. When Mr. Goodson left his farm there of course he had a sale, and they have a different custom of charging 2/6 for lunch and allowing wine. One of the company proposed a toast to Mr. Angerstiene [Angerstein] when the whole of the tenantry at once turned their glasses upside down. The act was significant of burning indignation. It has been said that for turning out Mr. Thorpe's widow of Otby he lost his election to one of the Kent seats in Parliament. Mr. Hobbes was one of the executors for Mr. Thorpe when the landlord performed this cruel and insulting deed that he could not submit to the aggravating repetition of injustice of being robbed of his following crop,[51] and I think his rent-day shifting some months earlier. Talk of Trades Unions[52] and other organisations, but is it not high time a grand and effective organisation was effected amongst the tenantry of this country in order to hold the selfish injustice of the landlords in check? Why should they be permitted to commit such outrages upon the tenantry without being called to the bar of public opinion? The rise that is taking place in labour and establishment expenditure together with a corresponding rise in rents and the unequal burden of taxation resting upon the land which the tennantry has indirectly to bear, I think the prospect for the tenant farmer is anything but bright at present. There is very little encouragement to the spirit of enterprize. Farmers will be tempted to take out of the land what they put in and not allow it to remain long dormant. Can agriculture flourish long on these principles?

Yesterday I sold 70 qr. Barley and 50 qr. oats, the one at 36/-, the other 21/-.

FRIDAY, JANUARY 12TH, 1872

Yesterday Mr. W. Dawson came to see us and bought the two Dutch beasts in the cow stable for £26 each. Mr. Ashton bid me £25 on the previous Wednesday.

On Tuesday last my wife held her annual Sewing meeting.[53] There were over fifty five sat down to tea. The charge was 3d. The sum realised was £20.

I do not reccollect us witnessing so many rhyme [rime] frosts in succession through any previous winter. There is seldom a tolerably hard frost without rhyme and hoar and often followed by alternate heavy rains. We had a pretty thick covering of snow the latter part of November and early in December.

The Dexthrope Verdant pony bred by Mr. Riggall out of the thick-set Let has been very unlucky. Uncle Arthur broke him in last Autumn to ride and then it turned lame. Mr. Kime thinks he has found the evil in its back and has applied some blister.[54]

I am thankful that though several bills have come in this Christmas they are considerably less than usual. They are numerous but the amounts are lower. The sadler's bill, Mr. Esberger's, Parker's, carpenter, and two or three others have never had such small sums attached to them since I commenced farming. My aim through the blessing of God must be to bring about a reduction of expenditure.

My barley and wheat stacks dissappoint me in the yield. There is about ten quarters less in each than I expected. The oats yield well.

The signs of the times in relation to the labour question are rather ominous. There is a strong outcry for an increase of wages. The working classes are combining in all parts of the country and demanding more money and less hours. I have paid mine 2/6 per day for two or three years past.[55] Last winter when other farmers paid 2/3 mine had half a crown.

SATURDAY, JANUARY 13TH, 1872

The changes which our climate is constantly undergoing represent the changes that are taking place in our own land. Look at the material change on the surface land, amongst our various institutions civil, political, ecclesiastical and religious.

Yesterday I paid my rent, £377/1/5 for the half year. Mr. J. H. Vesey always takes the rents now as the old gentleman is past business.[56] He has a bad cold and coughed a good deal during the afternoon. We have generally some interesting conversations upon agricultural matters. A good deal was said upon water supply by means of rams and wells.[57] Mr. J. Iles, who for the first year attends the rent day on his own account, remarked that one well had cost £300, the depth of which was 80 yds. I have heard old Mr. Mackerill and my neighbours speak of the difficulty and expense of obtaining water on our hills. I understand Mr. Nelson had to pay dearly for his well. He has now let his farm to Mr. J. King, some say for 45/- and others 40/-. There is about 5/- per acre tythe [tithe]. Mr. Vesey described the water supply machinery fitted up in connection with the new house at Welton now in building.

WEDNESDAY EVENING, JANUARY 17TH, 1872

Mr. J. Sharpley of Calcethorpe remarked at Eastgate that we should make £4 of our hoggets this Spring. Mr. Robberts paid me for 50 qr. oats at 21/- and 70 qr. barley at 36/-. It has been a miserably rainy and tempestuous day. Miss Meadows, our new governess,[58] has just arrived from Ludbro' station. I was not disappointed, or rather not deceived, in Rutter, one of Mr. Dixon's engine drivers.[59] I have learned today that he has been encouraging the men to strike.

THURSDAY, JANUARY 18TH, 1872

My two little darlings have retired into the upper schoolroom for the first time after a long vacation. Our previous governess, Miss Wright, went home ill last September, the day after our quarterly meeting.

Our blustering winds are driving away the clouds this morning, but the land must be soaked with wet.

I am afraid Miss Meadows will find the children in a very backward condition. They neither of them can read, and Denison will be 8 years old next March, Mabel 7 next June.

I have ceased to take milk suppers for the present. My health has not been good this winter though improving at present. My system of diet has undergone a complete revolution. I am practically a teetotaller though not pledged. My health has not suffered injury by that kind of sensuality. I am not sure nevertheless that I have taken a superfluous quantity of liquid such as tea, coffee, and milk. I am retrenching in my consumption of these things about half, also limiting myself in puddings and pies. Animal food is becoming more the staple of diet though Dr. Sharpley said he would leave that to my own discretion. I take three meals of solid food, breakfast, dinner, and supper, and a cup of tea at tea-time. The Dr. gave me a thorough examination and pronounced me pretty sound though he said I had not a pair of first class lungs.

At the close of the search into my case he remarked it was very hopeful and he could give me something to do me good. I have now taken 3 bottles of medicine and consulted twice. My boast of so long-standing is now gone. No longer can it be said that I have not spent 1 shilling in medicine for the last ten or fifteen years, though the boast has become a thing of the past and holds good up to this period.

My visit to Wheatley, my travels with Dr. Stovin, together with two or three complaints to him about the sensations in my throat have created a new era in my physical history. It has thrown a flood of light upon the state of my health. At present it is prospective of the entire renovation of body and mind.

My plans and purposes have many a time been more dazling than their fulfilment. I should like to cast a clear glance through all departments of literature, through all the branches of mechanical and agricultural industries, through all the leading events of the past and present. I should like a clear understanding of poor law and its administration, and to be able to solve the problem of pauperism and promote all remedial measures in relation thereto, without neglecting to administer the laws of nature and of God in relation to my wife, family and farm, that they may all be kept prospering in every kind of growth and accumulation. I should like to farm on a profitable principle, that I may be in a position to throw around my children all educational influences, that they may be fully equipped for life.

All this may through the blessing of my Heavenly Father be the outcome of the Wheatley visit. Thank God for the tokens of a more active and nobler career. A sound mind in a sound body is necessary for large accomplishment.

FRIDAY, JANUARY 19TH, 1872

T. Smith and Bratby were winter digging the garden yesterday. It has been in an untidy state now for sometime. Smith has cut and tied together the rasberry canes. He also is trimming the shrubberries and pruning the fruit trees. Our garden both front and back mainly consists of shrubs, and trees of larger growth. The brown beech, the massive elm, the mountain ash, the prick-holly, the box, the fir tree, the laurel and orchard fruit trees. These have grown around and overshadowed our dwelling. They stand in stately dignity in vigorous life and loveliness, sheltering and ornamenting our family life. They abound and flourish as to preclude the cultivation of many flowers. I sometimes wish the house had been evergreened by the ivy like Mr. Iles's. It is so exposed and damp. The white bricks are not impervious to the rain. The walls might have been umbrellaed by ivy leaves, rendering the house more homely and pleasant to the eye. I have seen both temple, home, and ruined castle completely clothed with this ever-foliaged creeper. It is a beautiful protection for a home; it gives it an aspect of comfort, respectability and beauty.

In reading this description to my wife, she remarks: 'It is too glowing. The trees are too close upon the house that it is too much shadowed. It shuts out the sun. If I were to give way I could hate the old house. Here I am shut up in it. The rooms smell fusty. They are close and unhealthy.'

Lizzie's health is very bad and the blame is thrown upon the house. Still, I tell her, love dwells within the walls, and Dr. Sharpley does not think it particularly unhealthy. The chief objection is there is no spring. We have to send to the village daily for water to drink. Lizzie remarks that this house is scarcely habitable.

SATURDAY, JANUARY 21ST, 1872

'Oh, Woodman, spare that tree!' Lizzie thought the house was too much closed up by trees and shrubs. They shut out the sunshine. They harbour the damp fogs. The garden air and ground are incessantly full of vapours. The evaporations are tardy and become unwholsome by their lingerings, thus holding obnoxious elements in solution. They have obtained a complete monopoly of the front garden as well as home sunshine. Yesterday and today this monopoly is being broken in upon. The axe has been laid at the roots of several, about half a dozen of the most encroaching. Their towering majesty is laid low. Even the prince of the garden, the brown beech, is beheaded by the saw. He looks squat, as Spurgeon said of St. Peter's at Rome.[60] The grace and beauty of these trees are sacrificed to sanatary [sanitary] laws. Sunshine in freeest access is necessary to domestic life and health. Whatever obscures the brightness of the sun's rising is obstructive to family growth. I may say that the pinacle pride of the two brown beech princes is wounded to death. They are destined to sit in the humbled attitude of busky gigantic shrubs.

We would like to have avoided the lower scale of ornamentation, though it is only bringing the garden into harmony with the locality. Most of the beauties which encompass and adorn the dwelling are of a miniature character. The site of the house is a miniature plateau, a minute bit of table rounded by a very circumscribed horizen. The horizen seems to touch the edge of the knoll and bound it to the eye. Hence, though the village is only two miles away, we must proceed to the verge of the hill before it comes into view. It will be seen that there is not much compass of landscape spread out before the eye.

Yesterday, too, I had some conversation with Rutter, Dixon's engine-driver, about the unsettled character of their minds and the unjust and ungratefull claims they were making. The strike system could not be legitimately applied to the agricultural districts. We are dependent upon the weather and many hours are lost in consequence of rain, etc. Agricultural duties could not by any possibility be fulfilled upon the nine hours principle being uniformly adopted.

Young Pride of the Isle arrived from the village last evening. He is a beautiful roan, rising two years old. By adding £4 to the £14 Mr. Gilberts of Fotherby gave me for Taffy (which was rising eight and bought at Lincoln Fair last April), I have obtained one stiffer and capable, if lucky, of carrying Denison (when broken and quiet) from now up to manhood. I hope Lizzie will find him a pleasure to drive in her phaeton.[61] It will be a great gratification if mother and son realise in it what they desire.

One reason for selling Taffy was he coughed so violently through last summer and caught cold by the slightest exposure. Another that it is not quiet in harness. Though Uncle Arthur broke it to harness it was not up to drive, especially in a four wheels. The young Verdant is rising four. He has been very unlucky during his youth, often laming himself. I think Mr. Kime has found the seat of the evil this time. He has blistered him twice on his back which has almost restored the soundness and uniformity of his action.

The man has come this morning for Mr. W. Dawson's black bullocks. We shall all be very curious to know the result. One thing is certain, they have made £12 more than the purchase money. They turn out as firm as rocks and I am mistaken if they do not weigh like lumps of lead. They must be full of sap. The quality of the keeping is so good. Sainfoin, common turnips, and, the last fortnight, two linseed cakes per day have formed the staple of their food.

THURSDAY, JANUARY 25TH, 1872

My mind and memory have experienced half a resurrection during the last few days. Mr. Beckerlegge of Grimsby arrived here on Saturday evening last as our missionary deputation for Binbrook, Ludford and Tealby. Our conversations have been of a most vigorous character. Our aquaintance has almost ripened into intimate friendship. The most desultory and various conversations past between us. His remarks called forth a thousand thoughts that had for years been catacombed in my memory. I believe God has sent him as a new manifestation of his goodness to me. By one or two suggestions thrown out he may have lengthened my life on earth ten, fifteen or twenty years. One is that the skin requires fresh air and that clothing should neither be air-tight nor should it fit close to the bodily shape. It should be loose and flowing. Hence on Sunday morning last I left off for the first time my under-flannel. Then incidentally in the current of conversation a reference was made to a button which had become unstitched upon his trousers. It was the main button, for it formed a substitute for braces. He referred to the advice which his Doctor has given him to throw aside braces as they tended to contract the chest, depress the lungs and hinder their healthy expansion, and prevent the legitimate appropriation of oxygen for the body's purification. I propose at once to avail myself of this kind of physical freedom. My own body shall no longer be subject to this binding force. The undue repression of an organ impairs the vigour of health. I have never been able to discover the cause of my physical depression. Perhaps it consists partially in braces and closely fitting vests. The removal of the vest instead of giving me cold has refreshed me already, and there is a prospect of a new biographical era opening up before me. How dependent is the mind upon the body for its energy and activity. Should a new stream of life and energy flow through my frame, a new lease of mental, moral, and spiritual activity and production will follow through the Divine blessing.

The blustering storms of wind and rain have not effected one tythe of disastrous chill upon my frame which I had suffered from to last Sunday.

The last two nights I have driven Mr. Beckerlegge to Ludford on Tuesday and Tealby last night. We had cheerful and jovial times together, being favoured with a moonlit and starlit sky. He appears very buoyant with expectation in relation to his future marriage.

FRIDAY, JANUARY 26TH, 1872

Yesterday was the last of the pig killing. We have salted down 4 for our own use.

Mr. C. Fieldsend sent his son Charles over to borrow our spare turnip cutter.

We are witnessing a long succession of November fogs this month. Torrents of rain have fallen the last few weeks. The great Nonconformist Conference is assembled during this week. The School Boards work disastrously to the great principles of civil and religious liberty. The Education Act must either be amended or destroyed.[62]

SATURDAY, JANUARY 27TH, 1872

This morning I have had sweet liberty in family prayer. My health improves every day. The spirit of meditation has possessed me for some hours in bed. For the first time this morning I have discarded braces. I trust my mind will be unbound and every faculty renewed.

At the breakfast table I told Denison a little story connected with my boyish horsemanship. I was riding the old dunn mare through the cow close in company with my father and brother. My conceit was rising within me in self-congratulations as I found myself accomplishing the jockey saddle-spring, when to my utter consternation I suddenly lost my balance and tumbled head downwards with my foot locked in the stirrup. While thus suspended, the mare paused and commenced eating turnips recently scattered over the field. Perhaps those turnips saved my life, as my father and brother were some distance on before winding round a plantation, and of course for some little time were not aware of my disastrous condition. If the mare had kept up her speed the consequences might have been very serious. Denison was speaking about his fall the other day from C. Fletcher's roan, Pride of the Isle, which he made [in] an attempt to ride round the paddock. The pony played up a little and the boy threw himself off. He said he felt so differently. He felt so much further from the ground.

Last Wednesday I bought the children a little book called 'Stepping Stones to Knowledge'.[63] He [Denison] said, after learning the first lesson, 'Papa, I like Stepping Stones', and he gave us the questions and answers both in succession, in the meantime his little face lighting up with pleasure.

I pray and trust the wing of Divine Providence may brood over my pair of young doves. Miss Meadows appears very genial and attractive with them. They don't come whining about their parents and complaining of ill-treatment, or injustice, or incompetence of their governess as they often had done of Miss Wright. They appear to have yielded themselves up to her authority and even enjoy their school hours as well as play. They are both cheerful and happy. God sparing and blessing me, I will train and educate them for Him. I will bequeath them to the world and to the Church prepared for the accomplishment of life's calling whatever that may be.

My dear wife still enjoys very poor health. Restless nights and wearisome days appear to be her constant portion. Her Providential path is darkened by the clouds of affliction. She is constantly speaking of her tingling nerves, her weaknesses and exhaustion, her inability for accomplishing life's duties. Her life is rapt in the impenetrable gloom of mystery. A character more wealthy in virtuous affection could not possibly be found. She is ever-ready cheerfully to resign her last modicum of strength for her family, friends and the church. Hundreds of times have her self-abnegating toils been concluded in sheer exhaustion. Notwithstanding her unique sufferings her nature is not soured, but the fragrance of her domestic and social affections is diffused and welcomed through every circle in which she moves. The elasticity of her nature is remarked by all with whom she is brought in contact. Her penetrating tact and sound commonsense never deserts her in time of need. Her intelligence in household affairs is most observant and acute. Nothing escapes her inspection. She can both perform and direct. In the varied art of cooking, perfection reigns. In arrangements, order and uniformity is a highly developed instinct. Any kind of confusion creates vexation. Under her maternal care the children flourish.

THURSDAY, FEBRUARY 1ST, 1872

The last day in the month of January has become memorable in our family history. My dear Lizzie and her son Denison took their journey to Matlock as they are somewhat out of health.[64] She has been the subject of a variety of physical ills during the last ten years. The first child, which never breathed, cost her months of acute suffering beyond the ordinary sorrow pronounced by God as the entail of Adam and Eve's sin. The next two, Denison and Mabel, are still living, but they came through the same gloomy avenue of affliction. It seemed like a continual struggle between life and death. However, though the first was an unfulfilled promise, the second and third are glorious fulfilment, and though the fourth and fifth are unfulfilled, there is one more in the womb, and at present the circumstances appear more natural than the last. Two months have elapsed and nothing disastrous has yet transpired. It is possible, through the blessing of God, Lizzie's health may be renewed by this pregnancy and in future be confirmed and consolidated. These numerous black clouds of illhealth are a deep mystery in our domestic life.

William Dawson paid me for the 2 black bullocks yesterday. He said they were ten shillings per stone. As he complained so bitterly, I gave him 10/- for luck.[65] I suppose there were some hoggets at Rasen last Tuesday made the extraordinary price of £4 each. I should think sheep have never made so high a price in Jan. before.

My waggon is carrying 20 qr. oats to Mr. H. Sharpley of Acthorpe and will go round by Louth to Mr. Barton for 17 qr. peas, 19st. per sack, at 42/-.

We are running the double ploughs again for a second course of turnip land ploughing.

The beef trade is rather slow just now and of course my blacks not being very well up must wait sometime longer. The crew beast don't thrive well in consequence of their exposure to so much wet and storm. We are extremely fortunate in the chalky locality of our sheep during the excessive wet of this rainy season. They are looking well and promising.

We are trimming our fruit trees and cutting down the hedge next Lodge Plot of Lodge Garden. The other hedge running along the road was cut last winter. I wonder what poor old Topliss would say if he could rise from his grave.

We have now ten men working on the farm, including the groom, four confined and three daily labourers,[66] two horse lads living with the foreman and, in addition to these, we have three boys, Charles Skelton, William Drew, and William Smith.[67] Amongst these there is an extra labourer, old Welsh, who was with Farrow and Bingham so many years. Smith and Bratby are doing the gardens, Drew and Welsh with the shepherd on the turnip land. The weather has been so bad we could not thrash; of course we are behind. There are 3 oat, 3 wheat, 2 barley and 1 wheat raking stacks still unthrashed.

I have a conviction that my complaint about my neck and chest is a slight attack of Rematism [rheumatism], though I am very sanguine about its entire removal. My kidneys are not nearly so irritable. I am not so sensitive to cold. I am less conscious of the action of my lungs. I still awake from a sea of dreams tumultuous. Sometimes my thoughts are wretched and desponding, at other times full of purpose and accomplishment. Fatige [fatigue] is a sensation almost unknown to me. I am rarely the subject of nausea. My taste for reading and thirst for knowledge becomes more vigorous. My love of the pulpit and platform is intense and enthusiastic. I am improving in the assimilation of my food. My nerves seem stronger and less excitable. I do not become so tremulous under exciting circumstances. Through the blessing of God the month of January just closed has proved to me pregnant with events of the most healthful character. I may possibly renew my youth like the eagle. How dependent we are upon physical conditions.

I trust every dormant power of mind and body may experience a noble ressurrection and be thrown upon God's altar of service.

FRIDAY, FEBRUARY 2ND

In attempting to write my autobiography, I find my life is interwoven with the agricultural and political life of the nation. I was elected by our circuit committee in Dec. last to attend the great Nonconformist Conference to be held in Manchester. Some of the delegates had arrived when it was decided to postpone it in consequence of the illness of the Prince of Wales.[68] 1880 delegates assembled last week for the purpose of enlightening the public upon the nature and consequences of the Education Act. It turns out to be a Popish Act. There is too much Jesuitical spirit impregnates. It hands over the education of the British Empire into the hands of the Church of England, and the Church of Rome. The Church is half Romanised. How is it that we are so slow in recognising the drift of this pernicious educational law? What does denominational education mean when supported by Parliament? Its truest exposition is in the growing predominance of priestly supremacy. Superstition will gain ground when reason and Scripture, sound doctrine, honest conviction, will be duplicated by dogma, tradition, and scepticism. The Bible will go down under the lumber of secular literature, of legend and science falsely so-called. The great anchors of the soul will be thrown overboard. The grand Nonconformist principle mainly exposited and defended was the inviolability of the human conscience and religion. The State has no right to encroach within the sacred precincts of man's religious nature. Denominational education lands us in superstitious idolatry on the one hand and secularism on the other. Let us look fairly in the face what kind of education the so-called religious education or sectarian education or denominational education really is. What is the quality of it? Are Ritualism, Materialism, Popery, by this very act to become formally nationalised?

SATURDAY, FEBRUARY 3RD, 1872

Yesterday was a lovely harbinger of Spring. A few birds gave us their virgin songs. How sweet their solos fell upon the ear. All nature looked grateful in its drippings as it glistened in the Feb. sun. Our Binbrook valley has not experienced so glorious a light for months' past. This morning the rhyme [rime] is again on the ground and gloomy mist and cloud hang around the sky. No two days alike in this ever-changeful clime. How like our domestic and social and national life.

Last night I read a portion of the Atorney [Attorney] General's address for the defendants of the Tichborne Estates.[69] Supposing the claimant to be an impostor, what a series of unprofitable tortures he has submitted to in order to secure his identification.

Today we are leading ashes from the village.[70] The effect of a liberal supply of cinder ashes upon the turnip crop is an amazing success. When the demand is created the supply is artificially produced by adulteration. Road scrapings are mixed up and a dear robbery is effected before the discovery is made.

Bratby has already caught 16 moles which he has hung upon a pole in his garden. It appears from Maultby's remark he is looked upon by the villagers as my keeper. My fields are almost threaded over and undermined with them. Phido has had a long holiday from ratting and rabbiting.[71] The last year or two Bratby and he have destroyed the greater part of them. We have not reared much poultry the last few years beyond what we required for the house. The yards presented a broad contrast during my Mother's life when the ponds were covered with geese and ducks and the yards were alive with turkeys, guineafowls, cocks and hens.[72] One summer we had six hundred heads. I shall never forget the family outcries about lost turkeys and their broods. In the beginning of harvest they would wander through the fields of standing corn and of course were in danger of a visit from Mr. Rennard. Of course it was necessary to ring the alarm bell when the turkeys strayed. A search expedition was at once set on foot.

Suppose the life of the farm had gone down in proportion to the yard, could my family have existed, and especially at an increased rental? The plumed life may have diminished, but through God's blessing the stackyard has grown. The soil of the farm is enriched and field life has unfolded and multiplied which, when compared and contrasted with the past, may compete with any farm in the County. Have I not appropriated most of the scientific discoveries of the day, whether mechanical or chemical, to the stimulus and renovation of the farm's hitherto wasted energies? Were we two brothers not early in life called out by the Landlord in consequence of Father's fits having weakened his mind and rendered him incompetent?[73] We were pushed forth without paternal help or experience to study and carry out the problem of rescue in relation to the rubbishy character and barrenness of the farm. The era of modern progress had set in and the Landlord, instead of turning us out in disgust, opened before us youths the opportunity of seizing hold of all improving appliances as they presented themselves for our service. We were wise enough to take time by the forelock. We grasped the prize held out and were saved from eviction, and not only saved from eviction but enjoyed the respect, the approbation, the encouragement of a thorough business landlord. He warmly appreciated through the succession of his annual supervising visitations every improvement effected. His visitations have ceased since the appointment of Mr. Vesey to the agency.[74]

This reminds me that the struggles of one quarter of a century of my life have brought me into practical aquaintance with the progressive character. I have played my personal part in the great arena of conflict with the barbaric medievalism of the past and in building up our modern civilisation. A quarter of a century of my own life of thought and action is woven into the warp of modern history. The threads may not be visibly identified, still there they are. Facts are stubborn things, they cannot be broken or annihilated. Facts are not effaced by being rubbed out of the memory. The ample wear of mental and physical power in stemming the current of these progressions and excitements has graven deeply upon my nature their importance and value to myself, my family, my country and the human race. The industries of life help to clarify our views and strengthen the sounder elements of our political, social and religious creeds. They impart a vivid reality to our opinions upon all matters vitally affecting the interest of humanity.

SATURDAY EVENING, FEBRUARY 3RD, 1872

Miss Meadows having retired, I take up my pen while in its autobiographical mood. My wife is not at home to insist upon my accompanying her to rest.

Mr. Keyworth, dealer from Lincoln, and Ash from Binbrook, came to look at my fat beasts. He bid me £18 for the young bull and £20 for the little Rushby heifer, also £24 each for 5 of the best black Dutch. I refused to strike the bargain though very tired of them. The cake wastes so rapidly and the sainfoin dwindles to small compass. Beef has declined in price 1/- per stone.

My mind today has been reverting to early days when the horse thrashing machine rang in my ears. I remember driving the horses while engaged singing the hymn, 'Victory, Oh Victory, etc.' It was one of the happiest days of my life. My religious experience was in its violet bloom. My joys were the virgin raptures of my recent regeneration.[75] God as my reconciled Father, heaven as my prospective home, the Spirit as my living witness, were no dim realities. I walked round that chair and cracked that whip with a bounding heart. The mounting of that machine was the mounting of Tabor to my spirit. It was a festal season which has followed me through life. I enjoyed a feast of spiritual luxuries. What was the avenue through which those memorable blessings flowed? How was the state of mind and heart produced? It was good to be there. Did it not happen through the instrumentality of Methodism? This bounding spirituality, this buoyancy of religious sentiment was the leading characteristic of early Methodism.

SUNDAY MORNING, FEBRUARY 4TH, 1872

I left my bed in time to walk to our Free Methodist hill of Zion 7 o'clock prayer meeting. The loss of sleep and bed comfort has proved a great gain in the spirit of prayer, of meditation, of heavenly taste and sensibility. My voice gained in clearness while joining the holy anthems of praise and thanksgiving. Three of us met at the altar of praise and the throne of grace, T. Giles, Robinson, the chapel keeper, and myself. The dew of Hermon fell upon my spirit. During my solitary walk I was the subject of impressions so personal and peculiar that language cannot embody and express with any degree of adequacy. The beauty of the dawn quickened new sensations within me.

WEDNESDAY MORNING, FEBRUARY 7TH, 1872

There is one advantage perhaps in living an agricultural life. There is more room for the development of the individual life. In a great forest of innumerable trees you find them grown to a uniform height, while the one standing out there solitary and alone has wider expansion and an eccentricity of growth all its own. The activities of the individual man are apt to become erratic but sometimes a more bulky development is the result. This reminds us that an education to be complete necessitates a wise balancing of social and solitary life. The trees cannot change their positions. Where they are planted there they must remain whether in the crowd of the dense forest or the solitary hedgerow or more open park. The time was when human life was more isolated, less social. Today the cohesive forces are being brought unduly into play, hence the danger of men growing tall but wiry. The large girth which comes from the growth of conscientious principles is not secured. In wiry tallness there is weakness and danger. Man's life must be alternated, social and solitary.

THURSDAY MORNING, FEBRUARY 8TH, 1872

Yesterday I attended Louth market, called at Eastgate. Mr. J. B. is still very poorly though a little improved.[76] He was not able to attend the Board on Monday and business moved very slowly.[77] Our Chairman is 79 years of age and his infirmities of memory etc. have become too numerous for a position of that kind. If he were wise he would retire. The board business was singularly distasteful to me for some time, and singularly novel. The whole subject of poor law, the embodiment of poor law, the administration of poor law, was perfectly new to me. I knew a Relieving Officer by name, a Board of Guardians, by name, and a Workhouse with its garden as it stood with cheerful looking front on Union Hill. But I had no idea of its interior construction or household arrangements.

Last week I dreamed that we were in the literal room where we weekly assemble and were diverting ourselves by grouping primroses and violets in little vases as a relaxation to our strained energies. The dream was to a large extent true. The chairman allows us too much leisure. There is not enough of determinate promptness in pushing forward the business.

I am not aware whether I shall have health and vigour enough of mind and memory to occupy a position of general influence in the Board. At present I confine myself mainly to the cases which arise from in my own village. The principal faculties required are acuteness of intellect, quickness of reccollection and aptitude in repartee, power to comprehend the details of law and apply them with justness to each case as it arises. The cases differ so much. There are the multiplied details of circumstance and character, and the precise adjustment of the scale of relief that the relief may be legally just without being generous.

Yesterday and today we have been carting ashes and sewerage from the village. The machine for thrashing has come into the stackyard but the weather would not allow us to thrash today. The foreman said that about 5 o'clock the rain descended in torrents. The clouds seem as inexhaustible in Feb. as in Jan.

My wife is now at Matlock and we correspond daily. I am glad Denison accompanied her. He is very kind to his mother and a great comfort to her in waiting upon and relieving her loneliness. Mrs. Smedley says he is a chip off the old block and his tongue is too large. Lizzie says in her letters, too, that the treatment is not very invigorating. His liver is covered with sponges and some evil kind of rash is making its appearence in that part. Lizzie gives very little information about her own case. In her first letter the account of the consultation with Mrs. Smedley was very brief. Perhaps there was some reason in the expression of her opinion or perhaps she felt embarrassed in the formation of a definite and decided opinion.

If there are a hundred servants against a hundred visitors the expences may well go up! It appears the establishment is infested with rats after which they have commenced a chase.

Lately I have been absorbed in the Tichborne case. I have read the greater part of Coleridge's address. I will not give my verdict yet but the evidence appears strong against the claimant. I think as the defendants hold the estates in possession they have the advantage.

Today I have read the virgin speeches of both Lords and Commons, being the fourth Session of our Reformed Parliament. Disraeli and Gladstone gave the two speeches of the House of Commons. They were mainly occupied with 'Alabama' claims.[78] The picture appears rather gravely.

Am now reading, too, 'Christian World Pulpit', also Wilberforce, now bishop of Winchester, formerly of Oxford, on Hebrew Heroes.[79]

FRIDAY, FEBRUARY 9TH, 1872

We have commenced thrashing today with a good weather prospect. How dependent we farmers are upon the goodness of God! The aconite and the snowdrop and primrose are greeting each other, I suppose to garland the bridal day of the feathered tribes. They have already sung their songs of courtship. They are said to pair off on the 14th of this month.

As I was retiring to rest last evening, some thoughts came into my mind respecting Art and Artists. Are they not fulfilling a great purpose in the Divine government? Do they not spread more palpably before the eye the great facts of history? Take the woodcut, the engraving, the painting, the sculpture. Look at the vast monuments of the past and present rearing their lofty and sublime forms before our enchanted view and we express our obligations to noble works of Art for giving tangible witness and illustration to the facts of history. Look at the historic personages which figure in stone and crown our halls of science, our town and city squares, which hang around the walls of our colledges [colleges] and art galleries. Throughout both East and West, whether in ancient Pyramid and Hierogliph or in modern pedestal and column, in modern type or old manuscript, on medieval canvass [canvas] or modern watercolour, you perceive men have raised up the immense boulder stone facts of history and planted them upon their tiptoe edges along the great thoroughfares of human life. The motive may not have always been pure. Mere worldly honour or national defiance may have formed the sordid element of the artist's motive. But to my mind it looks like the development of a grand scheme of Divine Providence. Men must be impressed with the glory and Divinity of fact. Myth and legend, with all other creations of the imagination which tend to becloud the mind and weaken conviction in relation to the stern realities of the panorama of this world's life, by the light of Art are doomed to dispersion.

WEDNESDAY, FEBRUARY 14TH, 1872

I have had a few days of delightfully quiet reading and study. I have taken the first two numbers of the 'Congregationalist', and highly interesting numbers they are.[80] They are rich in varied thought and instruction. In the evening I amuse Miss Meadows with the Tichborne case. The Atorney General's address has already taken 19 days and is still unfinished.

I had a rather severe trial of my temper and patience. Two of my confined labourers, Skelton and Drew, came to my door to ask me to raise wages.[81] I had been boasting in an innocent spirit that my men had not mentioned raising at all. I thought they so appreciated my conduct towards them in the past that they were manifesting their gratitude for magnanimous treatment already received. When Skelton found I had raised Drew 1/- per week, he at once caught an inkling of the strike infection and evidently came with a determination to seal a hard and fast bargain; while in the field last week he had left it to me. I raised Drew because he said the others had only 7/- per week when he was allowed to have 11/- per week and keep his own pig. When I told Skelton I did not intend to raise, he abruptly walked off and said, 'Then my place is at liberty'.

I came in the house confused with grief and consternation. I felt injured by ingratitude. I considered and followed him into the yard. He softened in his manner but held firmly to his own terms. He insisted for the harvest gratuity to come into the bargain. A fortnight of piece work, or, in case he should be called off to lead at the expiration of one week, one sack of wheat in lieu thereof. Labourers being so scarce I dare not let him go. A crystalisation is already commencing throughout this county. They are forming themselves into organic companies for the purpose of dictating their own terms, and forming exactions upon the masters.

In opening my mind upon the page of this diary, I have long thought that a day of judgment would some day dawn upon the tenant farmers of this country. Their immorality has grown rank and the smoke of their grossly servile prostration of patriotic and religious principle before their landlords has ascended up as an abomination into the nostrils of the God man in heaven.[82]

There are scores would sacrifice their consciences for a farm and now what do they behold? The breach is opening on both sides of them. The landlord on the one side and the labourer on the other are deserting him. He is met by rigid exactions on every side. He stands helpless without a spark of sympathy from any quarter. In the midst of increasing rents, heavier tradesmen's bills, higher wages, an annually increasing disproportionate and unjust taxation, the farmer is floundering aghast in consternation! As a class unable to organise themselves in self-defence, like a rope of flowing sand. Is there any wonder that the attention of Parliament is drawn to social questions when they are stirring society to its very foundations? Faith says in whispering tones, 'Truth and justice will win the day', but not before men and classes become just and true one towards the other.

THURSDAY, FEBRUARY 22ND, 1872

Last Sunday Mr. Cornish paid us his monthly visit.[83] In his morning discourse he gave to the parents present some very unsound advice. They were not to tell their children that God saw them and was angry with them if they committed sin. I think he styled sinning as making mistakes. The advice he gave contradicted the introductory part of his discourse. He said the perfection of Christ's character consisted in its roundedness. There were no protuberances, but an equal and harmonious development. Justice formed one of the grand catalogue of perfections. After such introductory statements as these, to advise parents not to present to their children's minds a single glance of Divine justice is a contradiction of a most glaring character. If the Divine justice is doomed to pass into obscurity our minister's sermons will become a mere cloud of words hiding one half of God's character. If there be not just dealing between man and God we shall soon cease to erect our law courts for the vindication of justice between man and man.

Yesterday we were conversing about our agricultural prospects. The price of wool nearly approaches 70/- per todd.[84] Inlamb ewes are making 90/- each. Farmers are nearly beat with their turnips. A great many shells are being ploughed in. Grass and seeds are equally abundant. They look as green and luxuriant on Ash Wednesday as oftimes in June. Mr. Sam Foster said he had made a note to a similar effect in 1846 and it turned out an abundant summer.

The panic among the labourers is somewhat waning; though a small riot took place in Horncastle last Saturday.[85] It originated in the pulling down of a stump orator by the police. His intention was to incite the labourers to strike. It was an indiscretion to interfere with him. The mob made use of every loose brick for the purpose of destruction. The fray ended in broken windows, etc.

I am now enclosing the gardens for Smith and Coney. My Lizzie will feel it a relief to have a little more privacy in her garden. It has always been distasteful to her seeing labourers' wives entering upon the seclusion.[86] I am reading Froud's [Froude's] 'Short Studies'.[87] They are studies of no mean order. He has spent his life in the study of the Elizabethan period. Some of the studies are worth half a dozen readings. There is great force and beauty in some of his paragraphs though very unripe in his opinions. He assisted me much in the thought of my address at Market Rasen last Monday night. I occupied the chair at their Missionary Meeting. The thought came with great force while I was speaking, viz. the material framework which our glorious constitution had formed for itself, this being one amongst the crowd of material transformations which the Gospel has effected and is still effecting in this beautiful land.

My Lizzie is ill in bed. She took a violent cold in returning home from Matlock last Thursday. What a life of protracted suffering to experience!

This evening I sold Mr. Sawyer 7 Porket pigs, half-bred Berkshire, for £27.

FRIDAY, FEBRUARY 23RD, 1872

Yesterday I called on some of the friends to solicit subscriptions towards our Aggregate circuit tea meeting at Market Rasen.[88] I find a vast difference in the spirit of liberality amongst the friends. I learned, too, how censures had been floating through the circuit in the vessel of conversation. Dr. Bray was one of the architects of the conversational vessel. This vessel, it appears, was weighted with several tons of censure to be unloaded upon the deputation for their self-denying labours because they happened to say a few strong words upon middle class giving. If we press too hard upon the poor we give offence. It seems impossible to touch the money question without creating censure. There is a morbid sensitiveness in relation to the purse. The mania of the present time is money making. Shoals of men are hasting to become rich. The wealth-creating spirit has taken too exclusive possession of large masses of the community. It is exercising the nobler spirits which ought to keep it in just subordination. The middle classes are increasing in covetousness in proportion to their wealth, and to speak in the mildest terms of condemnation is only to be paid back with the same and a hundred per cent interest.

Last night was another proof of the inexhaustibility of our winter clouds. What months of teeming rains we have experienced! We are salving our sheep throughout the flock for lice. It is the first time this kind of filth has made its appearence.

A series of rhyme [rime] frosts has accompanied this unprecedentedly rainy season.

Yesterday I called upon Thomas Surfleet. What a tongue he has! I noticed a struggling in his mind. He evidently felt hampered by his untoward circumstances. Things seemed out of joint. He would like a readjustment of things. He desires to better his condition by readjusting himself, family, home, shop, to a more favourable part of the village. He feels obstruction to his trade.

SATURDAY, FEBRUARY 24TH, 1872

Bright sunny days are rarely exceptional. All nature drips and assumes the garb of melancholy, save the aconite and snowdrop which begem our garden. They constitute the solitary smiling features which tint the earth with hopefulness.

Yesterday was Mr. Nelson's sale of Whyham. Two pens of Gemmersen lamb made 96/- per head, bought by Mr. Bingham of Swallow. Little cull hoggets from 70/- to 75/- each. Cows and calves over £30 each. Useful 2 year old steers £20 each. Turnip keeping 1/- per acre, grass and seeds the same.

There is one short study in Froude's book on the science of history. It is a most masterly and complete answer to Buckle's theory.[89] If man were a purely physical being and was subject only to material laws then a science of his history might be possible; but man is a moral agent and his actions cannot be calculated acording to the laws of self-interest. Even the science of political economy takes the law of self-interest as its axiomatic foundation. There is a higher moral law than this which, as a fact inscribed upon the page of history, thousands have obeyed - viz. the law of right. The fact that there exists a moral science which reveals a self-determining power, a self-creating power, an originating force in creating motive. This originating force constitutes the substance of his free agency. Man is not a vessel in full sail into which circumstance powers its winds. A Steam vessel even has in itself a power to contend with outward circumstances. This overflowing well-spring of living moral energy which exists in man's nature forbids the power of calculation. This is the source of historical surprises. The endless variabilities of history spring from this almost infinite source. And notwithstanding the outstanding difference which already characterise the long ages past, the present is still more fruitful, and tomorrow there may possibly ring round the globe one joyous or calamitous exclamation over some great unanticipated event as unlike anything hitherto inscribed upon the page of history. And what is all human progress if there is not some faculty or energy yet to be evolved? Perhaps, too, the evolution itself may come into collision and subvert for the time being the law of self-interest, so that even the very axioms of some of our sciences may be swept from beneath them that they may be replaced by firmer foundations. Man's moral nature bears contingent fruit. Every building newly erected is expected to manifest some degree of creative power. The poverty or wealth of a man's nature individually is tested by the originality of his creations whether in art, science, phraseology. This is a fund of dormant moral and intellectual energy which has been buried in the depths of man's nature for a wise and Fatherly purpose. This marvellous evolution is going on today.

WEDNESDAY, FEBRUARY 28TH, 1872

Yesterday I gave the paupers their tea. Miss Short provided hot plum cakes, and thirty of them partook of the repast. They appeared to enjoy themselves very much. I thought I could not manifest my gratitude to Almighty God in a more acceptable manner than by this charitable deed, being the great thanksgiving day for the restoration of the Prince of Wales.[90] I also gave George Shaw 1/- to cry the thanksgiving service as it was not announced from the pulpit last Sunday evening.

Mr. Hodson opened the meeting with singing and prayer, then gave an address upon the national sentiment of loyalty and, comparing us with the other nations, also made a few remarks upon denominationalism. When he concluded I mounted the little rostrum and followed a little in the same line. I told the people I observed the day because I had sympathy with the Prince of Wales in his sufferings. I hoped the day would never come when I did not feel deep sympathy with suffering, whether in the royal household or palace or the cottage of the poor. I did not stand alone in my sympathy. The whole nation was moved. A pall as thick as the clouds rested upon the country. We all gathered around that sick bed with a load of sorrow upon our hearts. We thronged to read each new telegram, and now we are rejoicing over the recovery.

We have national reasons as well as personal feelings. Look what a glorious constitution we now enjoy! It was not built in a day any more than St. Paul's Cathedral. It is the result of the labour of a thousand lives. How much legislative genius had been expended over it! Centuries of thought have been expended over it. Our ponderous statute-book is but the diary of our state builders. It has cost the blood and treasure of our grandest heroes. I referred to the pageantry of London all arrayed in her royal attire. The river, the bridges which span it, the streets all robed in crimson and gold. Thousands of bright coloured flags wave in the breeze. A grand stand in the park, balconies tier above tier for spectators to witness the royal procession and, to crown the whole, the thanksgiving service in St. Paul's Cathedral attended by 14 or 15000 distinguished personages. Both Houses of Parliament, the city corporation, with the notables from every christian church, all assembled for worship. Such a gigantic congregation has never before gathered under that ancient dome!

What about the moral and spiritual magnificance behind this symbolic display! My paper gave a gentle rebuke to the philosopher. These glowing symbols were for the kindling of emotion. National loyalty kindled to enthusiasm by artistic symbol. What then are the benefits of our heavenly government carried on by our Saviour King compared with all earthly governments and constitutions, and what ought our loyalty be towards Him who reigns over Queen Victoria herself and who has superintended the upbuilding of this state? God has sent me to call all peoples back to their allegience and to demand of them in his name loyal enthusiasm of a more exalted character.

The passage of Scripture which moved me to give the tea was the 14ch. of Luke, 12v. 'Then said he also to him that bade him, When thou makest a dinner, etc.'

THURSDAY, FEBRUARY 29TH, 1872

Rents continue to rise in all parts of this county.[91] The Biscathorpe trustees are raising Mr. Kirkham's rent up to £2 or £2/2/- per acre. Mr. I. Sharpley of Calcethorpe positively declares we cannot live on our wold hills at two pounds per acre.

I think fine days are on the increase, though the rain was beating against my window again last night. We are scarifying turnips by the roots. In consequence of the open winter the tops are quite luxuriant and unless checked they will soon extract the nutritious elements from the bulb. We have had a south wind most of the winter.

I have read the 'Preacher's Lantern' for February. There is a beautiful sermon by Dean Alford. It is mainly apologetic in its character, a style which the higher order of clergymen of the Church of England adopt. It is necessary that other sects should follow up their teaching with the experimental and practical. The doctrines of the church as established by law are too vague and various to establish the faith of the community.

FRIDAY, FEBRUARY 29TH, 1872 [MARCH 1ST]

Yesterday I attended our aggregate tea meeting at Market Rasen. There was a nice gathering in the Town Hall and a tolerable congregation in the chapel assembled about 7 o'clock. Mr. Colam occupied the chair. Mr. Crombie, Mr. Cornish, our own ministers, Mr. Lawton, the revivalist, Mr. Hirst from Louth, gave interesting and stirring addresses. Mr. Crombie gave us a bird's eye view of the state of the circuit, statistically and spiritually.[92] It appears there is an improvement in several places. In spite of the drain which is constantly going on from our several churches by removals we shall be able to report an increase of about 30 members and 60 on trial. God is answering prayer in sending us some pentecostal seasons. I trust we were moved to make some more powerful appeals to heaven for more liberal bestowments of Divine unction. It was a representative gathering to promote circuit feeling and strengthen our circuit bonds, to increase the vitality and significance of our church membership or church unity. We regard every society as a church who have obtained saving faith in our crucified Lord.[93] Our formal connectionalism consists of representation. No one class of men can form themselves into an hierarchy. But the freer the form of government, the larger amount of intelligence, ecclesiastical industry, wisdom and self-control is required on the part of members.

I must now refer to the great mystery of Divine Providence in not permitting our Binbrook friends to be present at our festive gathering last evening. They started off a cheerful company, about 25 persons, in Dobbs's carrier waggon drawn by my two chesnut horses, Tramper and Tipler. As they were descending Kermond hill the horses galloped away and threw the waggon over, and several of the pilgrims were scratched and bruised - scarcely a face but was disfigured more or less. They had evidently been dragged in the dirt. George Smith's back, Brumpton's leg somewhat injured, his servant girl's shoulder put out of joint, but no bones broken. I believe these were the principle injuries received.

This is perhaps the greatest physical calamity our Binbrook church has experienced. Is it a chastisement from God or a permission to the devil to attempt the frustration of our object? I would solemnly spread out the case before God that He may be pleased to turn it round to the eternal good of the church and town. How could we find our way through life when fastened up on such thorny laberynths [labyrinths] but by looking upward to the guiding star of Divine Providence. The overtaking hand of God grasping the calamitous events of life, individual, domestic and national, is the only firm thing the church of God has to fall back upon. This accident is pregnant with meaning. It is one of the thousands which have overtaken humanity. It forms part of the cloudy side of the Divine Government. Trouble and affliction come when we least expect.

Rain has attended the egress of Feb. and ingress of March. Though the clouds have poured their floods upon the earth, they still darken the heavens. The prospect is tinged with ill-omen for the Spring sowing.

SATURDAY, MARCH 2ND, 1872

We are this morning folded up in fog. We have not enjoyed much direct sunshine. It seems very cheerless when passing through so dense a medium. The temperature has been comparatively mild for some time past.

Yesterday I found G. Smith in bed, though not so much injured by the accident as I expected.[94] His back was bruised in the lower part 'somewhere about the couplings', as he described it, so the kidneys were not hurt. It appears he was partially unconscious for a considerable time. His power of recognition was paralised [paralysed] that he has no reccollection of seeing me ride up or Mr. Burkinshaw or Mr. Fieldsend or Mr. Fawcett, who came to render what assistance they could. It appears a man may be intellectually dead while he physically lives. My eye was more intently fixed upon him the moment I surveyed the marred and bespattered group, as looking more ghastly than the rest. It was a disastrous scene. The waggon thrown up on its side, the horses unyoked, the group of passengers blanched with dismay and dissapointment, bruised, torn, scratched, flesh rent, clothes rent, hopes rent, and all anxiety about consequences. Mr. Fieldsend was very kind in allaying the evils by sticking plaster and brandy, and by sending a cart to convey as many as were unable to walk home.[95] The catastrophe arose from the misconstruction of Dobbs' waggon.[96]

The thanksgiving day was exceptionally fine and gave universal satisfaction. I look upon it as a historical demonstration. It has filled up the whole space neatly of our historical press. The loyal valve of the national heart has opened wide and expression given in all beauteous forms. The day was adorned by the splendours of diction. The press in all its varied membership burst forth into moral and artistic eloquence. Every paper has rung out its enjoyment of the day and glowed intensely with the fire of loyal enthusiasm. The nation has scarcely ever mingled so much joy with its patriotism. The national belief is that God answered prayer and a national offering of thanksgiving has been brought to the altar.

The question arises, was it loyal feeling merely or religious thanksgiving which obtained the uppermost place in the human heart. I am afraid a good deal of carnality mingled with the offering. Officialism carried the day against moral and intellectual worth. The State patronises her favourite sect. The real grandeur of the day has the den of obscurity assigned to it. The representatives of one half of the nation and of its cream were said 'to be enclosed like wild beasts in a cage'.

WEDNESDAY, MARCH 6TH, 1872

Yesterday I attended a sale at Fulstow and bought a chesnut mare, 8 years old, for £30/10s. including duty and bringing home. I have now 3 beautiful chesnuts.

The weather has changed since last Sunday. Today is the fourth brilliant day. It is very cheering to witness such a grand dispersion of clouds.

I am reading 'Contarini Fleming' by Disraeli,[97] lent me by Henry Atkinson of Grainthorpe, also Dequincy [de Quincey] on the Lake School,[98] lent me by Mr. Crombie.

The trustees of the Free Methodist chapel met in the schoolroom last Monday to consider the best method of repairing and restoring the chapel. Clarke's disgrace in building the chapel so badly becomes more patent every year.[99]

We have commenced taking up our greentop yellow turnips. My brother George came over to dine with me last Monday and in riding through the field remarked that he had not seen so fine a crop of yellows on this farm before.

It is the first occurrence that our winter flock has proved inadequate to the consumption of our turnip crop, though it is general throughout the country. A Spring so abundant in keeping of every kind is seldom known to come round with the revolving year. It is almost unique in the annals of agriculture in England. Just fancy early in March seeds and grass a bite for a bullock! The contemporaneous history of this land is an ever brightening display of the Divine goodness. Every day ought to be a thanksgiving day.

My own health is considerably improved though not perfect in vigour. I am often experimenting in various kinds of underclothing. I have thrown off my Matlock body bandage.[100] My neck and upper limbs are not free from cold and stiffness nor my head quite free of singing, buzzing, hissing, obstructions in breathing causing a ratling in the nazal department. My digestive organs may suffer from defective mastication, my double teeth having vanished from my mouth many years ago. I am often astonished at the goodness of God in the comparatively good health I have enjoyed in the last ten years. The youthful period was anything but healthful. I had scarcely a strong organ in my frame, digestive organs especially. My physical life has been quickened and born up by the supernatural.

I think married life has exercised a beneficial influence upon my health. Perhaps my wife has suffered for my benefit though she has borne ten years of acute suffering,[101] and in consequence a heavy gloom at times enshrouded our dwelling; still she emits a compensating fragrance by her virtuous character. She has born a pair of immortals which are worth far more or far outweigh the suffering endured. I trust the little characters forming amid the moral influences as are being diffused through this home may ripen them into the very highest type.

THURSDAY, MARCH 7TH, 1872

We have formed some weather axioms by experience. Early winters as a rule are brief. Three times during the last 19 years has this been verified by observation. Severe frosts set in late in October and early in November but were succeeded by a green mild

Christmas. Such is the winter we have now witnessed. My heart shall ascend in praise to God that the time of the singing of birds has again arrived. With the dissipation of the clouds and damps the clarified air and brilliant skies are voçal with the cheery songs of thrushes and larks. We have one live lamb come as the harbinger of the young flock. We only just salved the flock in time. The tobacco water was ineffectual in killing lice. I hope salivation will prove more successful. We have never before wintered so few as eight horses of the draught type.

The long shadows of winter are rapidly shortening and all nature is waking up to new exertions. It is the grand birth season of the year. It is the budding and blooming season. This is the fifth of a brilliant succession of unclouded days. The cloud of agricultural despondency is breaking in relation to the Spring sowing season. How is a seedbed to be formed of flood and mud? Fact and imagination together have been at work in creating all kinds of impossibilities. However, genial breezes have already fanned the farmer's hopes as well as dried the ground. The bright weather is annihilating the imaginary impossibilities by its magical effects. It is a Spring triumph accomplished by the most high God in the grand order of His Providence. There is too much God-fearing and God-loving affection stirring the heart of the nation for the Almighty to forsake us in the performance of our agricultural labours. If He were to abandon the superintendence of our work we should fail in everything our hands find to do. Every shepherd has a Divine superintendent.[102] We have a Divine overlooker to glance through all departments of human labour. The more labour man puts into his work the more proportionate energy does God impart. Man receives aid from Heaven in proportion to his own exertions. God's power is more vigorously exercised where man's is most in play. God's universal law is co-operation, human and Divine. Each harvest is a monument to earthly and heavenly co-operation.

Dequincy [De Quincey] speaks of sales as forming centres where the peasantry in the Lake District met for gossip. We have in our own neighbourhood abundant opportunities of posting ourselves up in this kind of intelligence. A large number of auction sales are effected through the Spring and Autumn. When business is brisk an immense concourse of people gather and every kind of commercial as well as incidental intelligence circulates through the community. Some mouths open at sales that are sealed at other public assemblies, while others listen like silent pupils who are communicative elsewhere. Lunch is provided with stimulants at the more important sales; the latter often imparts an artificial and feverish excitement to the sale. It gives an undue briskness and vivacity to the bidding, and bargains are made at extreme prices. Some have to regret their folly on the following morning.

WEDNESDAY, JULY 10TH, 1872

Is it possible that four months can have elapsed without a single record of my biographical life?[103] Four months of blank page! What literary lethargy! Is it not a sin to keep a rusty pen?

I find the last note concerning my flock of sheep was that one lamb had dropped. What has been the fate of the three hundred and nine then in promise? Barely two hundred and fifty is the fulfilment! I have only witnessed one season for twenty years when the flock was so marked by disease and death. An epidemic fever proved fatal to about 25 of the ewes and about 100 lambs, many before, and others after, birth. The shepherd could scarcely speak of anything but disaster. Still there were many farmers whose flocks were more severely blighted than our own. It was no uncommon occurrence for 400 ewes to yield only as many as our 300.

In reviewing the weather during the last four months we forget the calamities and our heaviness is removed. Such an inviting summer to vegetation has never visited us within human reccollection. It is generally believed that England has not experienced a summer of such abundant pasturage. It is stated that for the last month has been produced a surplus pasturage enough to feed a third more stock than exists in the country at large. God has extended his bounty towards this isle to an unparalelled extent. There is some loving design overflowing the nation. Why this unprecedented yield of herbage on the part of England? My own fields have never had such a dense herbal clothing nor so thickly strewn with sheep. Instead of three being barely able to find satisfaction, 5 or 6 have enough and to spare on an acre.

And the gaiety as well as abundance is equally remarkable. Both grass and clover fields are a mass of blossom. It is a summer to kindle the poet's vision as well as cheer and gladen the farmer's heart. As we have never enjoyed one so rich in landscape beauty neither have we known one so profitable in sheep (of course, excepting the lambing season and this occurred in the early spring). I had a grand clip of wool. Having kept my he-hoggets, my flock's backs yielded me the extraordinary amount of 230 todds nett at 59/-, constitutes the sum of £680 into pocket. We had 605 fleeces weighing more than 80 twos and the rest threes.

THURSDAY, JULY 11TH, 1872

How beautifully the designs of Divine Providence are unfolding throughout the history of this globe. We have witnessed most striking fulfilments of prophecy. The church has settled down on the principle of cosmopolitanism.[104] Her eye and presence is penetrating into the distant populations. But it will neither be bombast nor egotism to declare that God's designs are unfolding day by day in me as a member of the most glorious community under heaven, the Christian Church. I form a contribution towards the ripening of those purposes. The more watchful and prayerful and energetic I am the more rapidly will the consummation be effected. I am endeavouring to throw my farm into the treasury of Christ. It has been tythed for a different purpose than rearing altars for priests and manufacturing fishing rods and creating all kinds of blasphemous popish mummery.[105] The Bennett's judgment has made it patent what the state can do for the heresies of the church.[106] This judgment has rung another great knell of doom to the establishment.

But to return to agriculture, I have effected a sale simultaneously of wheat and wool, 107 qr. of wheat at 59/-.[107] About Mayday time I sold my cull hoggets and barren ewes, the hoggets at 70/- per head, the ewes at 73/-, 39 ewes and 40 hoggets.

The turnip crop has for some time past presented rather a precarious aspect. The little golden winged fly has enjoyed a great feast in consuming [the] greater part of the first sown as well as greatly shattering the Horncastle fair sowing. These tyny [tiny] insects still baffle the farmer's skill notwithstanding the triumphant conquests already achieved over the natural world. Has not this one insect been an annual source of irritation and loss to the agriculturalist? Does this not form part of man's discipline? How disastrous have climatic changes proved in cutting off his purposes and plans, in thwarting him in his undertakings.

My wheat crops look healthy. They have just gone out of flower. The weather was very propitious for the flowering. The bulk is not large though perhaps larger than my neighbours. It is some years since the spring corn has been so much behind the wheat. It is only now bursting into ear. The oats promise to be very heavy and the barley in the medium. Loud thunderstorms have recently burst over this district, somewhat destructive to animal life. A new cottage was severely struck in Mrs. Bland's valley. Two bricks were chipped as with a chisel from the outer wall, others scattered from the chimney and some of the ornaments on the mantlepiece perforated and driven through the kitchen. Mrs. Tripp, a widow, who only the other day buried her dear husband, had a horse struck dead while grazing. Its mouth was full of grass. Calamity is still woven into the daily history of this world.

Thursday Evening
It is a daily enjoyment to roam through the farm and neighbourhood while vegetation is pushing its way on to perfection. I walked to the village this morning, visited our Free Methodist chapel, and beheld with pleasure the advanced stage of the repairs and restorations. Mr. Sumpter, the bricklayer, has completed the colour washing, whitewashing and plastering. He has coloured the centre flower and the beading of the cornice with orange and green. Parker is now engaged staining and varnishing the pews for the first time since the chapel was built. They were brushing on the last coat of varnish in the gallery. The harmonium is readjusted to the front pew. The player will sit facing the congregation. The awkward-looking chair-back is removed and the choral gallery remodified. George Smith is painting the interior throughout,

chapel, schoolroom, and vestries, etc. The chapel was shamefully built or it would not require so much repair in less than 20 years. The plaster has peeled off one side of the wall. I wish we had the funds to plaster the exterior walls of the entire building. Many of the joints along one side are sadly delapidated.

It is very convenient to have the old Temperance Hall to worship [in] while the work is being effected.

I regret we have not had a church register in which to insert the names of all who have been converted since the erection of our chapel. Scores have been born again on this little hill of Zion.

I called this morning at Mrs. Bland's new valley cottage for the purpose of ascertaining the amount of damage done to the cottage by the terrible thunderstorm which broke over this neighbourhood the other day. The lightening struck the chimney and chipped two or three bricks off about the centre of the outer wall on the southern end of the cottage. It pierced its way in a most capricious manner into the interior, broke an umbrella in the corner of the bedroom, scathed the frames of two or three pictures, almost obliterating the gilt. It perforated two tin canisters in several places which stood on the mantlepiece.

The devastation committed by the material elements upon man's property, possessions and work! These calamities are not without their moral lessons. The material elements may turn round upon man and become a cruel and bitter enemy. We are not to put too much confidence in the material elements. When God permits they may strike us dead. When the Almighty chooses He can arouse our fears and strike us with terror and alarm. The rumblings of distant thunder is already and has been through this afternoon sounding in our ears. I have thousands of times asked for the wing of His protecting love to overshadow my dwelling, family, household and farm.

FRIDAY, JULY 12TH, 1872

My dear wife and I were disturbed by another fearful thunderstorm. It seemed as if all nature were suffering from a wild throe of conflicting anguish. The heavens blushed with a thousand flashes. Successive bursts of fire electric flew from one horizon to the other. Loud peals of thunder broke forth in almost ceaseless successive peals. I felt perfectly calm in Christ. While the elements were wildly raging in frantic confusion my spirit was as unruffled as the summer lake.

We were fortunate in gathering our sainfoin while the sun shone. We seized one fine opportunity as it flew past on the wings of a few days. One day is only like the flash of a bird's wing. I think it is heating more than last year. The long stack is settling down into smaller compass.

During the last four or five months organisation unions have been effected among agricultural labourers.[108] There is an evergrowing agitation going on for higher wages. What a kind Providence! As work increases and labour becomes scarcer, machinery develops and more widely adapts itself as a substitutionary power. The wheel and axle is filling up the vacancy of muscle. The strain upon the muscular is lightening in proportion to the development of mechanical power and its ever-widening adaptability. These strikes will be over-ruled for good in proportion as they awaken mechanical ingenuity so as to make it more than ever fruitful in invention. If ever we are to see an earthly millennium the burden of toil must be lightened by the invention. The adaptation of mechanical to the replacing of muscular power must be still further multiplied.

Tipler kicked on the right hock joint.

SATURDAY, JULY 20TH, 1872

How multiplied are the anxieties of the farming life, and one of the greatest sources is the turnip crop. We were just recovering from the effects of the fly, and now the wireworm is knawing the root. I never knew them commit such depridation at so early a stage of the plant's growth. We have turned out the heaviest rollers so as to crush them if possible. The land is sadly flooded by the late heavy rains.[109]

How unfortunate our poor Tipler horse![110] He had the influenza very severely in the Spring, not able to work for several weeks, and now he stands upon three legs in consequence of a kick from one of the other horses. For nearly a week we doctored him ourselves, and finding that he only grew worse we sent for the farrier, Mr. Kime, who informed us we had aggravated the case by the application of hot water in fomentations, and that the joint was open and the joint oil was running out. He at once ordered a cold bandage and the incessant pouring of cold spring water day and night. The foreman sat up with him on Thursday and Coney last night. So much for the evils of popular ignorance! The laws of organisation and life in relation to horses' joints we were entirely in the dark upon. I am not aware that we have ever witnessed a case of open joint or the outflowing of its oil. I hope the inflamation is on the decrease. Yesterday he was quite improved to his expectations.

Yesterday I inspected our chapel repairs and restorations. J. Parker was screwing the number plates on the pew doors and Mrs. Maultby, the tailor's wife, was stitching the cocoanut matting for the aisles. It will present a transformed aspect to Mr. Hirst and the congregation tomorrow upon its re-opening. Mrs. Robinson, Bemrose, Lowry and Appleyard form the washing and scrubbing group. They finished the outdoor steps yesterday. While I was present they formed a group of tongues as well as hands!

The weather is all we could desire the last few days, since the abatement of the storms. The wheat looks promising. My own looks better than most in the neighbourhood. If the rolls only check the grubbs the farm looks first rate. To a kind Providence be all the praise.

We ought to be cosmopolitan in our ideas and sentiments while we have cosmopolitan men stand out before us and cosmopolitan literature spread out before our eyes. I have drunk large draughts of American sermonic wine from the kingdom of heaven. It is fresh and sparkling. Who that delights in saintly aquaintances can ever forget such names as De Witte Talmage, Dr. Cuyler, Rev. Theodore, Dr. H. W. Beecher, Bushnell.[111] Oh! for more of their heavenlyness of mind and industry of character!

What a beautiful breezy sunny and health inspiring morn is this. It promotes a joyful inspiration in the Christian's heart. A summer day like this reflects itself in the soul as in a mirror.

My own health (through God's blessing upon means) has permanently improved. My sleep is sound and refreshing, my appetite good, my bowels regular, which has not happened for twenty years past before this summer. My enjoyment of life and Christ intense. This is the key to human happiness. Oh that his life of devotion might continue further to increase! Christ is the charm of life.

THURSDAY, JULY 25TH, 1872

This morning we are thrashing the last stack of oats. There are very few mice. The weather is all we can desire for mellowing the grain. In my bedroom the thermometer stands at 72 degrees. We require scarcely more than the sheet to cover us in bed.

My dear wife is once more approaching her confinement and complains of a good deal of pain in her body and of extreme helplessness. This world has proved a very sharp grindstone to her. She has been ground by a great multitude of afflictions. Her sufferings have been very protracted and numerous. This is her sixth pregnancy and three have proved miscarriages or abortions.

Miss Dawson returned yesterday from her holidays. The children were let loose from the cares of school rule. They have almost been allowed to run wild at Dexthorpe and Snitterly.

The crops have improved the last few weeks. The fields glow with sunshine. The sweet milk is being pumped up the stem in large measure and filling the grain skin and swelling it out to plumpness. My harvest prospects are good at present. To God be all the glory!

Tipler is improving. What a beautiful instance of Divine Providence among the smaller incidents of my life. At first sight the circumstance appeared purely accidental. I and my brother and Dr. Stovin from Wheatley were strolling in the garden and in looking over the garden gate we saw the horse attempting to get up. We walked up to him and found matter was squeezing out of the wound caused by the kick the animal had received. The Dr. said the joint oil was running out and I must get an experienced man to dress it or it would soon endanger his life. I at once sent for Mr. Kime, he came and changed the treatment and has so far, with the blessing of God, been successful. Our ignorance had well nigh proved fatal. Whas a kind Providence!

Mr. Nicholson of Grimblethorpe shot himself the other day; left a widow and ten children, and she about to be confined. What a ghastly scene!

FRIDAY, JULY 26TH, 1872

I have just had an interview with my foreman, Charles Smith, and he states that his wife's brother visited them yesterday and gives a terrible account of the turnip crop in the neighbourhood of Driby. Many of the strong land localities are irrecoverably destroyed by the fly. Most of the fields in this district are patchy and imperfect. I think my own look as well as most I have seen, none so good as my first sown, the stackyard field.

We are hoeing in the 16 acre today, having finished the 11 acre. We took the lambs off on Wednesday afternoon. Some of them have not recovered from the effects of the distemper they had in the Spring. They are lame and crippled. Calamitous rumours are already floating through the air about the mortality of lambs. Mr. Harwoods, Mackinder, R. Fieldsend, etc. are losing a great many.

What a succession of sunny days! This county has been highly favoured with comparative exemption from thunderstorms. We have frequently heard thunder in the distance. The lightenings have spent their force upon other districts. Thank God our harvest prospects at present on the farm brightened considerably during the last two months. How it gladdens the husbandman's heart to see the labour of his hands established by Divine Providence.

SATURDAY, JULY 27TH, 1872

I have sold Dr. C. F. Stovin (my brother-in-law) Taffy, a pony of great strength, 5 years old, a dark brown with four black legs, not remarkably swift, rather sluggish, but sound in constitution. As I have to send him off by the first train from Louth on Monday morning, I must tie the address upon his tail this evening. He is so quiet that Denison can ride or drive him anywhere. I bought him a few weeks ago at Louth for £21 and the Dr. takes him at £25. Denison is talking of breaking Topsy into harness now Taffy is going. Topsy is three years old. Mabel is very reluctant to part with Taffy. She very much enjoys riding in front of me round the farm. We shall all miss him very much. His action is too clumsy to ride pleasantly being altogether void of elasticity. I fancy he is full of steel for wear.

We have had another repetition of thunder and lightening and pouring rain through the night. It has curled the corn about very much though the turnips were suffering for want of rain. This has been a summer of flood and drought in alternate succession. We are experiencing an exceptional summer of tropical heat and tropical storms. God never repeats Himself monotonously either in nature [or in His] Providence. We have never two Springs or Summers precisely after the same pattern. The variation appears to us almost infinite. How abundant is the Power and Wisdom that can accomplish such shifting combinations.

I never reccollect laying in warmth and comfort for a whole night with my feet quite bare. The last few nights Denison and I could dispense with blanket and sheet. We have had our cistern recemented this summer.

In my readings I seem to have given myself up very largely to sermon literature lately. I preach as a rule fortnightly. I have experienced some glorious times in the pulpit. Praise God!

We are enjoying a great abundance of rasberries, gooseberries and currents this season.

Antony Sharpley gave us a very lengthy speech last Monday night on the occasion of the reopening of our Free Methodist Chapel.[112] He recapitulated his compound boast that he was an Englishman, a Protestant, a Nonconformist, a Free Methodist, a Christian. Mr. Hurst unfolded the idea that a man was better than a sheep. We cleared a trifle over £14.

Mrs. Benn delivered up her sewing meeting money which, being added to what Lizzie had in hand, amounted to £26/5/-.

TUESDAY, JULY 30TH, 1872

Mrs. Beswick arrived last evening from Matlock to nurse my wife during her confinement.[113] Mrs. Smedley is still unable to attend her patients. Mrs. Beswick appears in capital spirits and says Lizzie is looking much better than when she saw her last. Her general health has improved during two months past.

Walter and the children are exceedingly merry and gladsome over breaking the little grey Topsy into harness. Denison comes running into my room in such glee, 'Papa do come and look at Topsy pulling the cart round the paddock.' Of course, papa must leave his writing desk under the pressure of such joyful importunity. I don't think it is likely to be much trouble breaking. How much the pony has improved in appearance and condition. I hope it will prove a good substitute for Taffy, with which I have parted so reluctantly.

I am sorry the wireworm continue so persistant in cutting the roots of my turnips. The crows have found them out and bill up the plants to find them. We were rolling a second time yesterday.

A cooler breeze wafts the heated community this morning and a thin vapoury cloud veils the sun. The name of God is stamped upon our seasons. The mind of man from all the experience of the past could not have invented a summer so unique as the one we have witnessed. We stand in astonishment at the originality of the Divine mind in unfolding such rich variety of seasonal changes. The testimony of the oldest man living will declare that our summer panorama has manifested a wealth of splendour alternated by a darkened terror unparalelled within the sphere of reccollection.

One of my foreman's wife's brothers has been over to spend a week with them. He is a shunter on the line at Peterboro, a quiet, good-natured, commonplace sort of man. He remarked the labourers are better off in this neighbourhood than his own. He kindly lent me a local paper just started from the Peterboro press in which is reported a speech on the labour question by the Bishop of Peterboro. Its pregnancy with common-sense is truly remarkable for a learned Bishop.

WEDNESDAY, JULY 31ST, 1872

Yesterday was a red-letter day in my spiritual biography. I rode to Mucton for the first time on a spiritual errand,[114] and a more joyous piece of jockey work I never performed. Though Mucton is only 4 miles from Louth, and as many miles as I have traversed through districts bordering upon this bright little town, I was quite ignorant of the road. The sun burst forth from behind the clouds where he had been lingering through the day just as my pony's feet touched the hill rising out of Little Cawthorpe. We had not ascended far before a sweet landscape panorama greeted my kindled eye. I never before felt such a correction of old impressions. My old creed concerning Mucton experienced a thorough airing and blowing. A little dirty sediment had settled down in it when a boy, but yesterday's breezes disturbed it for the first time. It was blown into dust and scattered.

Mr. Lawton in his kindly address punned the word Mucton or Muctown. However, the term has lost its significance, for a more tidy, cozy, happy-looking little hamlet could scarcely be found. A grand culture has been at work. I mean Gospel culture, the sap of all culture worth the name. Mucton has in possession the tap root of all education. The best and most powerful educational institutions are simply outgrowths. The Free Methodists have bought the old Wesleyan chapel and renovated it and I never more cheerfully joined in any re-opening celebration. The friends had intended pitching a tent amid the dense foliage of the wood close by the chapel. They were making active preparations up to last Friday evening, and the rains descended and the floods came and washed away all their plans and preparations.

Undaunted by this defeat they soon broke through the difficulty by an altogether new device. Labour not considered toil, they soon emptied Mr. Twigg's carpenter's shop. They lined the interior of the boarded shell with ivy, fir and beech from the roof to the floor at a great cost of time and labour. What a relief to the eye! The tables were erected, covered with beautiful white cloth drapery, this again adorned with pleasant crockery, and the whole crowned with substantial viands and all kinds of confectionary with the addition of the seasonal fruits. Over the door of this temporary sanctuary was inscribed in large coloured type the word 'Welcome'. A most grateful word to a visitor. When I stood up to address the beautiful audience assembled in front of me, I felt the ivy of my heart to shoot out in every direction. I shall not soon forget the pleasing countenance of Mrs. Twigg as she introduced herself to me at the teatable. Her face shone as she proceeded to express her grateful appreciation of the beautiful expanse which stretched away from her beloved home, and the delightful fragrance which issued from the neighbouring woods and difused themselves through the air. What a sublime novelty this re-opening has proved! It was a re-opening of the intellectual and spiritual pores.

Mr. Hurley occupied the chair and referred to our distinctive principles, which was dovetailed by Mr. Barker. He referred to the origin of our Reform movement, etc.[115] Mr. Hurley clinched the speechifying by a remark or two upon one great object we have in view as Free Methodists, viz. to bring the sum of truth down upon the doctrine of ministerial supremacy.

AUGUST 2ND, 1872

Yesterday I accomplished a feat in leaving my bed about 4 o'clock for Dexthorpe and Partney Fair. Lizzie prepared me a cup of chocolate the night before, which I found very refreshing. I mounted Charlie with a bounding heart and pierced the delightful avenue of over-arching foliage, the ascent and descent of the richly clad hills as they shone in the early sunlight with their thousand long drawn lights and shades. Our wold and marsh landscapes have each their peculiar charm and were peculiarly enjoyable on yesterday's early morn.

The myriad beauties disclosed to my eye were sweeter than honey or the honey comb. But the artistic was not the only pleasure. The agricultural prospect looked encouraging. The varied shades of fading green and shining gold betokened the harvest at hand. I felt as the husbandman alone can feel, that God was about to reach him the prize due to his year of anxiety and toil. How the faithfulness of Divine Providence was about to be witnessed anew by the whitened fields with their responding wavelets to the breeze.

The turnip crop is somewhat defective. The fields are patchy. My father-in-law's are exceptional in their comparative regularity of plant. My own have declined this last few days in regularity. The Dexthorpe farm looks exceptionally fruitful altogether.

I found Annie ill in bed and Mr. R. was carrying her breakfast. What appalling years of weakness and suffering the two sisters have experienced. The key to this mystery will only be found on the other side of Jordan's swelling stream. Mr. R. and I had some pleasant talk together at the breakfast table and as we strolled across the turnip field. We parted at the gate leading into the highway and [I] proceeded some distance when Mr. Mason of Rigsby kindly picked me up. We perceived the effect of the abundant season in the small show of drape ewes. There were several lambs, and prices ruled somewhat lower. Midling lambs from 40/- to 45/- and best from 45/- to 52/-. Mr. Hill of Winceby said he never knew so much disease among cattle and sheep simultaneously. Mr. R. bid Mr. Cussons of Halton 44/6 for 20 lambs. He gave us a receipt for skit in lambs, calves, etc: one table-spoon of whitening in a little water.

SAT. EVENING, AUGUST 3RD, 1872

Praise God another joyous day! Mr. and Mrs. F. Riggall lighted up our little circle with their presence. We had given them up as they spoke of coming earlier. Mrs. F. R. made Mabel a present of 15 young ducks. We had a little horse-dealing in the afternoon. Robinson brought me a chesnut pony to look at. I rode it round by the lodge and liked its riding, then called Mr. R. out for his opinion. He thought I might venture to £22, and we bargained. Afterwards Mr. R. bought it of me for Annie. We had him christened young Jerry; old Jerry was to be sent to be a companion in work at Wheatley.

Well, we have had a happy day together. They are dear parents. How they kindle up our domestic affections! Mabel became nearly wild when they entered the house. They lavish kindness upon us all. I told them I thought the year 1872 was likely to become a memorable year in our married life. We have balanced up our financial accounts and settled all for the present.[116] Lizzie appears quite cheerful this evening.

TUESDAY, AUGUST 6TH, 1872

Yesterday I arrived home from the Board about 4 o'clock after a fast of about 9 hours. I drove Topsy for the first time to Louth. Robinson says it is 4 years old.

On Sunday last Mr. Cornish preached his two fairwell sermons. He speaks of going to Driffield where he will appear weekly before the same congregation. He speaks too much of man's nobility and not enough of his shame, dwells unwarrantedly upon his greatness and heroism, not enough upon his misery and degradation. If he visited the sick and sorrowing more this exaggeration would be considerably toned down. The terrors of the Lord appear to be under eclipse in our modern pulpit. The Apostle says, by the 'terrors of the Lord we pursuade man'. Where are our pulpit artists who give any prominance to these. How can our congregation behold the goodness and severity of God unless faithfully pictured upon our pulpit canvass. Let the facts of ruin and desolation which have marked this earth with scars and stains be dragged once more from the oblivion of liberary record, and their awful lessons brought home to our own generation. Mr. Cornish's preaching is largely tainted with this fatal mistake. It is confectionary which produces a certain kind of dispepsea [dyspepsia]. It is moral granduer [grandeur] in theory but not translated into real life.

BINBROOK, WEDNESDAY, AUGUST 7TH, 1872

Yesterday we had a delightful meeting at South Reston, on the occasion of their chapel Anniversary. Mr. Samuel Foster of Great Carlton occupied the chair. Mr. Burt of Louth, my brother, myself, and David Bennett each delivered an address. It was an exceptional platform by the absence of clericals. I would to God that more laymen were called out to pulpit and platform labour. The choir, too, was quite a scene. A little girl presided at the harmonium. My eyes were riveted upon her nimble little fingers running along those keys. The energy and force with which those notes were struck, and the amount of musical harmony elicited from the instrument, excited all our admiration. The child appeared to have seen about ten summers! 'Out of the mouths of babes and sucklings thou hast perfected praise.' I think it was one of the happiest meetings we almost ever enjoyed. The light of heaven beamed in the countenances of God's people. Glory be to God!

I rode Jerry the younger. The first journey since the purchase, and perhaps the last. He has now gone to Dexthorpe. I sincerely hope he will meet Annie's requirement. As I roam along the green lane bound by the leafy hedgerows and here and there over-shadowed and embowered by winding lines of trees and woods with their expanding arms and unfolding drapery - how bold would these marsh and fen flats of Lincolnshire appear without this park-like luxuriance which blends with and surrounds the hamlets and villages which harbour our agricultural population. I might have said these sanctuaries tend to promote every kind of material development, intellectual development, moral and spiritual, etc.

THURSDAY, AUGUST 8TH, 1872

Mr. Crombie is very kind in posting me up in our Free Methodist Convocation intelligence by sending a Bristol paper.

Yesterday morning I carried my breech loader round the farm. Most things looked pregnant with promise and delightful to the heart of the husbandman. The thought struck the spark of gratitude into a flame of Praise and thanksgiving. The farm seemed all alive with joyous response to the husbandman's skill. It has broken into weighty fruitfulness under the magic wand of skilful industry. It is the seal of God upon our toil. My agricultural occupation of crow-tenting amid such pleasing associations attuned my soul to more lofty contemplation. In consequence of a temporary shower of rain I took shelter beneath the foliage canopy of a fine elm tree and while leaning against the massive trunk my mind was caught up with Paul into the third heaven. A bright vision occurred to me showing the utter futility and baselessness of sceptical objections.

What is the legitimate sphere of the physical sciences? The power of articulation is not in the air. The power of vibration is! He that planted the ear shall not He hear? Did not God create the air and endow it with certain properties? He that gave man the power of language and utterance shall not he speak? Man can imitate nature's sounds and forms and why not God? Infidel objections may be reduced to a very small compass by the fact that the whole of them may be pronounced as a limitation of the Divine attributes. Why, the Almighty could with one throw of his hand toss this ball

with all its observatories into the black oblivion of non existence.
How brightly the wheatfields glow and gleam, all golden in the warm sunshine. This is the bloom of health in the ripening. When the green becomes grey there is ghastly mildew. God in His kind Providence is warding off what He sometimes permits.
I have strolled to the village this afternoon and Mr. Barton and his two sons [are] busily engaged in building his butcher's shop, slaughter and firing house.
I think I may pronounce this a happy day. The dear children have been gay and my wife somewhat more cheerful. Turnip weeding and ploughing and sainfoin stack-thatching the staple work of the farm for a few days.
We witnessed an indescribable charm flung across sky and field by the setting sun. The beauty of the ripening wheat was intense. I was reminded of Rosa Bonner's [Bonheur's] harvest scenes she has reflected on canvass frames and hung in the Leeds Infirmery [Infirmary] which was opened by an Arts Exhibition.[117] A sight so lovely as this evening can only fill the eye about one or two hours in the year. It is the most transitory stage of ripening. It is here as in the human face, where there is the bloom of health physical beauty shines. Disease fades the golden glory on the field as well as the rose upon the cheek.

BINBROOK, SATURDAY, AUGUST 10TH, 1872

Yesterday I mounted my bay steed, Charlie, for Benniworth Sabbath school Anniversary. After a pleasant chat at the tea table with my brother, Mr. Colam and Longbottom, I took a short solitary walk towards Willingham. When I returned the singing had commenced. My brother called upon Mr. Colam to pray, in which he was led out very fervently. George was called to occupy the chair. David Bennett, Mr. Longbottom, myself and Colam addressed the meeting, which the people appeared to enjoy exceedingly. David Bennett made reference to Dr. Livingstone, whom Mr. Stanley has had the honour of bringing out of his obscurity.[118] He has considerably enlarged the sphere of our geographical vision. He has discovered an immense watershed of 700 miles extent, covered with lofty chains of mountains 6 or 7000 feet in altitude feeding great lakes and rivers and fountains in abundance. He has forced his way through trackless regions of grassy luxuriance, grasses as tall again as himself, also through boggy districts where he has sank up to his hips. The excitement arising out of all these geographical discoveries in opening up a new continent larger than Europe before the delighted eyes of all civilised nations has not blinded his comprehensive vision nor diverted his mind from the main object of his explorations. The horrors of the slave trade with its thousand attendant miseries move his philanthropic compassion. The development of the Missionary spirit advances in the midst of his other successes. Dr. Livingstone is accomplishing the most valuable and splendid achievement the world has yet known. He is giving a fresh impetus to cosmopolitanism which it is the sole glory of Christianity to have created and fostered.

This is a summer of floods. England has scarcely experienced such copious baptisms from the skies. Many districts have overflowed several times by the incessant pourings. May it please Heaven in mercy to send us seasonable weather for the harvest. Praise God we are under the consoling Promise!

I met with Hay and the Isaac Sharpleys of Calcethorpe and Boswell in Uncle Isaac's grass field.[119] They were taking a walking survey of the smiling fields of his own farm. His turnips look about the best in the county, according to the testimony of Boswell Isaac. One can never ride through Calcethorpe without being struck with admiration at the almost unparalelled skill in the perfection of cultivation. Cousin Isaac can say as scarcely any other man can say, 'This one thing I do.' He is nearly as ignorant as a Hottentot on most other subjects. He said he had written a letter to me about the penshioned [pensioned] medical officers.[120] He thought the penshion did not amount to much. Why is not Fawcett over sixty? When does he realise it? In about 5 years.

The clock struck 12 last night before retiring to rest. One short sound sleep of about 5 hours and up I spring. I might have had ten for the vigour I feel at this moment of mind and body. Praise God for health and soundness of constitution.

We are dipping the lambs today.

The morning is breaking and sunshine stealing through the clouds.

Last night the black shadows of the trees enshrouded me as I dashed through Biscathorpe. I told the Benniworth friends that thousands of poor wretches packed in the large towns would be thankful to be transported into these lovely sylvan districts. What mean all these restless picnic excursions? Why there hearts would dance for joy if they could exchange their garret-like dwellings, dismal with smoke and damp and squalor, for your smiling cottages, all rose-covered, honeysuckled, and ivy-wreathed, shining in the full glare of the summer's sun. I love these villages. It is an exquisite pleasure to roam about through and amongst them in Mission tours.

My admiration has been much struck with the manner in which the Louth friends have turned the romantic spirit of excursions to a missionary account. They are wisely adapting themselves to the times by bringing the picnic spirit into the service of the church. Our rustic dwellings are blooming inside and out. Thousands of geraniums, fusias, and other flowers have gazed out of the windows of the poor and caught my ravished eyes. Flowers of every variety rivet my eyes each succeeding summer with an increased intensity of delight.

After driving my two children with Topsy and basket phaeton to the village,[121] I held a conversation with Mr. Fawcett upon his medical salary and prospect of forthcoming pension. He requested me to look into the real facts of the case as to what it is.

I have experienced an even flow of physical energy quite

exceptional considering my enthusiastic platform labours, succeeding long ride home and short sleep of last night. As a rule nothing exhausts me more than public speaking. My moral and spiritual victories reflect back upon my physical frame in improved health.

We have imported one truck load of coals, or as D. Bennett styles them, 'black diamonds'. C. Smith has taken 1 ton 2 cwt, and amount in total is tons 8 cwt 1.3 qr. The first price fixed was 21/-. About a fortnight after, Mr. Cook came to me in the market and asked for one more shilling per ton as prices had advanced. These have been ordered now several weeks and the second truck is not yet arrived. The one arrived has considerably less overweight, only 1 cwt 3 qr.

The advance in wages appears to have nearly moved round the circle and most things are enhanced in price.

The clock has struck nine, and I am beginning to gape. Oh, may God prepare me for tomorrow's worship and make me a true leader of his saints and an anointed preacher of His word! We must have sinners converted.

MONDAY, AUGUST 12TH, 1872

Yesterday for the first time I preached at South Kelsey. Text 2 Kings 7ch. 1-20. A great sheet of God's wrath seemed to blaze in the eyes of sinners.

We experienced another heavy rainfall yesterday morning. What a variable climate. One day the air still and clear, another it is hazy and damp. One day miasma sleeps over our hills and vales and lingers about our dwellings. Last night as I commenced my journey home, the wind gently sighed through the trees which looked like globes of black shadows darkening the space they fill.

TUESDAY, AUGUST 13TH, 1872

Yesterday I attended the Board. We again sat on committee upon the medical salaries. The law was propounded upon medical pensions.

I sold a little heifer for £8, which cost £6/10 at Spring, also 25 weathers [wethers] at 70/-.

Yesterday we commenced harvest. The wheat crop good. This morning a gentle rain and no progress. The men congregate at my court gate for a bargain.[122] They agree to hand rake the wheat, open out hedges and pits by rakings, etc., finishing for 7/- pr. acre. A great many Irish are over.

Since breakfast I have been leading out Denison's mind in elementary geography. He is pleased with his new book on the subject by the author of 'Peep of Day'.[123] Its discriptions [descriptions] are given in simple and attractive language. Geography is perfect in proportion as it is graphic in describing the grand framework of the globe we inhabit.

I have lately [been] reading for my own spiritual profit 'The

Christian Age'. Its pages flash all through with genius. It has done both my head and heart good. What a mighty original is De Witt Talmage and what an inexhaustable is Beecher.[124] What summer freshness in his productions. Then the latest number of 'Preacher's Lantern' supplies me with many Bible lives left out of Beecher's teaching. In the 'Christian Age' shines the American Orion in the sky of Christian oratory. In some respects such a constellation was never known since the Apostles.

One word upon my own personal autobiography. Sleep refreshing, appetite good, spirits cheerful, amid bountiful surroundings, with growing domestic affections, increasing faith in God and His Christ's Providence, a clearer view of the Atonement and its relation to the moral government of God. A stronger desire to be useful in lifting me out of sin into God, into Christ, a richer experience of pardoning and sanctifying grace. A clearer consciousness of God's pleasure in my pleadings through Christ for the advance and growth of His kingdom in the world. An ever-brightening view of His providential government of the nations blended with the grand central purpose of man's eternal salvation. It is this expansion of vision which broadens and strengthens the shield of my faith. What a remarkable season I had at South Kelsey on Sunday night last. The power of God came down in an eminent degree.

Tuesday Evening

There are not only red-letter days but red-letter years. The reason I write in red ink is that this, 1872, is a perfect mystery of blessing. I feel a luxuriousness of Divine good growing in me and around. How delightful to follow the reaper once more and see the fine wheat fall upon the board over the charming sycle. Could our forefathers imagine a sycle drawn by horses! It is a sublime ringing out of human invention in the sound of these machines! My wheat crop is beautifully ripe; no blight has blackened its straw nor shrivelled the grain. These harvest scenes have kindled the eye and imagination of some of our greatest painters. What a scene of active industry are those family groups eagerly tying up the sheaves! It is the workmen's season of opportunity. His earnings are ample in proportion to his strength, skill and activity. He advances from sheafing to shocking. I remember many years ago the romance of the harvest field awakened in me a sense of the picturesque as I laid in bed in our little front bedroom. One or two rough canvass pictures or skeleton diagrams of Pyramids hung upon the walls. I was an enthusiastic student of Egyptian life and architecture. Of course pyramids were amongst the Egyptian wonders uppermost in my thoughts, and, in looking out of my window one sunny morn, those shocks of oats standing all golden amid the shining glories all circumambient, suggested the idea of pyramids in miniature.

Surely there can be nothing more crowded with romance than an agricultural life when characterised by devoutness. What a red-letter day of holy enjoyment has this been! The Methodist Recorder has proved a fount of blessedness to my soul today. These Conference numbers are truly heavenly.

THURSDAY, AUGUST 15TH, 1872

A copious dew and harvest sunshine this morning. Intelligence has come from the South that the rain has injured the Kent and Essex wheat.

Yesterday I had tea with Hay Sharpley. Septimus had tea, too. Of course, a very animated conversation ensued. The topic preachers and preaching. We place Mr. Cornish very low in the scale of usefulness. We pronounced him as a faint echo of Bushnell and D. Thomas. I referred to Mr. J. B. Sharpley, deceased,[125] as the greatest theologian Louth has ever had the honour to possess. A vacancy which may never again be filled up. His was a sound and robust theology. I said my assurances were deepened in relation to the importance and weight of the Methodist theology. If a lax and false catholicity induces us to cut off the sharp edges and points of our Methodist creed there is an end to conviction of sin, of righteousness and of judgement to come. When we cease to make sinners feel they have no share in the blessings of new Covenant.

FRIDAY, AUGUST 16TH, 1872

Yesterday Mr. Turner and Baker and two others came punctually at 8 o'clock for the purpose of drawing my drape ewes. He gave me 57/- fast and 58/- if he could afford it, also 35 of my best weathers [wethers] at 70/-, also 13 cull rams at 70/- fast and 71/- if do..

Of course my engagement to meet my brother to dine with Maria at Grainthorpe Hall. We found the little daughter very unwell and Maria a good deal depressed, having had considerable anxiety and loss of rest in consequence.

After dinner my brother drove me in his gig to farm his grass land at North Somercoates,[126] then to South Somercoates. We arrived soon after three o'clock and Mr. Andrews, one of the leading men in connection with the Free Methodist church in the village, conducted us to the intended site for their new chapel.[127] We surveyed the two stones with the inscription of Mr. G. Stovin upon one and Mr. Kirkby upon the other. We also inspected the new Parish schoolroom evidently built to fulfil Government requirements with regard to area.

While here the Louth friends arrived and after shaking of hands and the usual greetings and how do you dos, we decided to form a procession from the old chapel to the new site before commencing the ceremony.

SATURDAY, AUGUST 17TH, 1872

The blind son of Mrs. Hall, recently deceased, presided at the harmonium. Mr. Hirst gave out a hymn, we sang and prayed, and continued to sing as we walked along the street until we were gathered at the site, when Mr. Hirst read appropriate portions of God's Word and Rev. Biddulph offered up a beautiful prayer. After imploring God's blessing, our stone masons for the time-being commenced their work. Mr. Colam introduced my brother to lay the first stone, upon which he laid a five pound note, then Mr. Kirkby to lay the second (he also laid down the same amount). This work being completed, suitable addresses were delivered. My brother spoke of the admiration he felt in travelling about through these villages in seeing Methodist chapels. He had seen some villages without a single Methodist chapel of any kind and had witnessed the disastrous immoral character of those villages in consequence of that lack. He saw one village of this kind where people congregated on the Sunday evening outside the public house to drink and profane God's holy day. The presence of Methodist sanctuaries drove the remaining sin into secrecy. It was not so glaringly impudent and contaminating.

Mr. Colam now invited those friends who were wishful to have a hand in laying a golden or silver or even copper brick. I took the trowel in hand and laid a half sovereign brick.

My mind lingers with restrospect pleasure upon this scene and ceremony. I believe immense issues have grown and are now growing out of these Divine nurseries. What angelic joys run in streamlets through our social circles from these sanctuary fountains; civilisation flows forth from them. How stagnant would villages become without them. How barbaric the populations would become were they removed.

As we stood up these ever memorable planks we had a most picturesque view of the Wold hills touching the horizon in the distance; also a pleasing photograph might be taken of the cheerful village in the centre of which we stood. It has a beautifully suburban appearance.[128] The chief almost contiguous object before us was the eccentric-looking church marked by all the wrinkles of antiquity. Its spire rising like a tall spear from a squatting tower into the heavens would constitute it an interesting object to the mariner as he sailed towards our shore. On the left stands the parsonage, so snugly embowered in its leafy shades. The crescent form of the village and its scattered homes taken by the turn of the highway, blended with trees, shrubs and flowers constitute a pleasing photograph to eye, especially as the sun poured a few transient gleams down upon the ceremony.

These fine blocks of white stone inserted into the red brick front will add to the cheerful appearence of its noble little front. May the Divine blessing ever rest upon this unassuming little conventicle. May the shekinah dwell here. May scores of souls be born here.

Who would not praise God for so brilliant a harvest day as this.

While numerous complaints are spreading respecting blighted wheat in the fens and other contiguous districts, also of the injury done by continuous rains in the counties of Essex and Kent in sprouting their fine quality white wheats, it is a matter of great thankfulness to traverse my own fields and find them free and sage. All being well we shall finish wheat cutting today.

The last two mornings I have held a little conversation upon the European countries they [Denison and Mabel] are having lessons upon. I am pleased to find their little minds and memories take such firm hold of these interesting lessons.

When Turner takes the 110 drape ewes, we shall still have remaining on the farm 680.

A larger tea party assembled last Thursday evening at South Somercoates than was expected, being harvest time. After tea some of us took a stroll into the churchyard and formed a group in conversation upon the education question. My brother still adhered to the opinion he formed at the outset of the controversy, viz. that the Bible ought to be read in the schools, while some of us thought it would seal more firmly than ever the church and state, etc. Such were some of the chief of our meditations among the tombs. I then, according to general practice, took a solitary walk for purposes of prayer and mental collection. On my return I found the chapel beautifully filled. Mr. Colbridge occupied the chair and a joyous meeting we had. We all seemed under a gracious influence.

MONDAY, AUGUST 19TH, 1872

Praise God; in answer to earnest and faithfull prayer sombre nature brightened up her countenance early on Saturday morning last and this is the third day of almost cloudless splendour. We commence leading wheat today, and it comes home in fine condition. Oh, how my soul revels amid the glowing scenery created by this glorious summer. My own home surroundings never before appeared so intensely charming. My heart has expanded with light, joy and love under the general influences of this unique Paradisaical season.

It is a remarkable harvest inasmuch as the wheat is cut, raked, and finished, and d.v. will be led and stacked before a single ear of Spring corn is cut. This is another of the thousand proofs of God's Providential working. A christian farmer has a fine opportunity of studying the evolutions of Natural Theology in all their multiplied variations. The effects of the seasons upon my own farm, upon the land, the crops, manifests Divine originality of design and conception. Unforeseen events, unexpected events, sometimes surprises of a pleasing nature, at other times the source of alarm and anxiety and distress, are ever and anon happening. In looking round my farm I am gazing upon a part of God's dominions.[129]

This morning I rode Topsy to the village, enquired for my letters and had to sign my name as the recipient of a registered postal parcel. My curiosity was at first a little excited to know what the contents could be. It was my electric belt.[130] May heaven's blessing make it instrumental in the invigoration of my frame.

I had some conversation with the Blanchards about a machine and about our preachers. We agreed that Mr. Cornish's style of preaching would never convert sinners.

On the way home I opened the 'Daily News' and read Mr. Stanley's speech upon the results of his expedition in search of Dr. Livingstone. He described the search, the discovery.

WEDNESDAY, AUGUST 21ST, 1872

Yesterday morning I mounted Topsy about 5 o'clock. The little animal gave me several sudden jirks [jerks]. He stunted, gibbed and flew from one side of the road to the other. Its strong-headedness and obstinacy was almost unbearable before I reached Sotby. This is the third day of uninterrupted wheat carrying. I suppose the barometer gives way somewhat.

I have girded myself with my electric belt for the first time today.

Horncastle Fair was slow for lambs and midling store sheep. The best lambs are making no more than a month ago. On my Rent day in July reports were circulating of Mr. Briggs having sold 300 lambs at 48/-, and Mr. Vesey had taken some lamb rent which made 45/- each.

As we extend our information of the harvest prospects, they are anything but encouraging. My own wheat promised more than it performs. The extreme wet has shrivelled a large proportion which one time promised to be bold.

In returning home from Louth market with Topsy and phaeton, I took advantage of the opportunity to read a portion of Dr. Leifchild's book on the higher ministry of Nature.[131] It is evidently the work of an independent, original, comprehensive mind. It is full of gems of thought. His reference to the uncovering of the Egyptian mummy with the dead leaves under his arm and the reflections are rich and beautiful suggestions and call to mind the Egyptian memorials of the old nation which I studied many years ago by means of books and diagrams.

What a sacred thing a farm is when consecrated by the Divine presence! When that shekinah is recognised in our fields and woods agriculture ceases to be a purely secular pursuit. Each hill will constitute an altar step to Calvary and paradise.

This is a day of satisfaction or partial gratification of book hunger.

THURSDAY, AUGUST 22ND, 1872

The summer still mentains its character of alternate excesses of sunshine and rain, of bake and flood. This morning the rain literally pours. My foreman says the barometer has not given way much, and his wife thinks we shall not have much more rain. The clouds are breaking already.

I have inspected the work of my little family school. I generally receive a smiling welcome from my pair of young doves. Mabel is reluctant for me to leave the room. We are a very happy family; though my dear wife is a great sufferer she is a cheerful and patient sufferer.

Labour being so plentiful we have no trouble in gathering our harvest. Though my home is not in the crowded city, surrounded by the granduers [grandeurs] of architecture, nor in the compact village, still we are free from the smoke, the strife, and envyings, the vice and corruptions incident to human crowding. We have facilities for reflection and meditation, reading and storing our minds with lovely thoughts and images, with facts national and international. We have communications from all parts of the globe. If cosmopolitanism progresses during the next half century as it has done the last, our nationalities will be merged into one vast federalship.

I see Mr. Gladstone has enunciated his intention to launch another gigantic measure for the extension of representative government from cities and large corporation towns into the counties and parishes, as well as to rectify the injustices connected with local taxation.[132]

Thursday Evening
According to my wife's account, the bread and meat consumption of my household has considerably increased since last May day. Our maids are not economical. A grinding of two bushels barely lasts a fortnight.

I took a walk to Binbrook and had some conversation with Mr. Burkinshaw. I asked him whether Mr. Huntley was proceeding with the case of compelling the parish to pay his law expenses incurred with Wallace.[133] Mr. B. seemed in the dark about Mr. H's designs. This question led to further remarks of an historical character. He referred to the parish meeting when Mr. H made an offer of land for a burial ground on condition that we took the responsibility of the final settlement of affairs with the builder.[134] Mr. B. proceeded to speak of the control Mr. Denison Junr. had exercised in the erection of the church.[135] Nothing could be done without the approval of Mr. Denison. He increased the cost of the church about £400, the total being over £6000, and when the time of subscription payment arrived he refused to cash up the £125 promised by himself and father because he disapproved of the altar step.

FRIDAY, AUGUST 23RD, 1872

This morning has brought with it its sad intelligence. Mr. C. Smith's wife's brother, who was over here on a visit from Peterboro, while engaged in his shunting duties was smitten down and run over by a steam engine last night. Accidents of a calamitous nature are of daily occurrence. 'Be ye also ready, etc.' God looks upon human life and property as a small item compared with moral and spiritual character and his spiritual kingdom.

After the heavy rain we have again a fine breezy morn which admits of further harvest operations. The hands are collecting and marshalling. The scattered forces of horses and men and boys are being rapidly concentrated for rickyard importation. The rain has thrown us back in review of the work hastily and rudely done. We have raked down the half dozen stacks already reared, and made them still more secure against future inroads of wet.

Praise God for the blue, green and gold, the shining contrasts which always refresh and delight us, especially in the meridian of harvest! Both taste and pocket and religion flourish in the midst of their genial influences.

Parker is engaged in the work of stable renovation. Racks repairing, cribs making, standing and rearing new door, and frame fixing - these form the staple of his handywork today. Oak spills, caps, posts, threshhold and deal for door frame, cribs and crib-caps, are the materials he has to mould, smooth, fashion and joint. The most elementary workman manifests design and skill in every fresh execution. Even a horse stable and farm stedding as a piece of workmanship is pregnant with design and adaptation. Perhaps as much building ingenuity may be manifested within the compass of a well-contrived farm house and premises as mechanical skills in the construction of a watch. The two kinds of work may be quite distinct while the principle of design may be precisely similar.

The principle of design runs through all man's work. Man has stamped his purpose upon every execution whether sacred or secular. This forms part of man's dignity. The more complicated man's designs in his varied workmanship, the more he resembles Deity in His natural attributes. His progression in this is his progression towards natural perfection.

SATURDAY, AUGUST 24TH, 1872

Last evening I experienced my Autumn attack of diarreagh [diarrhoea]. Thank God I feel much better tonight. How thinly scattered are my diary pages with jottings of failing health.

Yesterday I drove Augur in waggonette to Louth station and met with Annie, John and Lizzie Lois Collett. This morning John and I walked together in the glorious sunshine. He read aloud a large portion of Gavazzi's speech delivered on the occasion of the first great public debate in the ancient city of Rome.[136] No sooner does Rome become Italian than Protestantism challenges Popery in open and free discussion close by her citadel outside the gate of the Vatican.

A sack of wheat was sent to the mill on Thursday and the flour has come this evening.[137] My Lizzie says it ought to last a month.

TUESDAY, AUGUST 27TH, 1872

Today we commence our Spring corn harvest in good earnest. The reaper is cutting oats in 37 acre above lodge. The crop is so heavy and laid and curled and twisted that we must turn the main part of the field to the scythe.

The loose hands are weeding turnips and thatching wheat stacks.[138] This evening Denison and I have each climbed the plum trees; the fruit is neither plentiful nor fine. There are more greengages than red plums. The apples are a miserable crop.

The ravages of the potato disease is stated to be as fearful as ever was experienced. Dr. Hooker has stated that the starch is not injured by the disease, and by grating the bulb and cleansing the starch in a tub of water it falls as a sediment and may be economised as rice or arrowroot or any other farinaceious materials in the form of puddings or gruels.

I am thankful that perseverance with a restricted diet has allayed the internal agitation I have felt from the effects of diahrea [diarrhoea]. I think it has been the most protracted attack I have experienced for years past. It reminded me of my Father's frequent prostration from this kind of disorder.[139] We have conversed with Mrs. C. Smith upon the sudden death of her brother. The silver lining to the cloud shone in the fact that he was conscious two hours before he died and gave testimony to his acceptance with God and his joyful anticipation of soon being in heaven. He was a Free Methodist and the mainstay of that now mourning church of Peterboro. Surely this awful visitation of Divine Providence will drive both minister and people to more humble, earnest and faithful prayer.

WEDNESDAY, AUGUST 28TH, 1872

This morning dawned with a clear sky and the day advanced with dry, healthy and cheery breezes, highly favourable for harvesting. The reaper has run in bridle road 20 acres. The tyers have been mowing that portion of the 37 acres of oats that the reaper refused to cut, at 13/- per acre.

Poor Phido has met with his death in the harvest field today. James Drew nearly cut off his head with the scythe. He was indeed a treasure. We have never had so little vermin for he allowed them no rest when his keen nose caught their scent. The poultry and other places used to be infested with them before he came.

THURSDAY, AUGUST 29TH, 1872

Another fine blowy harvest day. The bridle road 20 acres barley is finished reaping and tying, and part of next 20 acres.

I have spent this day at home and on the farm. Farming, reading, playing at croquet with Miss Dawson and children, also riding out with them, I on Charley, Denison on Topsy, and Mabel on the Donkey, have formed the chief occupations of today.

I have read Mr. Clifford's address delivered at Nottingham on the occasion of the General Baptist Association, a magnificent production, full of information couched in rhetorical language. It is a beautiful reflection of the times. It manifests clearsighted intelligence, original eloquent power of thought and utterance, combined with good common sense and practical wisdom. He exposes with a master's hand the theoretical and practical errors which have cursed our age. His remarks upon communism as having been placed in the great American laboratory. Scores of experiments have been tried upon the vast and open fields of America by communistic communities and failure was inscribed upon their attempts. There has scarcely existed a solitary case of success. It must be a deeply interesting book of Mr. J. H. Noyes- Trubner, 1870, 'History of American Socialisms'. It would prove a treat of a high order to posess the book and study it.

Thank God this has been a day of improved health!

SATURDAY, AUGUST 31ST, 1872

This was a showery morning, which has hindered the reaper. In fact showers have cut the harvest day short at both ends. Such rapid dispersions and gatherings of clouds I scarcely ever witnessed. The elements are ever unsettled and threatening mischief as well as bright and promising. Money seems to flow like water these fortnightly payments.

T. Smith has drawn	40/-	
Robinson	20/-	20/-
Dobson	20/-	
Bratby	40/- [140]	

This morning I received a post card from Mr. Crombie informing me that Mr. Berry, our young minister, had arrived at Market Rasen and D.V. would come to Binbrook tomorrow to preach his first two sermons in our Free Methodist Chapel; also that the Rasen friends had consented to allow Mr. Lawton to hold a fortnight of special services at Binbrook. He also gives me an invitation from the Rasen friends to attend their reception service on Thursday night next. If God spare me and permit me a favourable journey, I hope to be present on the occasion. My heart burns for a revival of true and vital godliness and for an aggressive outbreak upon the ranks of the wicked one. May God give me a word of encouragement to our circuit ministers![141] The work of the itinerancy will assume a virgin aspect to Mr. Berry. He has passed through the gate of one examination into an entirely new field of labour. How great the contrast between the great Leeds and small Rasen. I wonder what the feelings, thoughts and sentiments will be excited in his spirit by this transition. I conclude that for a time at least God has called him forth from the busy turbulent scenes of city life into the more quiet and rural district. He has come forth from a great centre of art, science, industry. I shall [not] soon forget my visit to the Leeds Infirmery when opened by the various exhibitions of Arts.[142] It was there I spent a good round sum in an opera glass to strengthen my aching and bloodshot vision.

In returning home from the Louth fat stock market I read the latest number then issued of the 'Local Government Board Chronicle' upon the new Public Health Act,[143] which was introduced for the first time into our Board last Monday. It appears to constitute a germ of new responsibilities, duties and expenses. How the great statute book is opened for the study of all classes, clerical and lay.

TUESDAY, SEPTEMBER 3RD, 1872

The water continues to fall from the clouds as from a resevoir. It appears to stream down in pipes instead of showers. It was so through the early morning of yesterday and harvest operations are considerably retarded. Nothing was done until late yesterday afternoon.

The oats are all cut down mainly by scythe and the rest by reaper.

This morning I heard the ring and clatter of reaper about half past five. The morning dawned in clear sunshine which is now shaded by a thin curtain of cloud. May Heaven bless the work of our hands!

When we arrived at our little Sanctuary on Sunday morning last, Mr. Berry was at his post of duty. He has a very youthful appearance. Hair, eyes, complexion, dark; rather slim in build; a modest though confident manner. Earnestness without animation. An intelligent discourse, though overladen with material ornament. It made a deeper impression than the night sermon. In the house he is pleasant company, not so dogmatic as Cornish.

Tuesday Evening

My Lizzie is now bordering on her confinement and has this morning and during the last few days experienced hysteria and corresponding weakness and melancholy. Mabel is receiving treatment from Mrs. Beswick for ringworms which seem very obstinate.

Today I have studied the 'Local Government Chronicle'. It contains an exposition of the provisions of the new Public Health Act. The object of this Act is to create a new Sanitary authority centreing in the Board of Guardians, combining together the Sewage authority, under the Sewage Utilization Act, also the Nuisance authority, under the Common Lodgings and Houses Acts, the Diseases Prevention Act, and the Bakehouse Regulation Act, forming one rural authority. It has a further object in dividing the country into districts for sanitary purposes.

But in more closely reading, it might be inferred that I was restricting the application of the Act to one class of districts, viz. the rural, whereas it extends to the urban authorities and districts.

Today I visited Binbrook on Topsy for charitable purposes. I might have been a paid pastor for I performed, though very imperfectly, some pastoral duties in visiting poor John Orby, 73 years of age. His chief infirmity is palsy. His physical self-control is almost departed. He is very cheerful and happy, no fear of death. The old lady is full of trouble and strongly condemned Mr. Fawcett for his non-attendance when called for.[144] The old man might die, for what he cared, so long as he could have his shooting. Her complaint was long and loud of his carelessness in making no response to her application. Wyleman, 73 years of age, lodges with them. He finds no peace of forgiveness, no comfort of the Holy Spirit. What a gloom settles upon these old men who have lived lives of sin and ungodliness! What blankness and deadness of countenance is manifested! His features have never lighted up with heavenly radiance.

I met with Surfleet with a bucket of potatoes, and we entered into conversation upon his absence from class.[145] He likened me to the priest who passed by on the other side not caring what became of the Samaritan.

WEDNESDAY, SEPTEMBER 4TH, 1872

I wake early in a morning with considerably more vigour of mind than of old. Reading, study, prayer and praise are the chief delights of my soul. My mind revels in almost every kind of literature of a pure type. Dr. Leifchild is a master in the Theology of nature. A more masterly refutation of Darwin and Wallace's theories of natural and sexual selection as accounting for the myriad evolutions of nature and especially the evolution of man's intellectual and moral faculties.[146] The Dr. gives an extract from Reid's 'Intellectual Powers' which reminded me of a stage in my own intellectual history when I devoted my whole energies to the study of the logical, moral and philosophical subjects.[147] I was an enthusiastic admirer of Reid. I read his 'Active Powers of Man' and was much disappointed that his 'Intellectual Powers' was out of print at that time.

This morning we have a temperature of 68 degrees. More rain in the night. At present the sun shines and sweet refreshing breezes come into my open window. My dear wife loves an open window. This is her only access to pure air when she cannot have her scarlet reclining board in the garden. Her health is not quite so good the last week or ten days. My two little doves have taken their music lessons before school in anticipation of riding in the phaeton with me and Miss Dawson to Louth.

What shall I do with all the rabbits and vermin on the farm this Autumn now the keen scented Phido is no more? He could scent a rabbit down into the solid earth perpendicularly a foot and a half from the surface. Bratby followed his nose with the spade that depth and there found the animal. The rabbits have poured forth from the Hall plantations from two sides of the populous square, and much damaged the 12 acre barley, the 6 acre wheat and the old 9 acre turnips.

This is one of the social injustices of this age. The Skallows Hall was for some years empty and Mr. Denison gave my Father the offer of it.[148] His refusal has turned out a great mistake. The rabbits harboured in the Hall plantations have at least taken the extra rent out of my farm produce. The Hall is more commodious and convenient and comfortable as a middle class home than the one in which we now reside. We should have experienced none of the selfish encroachments on the part of the Wrights. We lost, too, three grass fields adjoining, amounting to about a total of 9 acres besides large gardens, besides liberties and priveledges [privileges] and pleasures.

My shearling rams are in a fearfully crippled condition.[149] It is painful to witness the amount of suffering the poor animals have to endure, and all on account of man's sin. No man can look sympathetically over his crambling flocks and herds writhing in the anguish of physical pain, with tongues like pieces of raw flesh and feet a mass of fevered corruption without feeling regret and remorse concerning his sins which have produced such a train of diseases through the ranks of animal life.

THURSDAY, SEPTEMBER 5TH, 1872, 10.30 a.m.

Temperature 68 degrees. Denison and I have ridden to the village and back since breakfast on Charlie and Topsy. A fine refreshing breeze with alternate shade and sunshine passing over the landscape rendered the ride very delightful. The joys far outbalance the sorrows. My career as an agriculturist is widely eccentric. One day I mount the pulpit and platform and pour forth a torrent of rude, sometimes incoherent, eloquence. Another day I plunge heart and soul into my dear children's amusements. I generally cram my pockets with the current religious literature and stroll along the shady and retired walks through the farm, the trees of which have formed tabernacles for worship and meditation. There is scarcely a sod on the farm which has not felt my foot. Some of the fields enclose the grandest reminiscences of reading and study. How strong and lively is imaginative memory in relation to an oblong grass field now in the occupation of Mrs. Drake, closed in on three sides by a plantation. The teaching of Bushnell's vicarious sacrifice was, in that woodland monastery, indelibly impressed.[150] It was there I perused Trench's 'Study of Words' and Dean Stanley's 'History of the Jewish Church' where he introduces J. S. Mill among the prophets as equally under Divine Inspiration.[151]

Nearly every room in the house, every walk in the garden, every open field and shady grove, is alive with literary associations. Some fields are clustered with bright conversational associations. In one word, this farm for twenty years passed has formed my study and liberary, my pockets the bookshelves, my hands the desk, memory the writing paper.

Yesterday I had some conversation with Hay Sharpley at Eastgate. He appears to have enjoyed his visit to Oxford and Leamington very much. He spent a fortnight at Oxford. He felt a little disappointed as his expectations were raised so high. He felt a measure of gloom to rest upon the old place. He felt the necessity of great changes being made in the re-arrangement, re-organisation, of the whole system of study in the University. It is too exclusively classical. He would reccommend a couple of colledges to keep up the classical department, but the physical sciences ought to be largely adopted by the main portion of the colledges. The majority of the colledges ought to be freed from the nightmare of ecclesiastical control. Mr. Gladstone has authorised a commission to examine her property and financial condition, her income and expenditure. Hay thinks we have not seen yet the issues of the Ballot reform bill.[152] How Hay's conservatism is breaking up. His mind is fast becoming liberalised by the influences of modern society. It is interesting to observe the progress he has made in political and social opinion during the last two or three years.

According to our weather table, we have a midnight change in the moon. This is considered prophetic of a dry change: the nearer 12 o'clock at night, a dry change, and nearer 12 at noon, a wet change. I have prayed for some time if in harmony with God's will we may have fine weather to gather the barley harvest.

FRIDAY, SEPTEMBER 6TH, 1872, 10 o'clock a.m.

Denison and I have taken our morning ride to call upon Mr. James Iles.[153] I discovered it was some money he wanted of me for which he called twice yesterday. He said he should order woodman Smith to apply directly to me for plashing and other plantation woodwork fencing expenses. The Landlord finds the wood, stakes, etc. for plashing and fencing, and I have to pay half the labour.[154] This morning I paid the sum of £1/1/7. My farm is vastly too much smothered up with hedgerow trees, plantations and hawthorne fences, etc. which swell my expenses to a very considerable extent.

I have learned this morning that the old Parsonage ajoining me is let but is not known to whom.

Temperature in the room 66½ degrees. Another beautiful breezy morning. It seems to blow health into my frame.

The wind and sunshine are so beautifully drying the Spring corn which was finished cutting on Wednesday last. Who would not praise the God of all our mercies? My own heart shall rejoice, sing, and give praise.

The acknowledged immoral condition of the servants and the broken and disorganised relationships existing between them and masters and mistresses.[155] Authority, human and Divine, appears to be clean set at nought. Obedience, whether to God or man, is well nigh repudiated. Both morality and religion are trampled underfoot. No kind or degree of good treatment produces corresponding industry or decent behaviour. Shrinking from work except for self is fast becoming the order of servant life. Every advantage is taken in this house of my dear wife's affliction. In her absence all manner of misconduct, extravegance, waste of time and substance, light and rude and immoral conversation, false representation of the authorities, slipping of work, uncleanness. What a rampant spirit of murmuring discontent pervades the culinary department of the house! Last night in the yard the two waggoners were lewdly singing an obscene song. I felt it my duty to hush them.

Better wages and better living and more kind treatment does not in the least change their moral dispositions. The intensity of moral corruption only luxuriates and fattens and becomes more gross in proportion to the increase of material prosperity. Luxuries are only a richer soil for sin and iniquity to grow in unless the carnal nature is distroyed by supernatural power. It is only the grace of God which can transmute our life's surroundings into subservience to purity and godliness. The salt of grace alone can stop the progress of decay. Oh, for a larger measure of this seasoning power! I would want and plead for it. Glory be to God it may be obtained in overflowing abundance!

SATURDAY, SEPTEMBER 6TH, 1872, 8.20 a.m.

We carried the first sheaf of barley home yesterday. One or two slight showers fell during the afternoon but not to stop our proceedings.

I asked the shepherd about the rams. He thought they had the foot and mouth disease but now improving. I told him about half a dozen receipts reccommended for lameness.

This morning does not indicate much influence exercised by the so-called dry change of the moon. There is no importation of corn into the rickyard at present as more rain has fallen.

Tipler's hock is so far recovered as to admit once more of the collar. Old Jack has enjoyed about a month's run but is not yet quite sound; he plants the foot of his lame hind leg more firmly. A few weeks ago it appeared well nigh useless to him. Perhaps he has done more continuous hard service than any horse upon the farm.

Yesterday afternoon I mounted Charlie for Rasen to see Mr. Crombie to inform him of the intended invitation to Louth circuit. My journey was of no avail as far as my main object was concerned. Mr. Crombie has accepted an invitation for Harro[w]gate. However, we enjoyed a very pleasant cup of tea together. It was a tea party in miniature. The more tiny the group the more social they are to me.

It appears Mr. Berry is a solitary dissenter in his own family, the rest being members of the Church of England. He numbers four at the tea table. His friends were strongly opposed to his coming out into the ministry. His father refused to accompany him to the station.

I trust memory will be invigorated by yesterday's journey. I have had many a bright thought on the saddle, on wheels, on stroll, on my bed in the night watches, further out on tour, in public libraries, in steam vessel, in railway carriage, in public Town Hall, under Temple dome, etc. As I descended Kirmond Hill, a new revelation flashed upon my mind on law idolatry. How fertile has the human mind been in its creations of rivals to God's Throne!

TUESDAY EVENING, SEPTEMBER 10TH, 1872, 7.30 p.m.

Last Sabbath I rode Charlie to Snarford Bridge and preached twice. Afternoon from Psalm 36, 6v. Night from 2 Kings 7ch. 1.2v. I don't remember a home Missionary journey more charming. The day was fine. A cool and pleasant breeze fanned my cheeks and refreshed my lungs. As I ascended the hills landscape charms greeted my eye, richly wooded. Rarely have the lanes presented so meadowed an appearence or the fields more dressed in living green. I can scarcely think of any objects I passed without a revival of pleasure felt so vividly on the occasion. I cannot call up the lovely photographs without gratitude to God. I can see in imagery while writing in this room, lovely objects and masses of objects, animate and inanimate, which then filled my vision. One portion of the roadsides were lined with ashes and elms, another the tall and stately poplars with the bright green and delightful rustlings of foliage both to the eye and ear. The long journey was broken of all tediousness by the variety of scenery. I passed through Ludford sixhills, descending by the Legsby and Bleasby Moors to Lissington, Wickenby and finally to Snarford Bridge.

1872 MEMORABLE
WEDNESDAY, SEPTEMBER 11TH, 1872, 5.30 p.m.

My dear Lizzie was confined this morning about 12.20. While I was at Louth market she gave birth to a manchild.[156] This presentation of another son creates a new era in our domestic history. God has given him a splendid physical organisation. He has laid the foundation of a grand physical manhood. He has a face wide open already, a broad back, an expanded chest, and other limbs well formed and elegantly knitted together. He is an admirable piece of Divine workmanship. I found the new immortal in a widely different place from where I left him. He was born some time before Dr. Higgins arrived. The nurse said he just peeped in and felt the mother's pulse and pronounced matters all right as far as can be seen at present. It must be favourable to have a good pulse under such circumstances.

We have been kept in suspense some weeks. He has received a kindly welcome from his parents, brother and sister, and general pleasure seems to prevail upon the first introduction. His visit into this world will constitute the present year the most memorable since Denison and Mabel were born.

THURSDAY, SEPTEMBER 12TH, 1872, 8.35 a.m.

Yesterday I bought a four year old mare of Robinson as I was riding to Louth. Yesterday Denison and Mabel and Miss Dawson drove to Louth in the phaeton and Topsy. While we were at Louth the new olive branch made his appearence in the world for the first time. He is a portly babe and capital sleeper.

Lizzie has suffered a good deal of after pain and weakness. She has passed a long and dreary night hearing the clock bell every hour until 4 this morning, then dozing a little until 6. Her pulse is about 100. She gives her strength to the young sprigs. Her system seems to have lost its conservative power.

The weather-table prophets are confirmed and endorsed by three fine days in succession during which our barley is coming home in good condition. Praise God, Oh my soul! My heart should overflow with gratitude for fruitfulness indoors and out. May this house form a crystal conservatory from which shall issue characters of godly type and build.

MONDAY, SEPTEMBER 16TH, 1872

Our harvest is gathered with the exception of barley and oat rakings. My soul shall praise God for the beautiful weather we are now enjoying.

Last week was pregnant with Divine gifts. With an addition of a new member of the stock coming forth into the world, a bright and green and tender olive branch, the week has proved productive of some large blessings.

On Wednesday last I bought a mare, four years old, for £29. On Thursday another strong mare, 5 years old, £33, and changed Topsy away for a two year old pony, rather pretty in shape. Robinson valued Topsy at £12 and his own at £21. I gave the difference of £9 in exchange. We have named the first mare Rose, the next Pink, and the pony, Fanny.

On Friday I went to Louth Fair. Mr. Mason is very successful with the new Friday's auction. After looking at the auction mart for fat sheep, I walked leisurely through the beasts, and Mr. Marshall of Grimsby wanted to sell me 20 beasts. I looked through them and thought they would suit my purpose. I found three not so good as the others. Seventeen of them were splendid cattle, about 2½ to 3 years old. He asked me £25 each. I asked him for £5 for luck in consideration for the three inferior ones. He offered £2/10, which I ultimately accepted. It appears one of them is unsound and Mr. Marshall is coming over this morning to look at it.

On Saturday last I rode Charlie to Caistor Fair and bought of Mr. Tuffy 100 lambs at 53/-. He gave me 20/- for luck, also 30 lambs at 10/- over 46/- each. Mr. Brown of Thorganby kindly consented to lodge them for me until this morning. Skelton will fetch them and spend most of the day on the road.

After the Fair on Friday, I drove the new five year old mare, Pink (she is a little too heavy for riding) to Market Rasen to attend our Free Methodist reception service. Mr. Berry received a very kindly welcome from those who were present, though a miserable attendance. It was an interesting meeting.

MONDAY, SEPTEMBER 23RD, 1872

The temperature has come down the last two or three days to about 54 degrees.

Being from home a considerable portion of last week, my diary notes are scanty. Denison and I drove Pink, our new 5 years old waggonette mare to Dexthorpe on Tuesday evening last, where we met from all a fragrant welcome. We retired early and rose early to attend Partney Sheep and Ram Fair. Mr. Riggall bought Mr. Wright's lambs of Aswardby, at 52/-, also Mr. Harwood Mackinder's best shearling Ram at £30/10. There was a large show of sheep compared with the other Fairs. Edmond Mackinder gave me the offer of 10 beasts which he said he intended showing on Thursday morning. I found him a very free seller and we had very few words to the bargain. The price was £25 each. We have had high prices too, amongst foals, from £20 to £30 and even upwards.

The past week has been highly favourable for thatching. I have not a single roof injured by the wet, and last year all were more or less seriously damaged. I think, upon a survey of my stackyard and Mr. Riggall's I may safely pronounce them exceptional in filling [a] larger area than most in the surrounding districts. We have neither of us tested the yield. The majority of rumours are of a complaining character in reference to the smallness of bulk which is gathered off most farms and also the lightness of yield - say from two to three quarters per acre. It is emphatically pronounced a deficient harvest throughout the country.[157] The potato crop is a complete failure. The disease has destroyed this grand bulb to amount of £40,000,000 sterling. Famine seems to stare some of the poorer people in the face. They have a dark winter before them. When will the people learn righteousness under God's providential chastisements.

Tipler horse continues to improve from his relapsed hock. Rose, the new harness mare, 4 years old, has had the misfortune to receive a stroke on her near fore knee, which is considerably swollen.

I must just mention one circumstance to the credit of Mr. Marshall of Grimsby, who very honourably accepted the return of an unsound beast.

We are busily engaged ploughing seedland for wheat. I am about to act upon an impression that next year will be a favourable season for a good wold wheat crop. We have already turned up Cadeby lane 33 acre, also Top 18 acre measuring 20 acre, and greater part of black pond field. Never since I commenced business have we ploughed down such abundant pasturage. We have manure hills led out for the purpose of spreading upon the wheat land, but we shall transfer it to another part of the farm. My brother remarked it had been well tried and found to be of no benefit whatever to the wheatcrop but sooner on our hills promoted the blight on our wolds.

WEDNESDAY, SEPTEMBER 25TH, 1872

Today I have ridden Charlie to Market Rasen Fair. It was an incessant downpour, something like Wragby September Fair last year. The high road leading to the sheep Fair, usually filled with cattle, was a blank on account of the inroad of the cattle plague once more into the country.[158] It gives a melancholy aspect to a Fair when minus cattle. I felt thankful the stacks were all thatched while being drenched in the torrents of rain. I could not say with Cousin Isaac of Calcethorpe that the seeds were all ploughed.[159] We have 36 acre still to plough.

This morning on the road to Rasen I have read a portion of a paper on the United States' methods of dealing with the poor. Charles Dickens was no great admirer of our poor law system, but largely expressed his admiration of the American pauper institutions. It appear they made a special distinction between one class of paupers and another. I think of ordering 'MacMillan's Magazine' for November last[160] as it contains the information drawn by the 'Local Government Chronicle'. Great care, skill and attention must have been paid to the poor of every species or class, while charitable institutions of so multiplied and various structure in the cities of the Atlantic seaboard. Those rocky islands outside of Boston and New York must be intensified in their romantic interest by being crowned by charitable erections.

THURSDAY, SEPTEMBER 26TH, 1872

This morning I have spoken my mind freely to Tom Smith. I said, 'Look round the farm and see the backward state of the summer work', what we term distinctively labouring work. We have employed an extra labourer and still scarcely any of the hedges are trimmed and there never were so many buck thistles run to seed.

Mr. Paget, Mr. Wall, and another stranger gentleman, have arrived this morning, before the time specified.[161] Coveys of birds appear to abound, and they have gone forth along their career of sport through our abounding turnip covers. It is a fine, dry, cool, breezy morning for them. I have not lately heard the chuckle of the pheasant. They don't increase so rapidly as the other game. If our wold farms are to be over-run with game, we may put up our shutters and emigrate. The advance of labour, of trade, and rents, and a more extravegant expenditure on our family and household life will not admit of an increase of game. There are already indications of tenant farmers turning round upon their landlords. Mr. Cole and Robson are examples in point. I have a conviction these hills cannot be cultivated long at the rate of loss sustained by a large number of tenantry during the last few years. In my own case it is a hard struggle.

SATURDAY EVENING, SEPTEMBER 28TH, 1872

The temperature has risen a few degrees the last day or two, with equanoctial gales and torrent showers. We have little more than 20 acre left to plough for wheat.

We have commenced the renovation of the crew fences today. Coney has taken 90 weathers [wethers] to Torrington for Wragby Fair on Monday. Septimus kindly consented to lodge them for me tomorrow.[162]

I settled with Bratby for pitching, 9d. per acre for wheat and 8d. for Spring corn, this afternoon. Paid 5/6 per day for leading this harvest. Paid Welsh, seen off tonight. Drove Pink and waggonette to Ludbro' station to meet Annie and Mrs. Frank Riggall Jun., also back again this evening. Aunt Annie brought a beautiful white robe trimmed with blue satin for a present to my baby boy.

TUESDAY, OCTOBER 1ST, 1872

Yesterday I rode Charlie to Wragby Fair. I breakfasted with Septimus and Mrs. J. B. Sharpley Jun. of Torrington; also returned from the Fair and dined. They were kind enough to lodge me 90 wether shearlings. Septimus drove me in his gig. We found a very brisk trade for sheep; mine penned well. They presented a healthy and attractive appearence. They had good frames and skins and pretty sound on their feet, which was a good recommendation in the midst of such prevalent lameness. Some judges pronounced them the best male shearlings in the Fair. My brother kindly said he advised me to bring them to Wragby as he thought they would gain me some credit and meet with a good demand. I was congratulated by some dealers upon the improved character of my flock of sheep.[163] One of the Smiths said he bought my drape ewes at Partney Fair the second at 64/-, and they were doing remarkably well and answering his purpose in a most satisfactory manner. Morley and Reece bought my wethers at 74/- per head, being a total of £333, a neat round sum for ninety sheep on the last day of September. Before they were shorn Mr. Ashton and Cuthbert bid me £4 each. I have never experienced so much summer profit arise from sheep.

I confirmed my reputation, too, at Wragby Fair as a salesman. Mr. I. S., Calcethorpe, said I had taken the first position as such. C. Sharpley said I had done my business well.

There was one very novel feature connected with the Fair. No beasts were shown on the Saturday on account of the cattle plague reappearing near Pocklington in Yorkshire. On Monday Mr. Weightman of Wragby sold 170 fat and store beasts by auction. He employed Mr. Walter to sell for him. No one seems deterred from purchasing at high rates.

How different our home appears since the advent of young Francis Riggall Stovin. God has sent him in the midst of a comparatively prosperous year. If he opens for us a more successful series of years in the order of Divine Providence he may prove a blessing. At any rate [he] forms a very important accession to the family and has already broken in upon his parents' ordinary routine of domestic life. He seems to have revolutionised the whole household. Every other interest has more or less to bend to his. At present his sway is almost royal.

I met Mr. Kime, our Binbrook Farrier, this afternoon in the pleasure ground. He asked me if I would have Tipler's hock fired by a new method which he described as 'prick firing'. I told him the horse was in his hands and to do what he considered best. He fired old Jack's hind legs on the old method. The new method leaves no mark or scar after the healing process.

TUESDAY, OCTOBER 8TH, 1872

On Saturday last we put the rams to the ewes, the youngest flock of breeding ewes I have ever had. We are mending the crew fences. On Friday last we finished ploughing seeds for wheat. Having ripped the fields into furrows, we now tear it in pieces by the sharp teeth of the arrows [harrows], and tough work it is this season. The month of October has brought with it the rime frosts and first tints of Autumn. I scarcely know whether the lustred green foliage of more brilliant summer or the more humble green and gold of Autumn kindle my sense of beauty most. How precious the Autumn evenings make homes feel! The novelty of the first evening fires and lighted lamps throw a charm over the family tent. It is the domestic era of newly created socialities in Autumn and winter preserve the delightful prospects of enlarged literary feasts.

On Sunday last I rode Charlie to Owmby, preached twice at Normanby. Being no moon, I remained all night. The Holy Ghost fired my soul in an unusual manner while in the pulpit. How much more deeply nature photographs her forms and features when the inspirations of God abound in my heart. My imagination is susceptable of a deeper dye while riding through the village-dotted landscapes, the parks and gardens. Some are said to be natural poets, born poets. The poetry of my soul is mainly of supernatural creation. Grace has changed, transformed my experience of nature, of history and of the Bible. It illuminates the sky, the earth, every path upon which I tread whether along the hard pavement of the city or the green lanes of the country.

My little boy, Denison, in coming in to school, seeing me writing with red ink, requests rather cantingly to be allowed to do the same thing. Both Mabel and he are off in search for a suitable bottle. In the bustle he has knocked over mine and blotted my diary. I pray God that he may be preserved from making a worse spill in future life. I trust he may never besmear his character.

WEDNESDAY, OCTOBER 8TH, 1872

We have still alternate days of sun and rain. No doubt it now becomes mercifully advantageous for the future wheat crop. As a rule (other elements of the season being equal) we consider a rainy Autumn fertilises our wolds for wheat. My own observations confirm this statement.

Last Monday evening we met a good congregation at Ludford Chapel Anniversary. Mr. Berry, G. Taylor, and myself (as chairman) addressed the congregation. It was a very cheerful service. I denounced hollow formalities and exhorted the people to wake up to the earnestness and life of true religion. At the close of the meeting I referred in a somewhat complimentary manner to Mr. Taylor's speech. He gave some startling statistics upon the heavy cost of drink to the whole of the population of this realm. He mentioned the sum per head. He referred to a distillery at Edinburgh absorbing an enormous capital and only employing about 100 hands. In any other branches of industry the same capital would employ tens of thousands more labourers than are occupied at present in manufacturing the leading poison of human life.

I drove my wife, babe, Lizzie Collet (who folded the young in her arms), Denison and Mabel with Pink and waggonette for first time yesterday since the birthday. Mother and babe enjoyed it very much. The sun cheered us on our way. Lizzie Collet brought a little fancy register book for the entry of her nearest friends and relations, requesting me to insert my own birth. This circumstance has led to the reproduction of my Bible family register, which my procrastinating pen had not touched since Denison's birth. Three generations are already memorialised in small compass. The expansion of these lives in literary representation would fill many volumes. Human biography, even of the most ordinary type is a widely different composition from that of even half a century back. The activities of men of ordinary standard education is much more mulitfarious in their character.

BINBROOK, SATURDAY, OCTOBER 12TH, 1872

The rain is again pouring in streams upon the earth. We are prevented from proceeding with our usual wheat sowing. On Thursday last I drove Miss Dawson, Denison and Mabel with Pink in the gig to Woodhall Spa.[164] We left the gig at Horncastle and took train the rest part of the journey. I returned home alone in the evening. The morning was bright and favourable though very chilly. All nature looked slattern and forlorn. All nature seemed to bear the impress of fatigue. The year looked worn out and exhausted by its past luxuriances. Having handed over her treasures into man's storehouses, she appeared about to fold up and husband the remainder of her strength and quiet down into winter's sleep, and wait for the resurrection power of another Spring.

I generally carry a journal companion of some kind. Paxton Hood's 'Preacher's Manual' afforded me some stimulus in the intellectual and Divine life, though there is an over-drawing of John Henry Newman's abilities and attainments.[165]

When the children complained of cold feet, I allowed them to run two or three times along the journey. We were very fortunate in catching the train, and arrived at Mrs. Fixter's West cottage when the rain began its regular downpour, which continued through the former half of my return journey. I left my little darlings in a comfortable little room. The walls were nicely decorated with engravings and chromos,[166] mainly of a Scriptural and religious character. The exceptional chromo represented our past and present civilization. Those objects which stood most prominent on the picture was an old farmyard and antiquated house, much bitten and chipped with the tooth of time. In the yard stood a fractured, worn-out stage coach used as a hen roost. The wheels were denuded of tire [tyre] and both loosely leaning against the body. The door broken off its hinges in a like position. It looked a very homely haunt for poultry. It was rendering a totally different kind of service from the one become obsolete. Further back in this striking picture is represented the glorious contrast. A neat, pretty modern-looking railway station from which is issuing the gigantic iron horse panting with fiery breath and full of metal, with his long train of coaches flying past the old coach and farmyard, rumbling and screetching, startling the sleepy populations out of their dreams.

What is the Allmighty about to accomplish by these material remodellings of England and Europe's life?

THURSDAY, OCTOBER 17TH, 1872

On Monday last I attended the Board after a fortnight's absence. A small attendance and light relief list. The first meeting of the Legal Sanitary Committee for the administration of the new Public Health Act.[167] We had an urgent call from the Inspector to take prompt steps in ordering the removal of several most offensive nuisances. The building committee also walked round to survey the vagrant wards and devise new plans for their improvement.

On Tuesday I drove Pink in gig to Horncastle and took train to Woodhall Spa intending to bring back the children and Miss Dawson. They were on the platform ready to greet their Papa. We had a very cheerful and happy little walk to Mrs. Fixter's lodgings. They were not satisfied without showing me the golden eagles in the Hotel gardens. They really are dressed off in brilliant plumage. When we reached West Cottage Mrs. Fixter declared the children were not cured, the time was too short. The Dr. said they would require another week to be of any service to them.

FRIDAY, OCTOBER 18TH, 1872

The sowing for the ensuing wheat harvest progresses, though slowly. The soil is anything but free. The dripping rains have solidified and clayefied its substance. It is difficult for the drill coulters to pierce deeply for a fruitful deposit. Farming is a constant battle with the seasons in order to secure a proper mechanical preparation for a profitable crop. We can accomplish nothing in life of any permanent value without difficulty. We have modified our order of sowing the fields according to the time of ploughing.[168] Our former plan was to sow those fields first which were ploughed before harvest. This year we are leaving these until nearly last. Today we are bringing the bullocks into the shedding. They are some of the finest cattle I have ever housed.

FRIDAY, OCTOBER 25TH, 1872

Another downpour of rain yesterday. We commenced harrowing foot road 20 acre for wheat sowing, but were compelled to leave it.

Today we have sent four horses and waggons to Mr. Coatsworth of Grimsby for cake.

Fallowing in lodge plot.

Mabel's ringworms are very obstinate. Their treatment at Woodhall has not cured yet. I think of trying some ouslich and cream and washing with soft soap. Baby has frog, but somewhat better. Lizzie speaks of sending Mrs. Beswick home. She does not consider her an experienced nurse for a confinement.

William French of Binbrook has taken our groom's place and came last Wednesday. Wages at the rate of £13/0/0.

October is nearly gone and no corn thrashed.

I am afraid the firing of Jack's hind legs has not made a permanent cure.

Store sheep are down in price about 5/- per head. Our bullocks appear to thrive well on cotton cake and oat straw, a year old.

I have read the Congregational Union address upon the position and function of the Dissenters in England.[169]

Bratby and Smith trimming hedges at 3½d. per chain.

In changing from linen shirts to flannel, I have taken rather a severe cold in my head. It is several months since taking cold; perhaps I have never been so impregnable for many summers past as during last.

My dear wife is still very feeble. She made no attempt to walk for nearly six weeks after her confinement, but the other night she sank down at the foot of the stairs completely exhausted.

We commenced feeding baby for the first time on Wednesday last. A teaspoonful of lime water in milk and water, a little more than half milk.

I think I promised to take Mr. Hirst a bushel of small corn and he would accommodate me with a volume of sermons by several eminent ministers, also Dr. Hannah's theological lectures. Mr. Hirst gave me his ideas of plagiarism.

I have lately been purchasing some illustrated books on painting and natural history. I am reading a borrowed work from Antony S.,[170] May's 'Constitutional History'. I must quicken my way through it or shall be having enquiries about [it], also Disraeli's

'Contarini Fleming', also Mr. Crombie's De Quincey's 'English Lakes'. Having visited those Lakes, the book is very interesting. It revives memory and old associations.

It is many years since so little wheat has been sown in the month of October.

Yesterday I made a call upon Mrs. Short. Miss S. was very polite and said she thought they would be able to secure 14 trays for our C.A. tea.

I had a letter from Mr. Bond, Free Methodist Minister.[171] He very kindly assured me that in case the negotiations now proceeding with another circuit did not succeed, he would entertain the question. He is reading Tyndal v Darwin and is both delighted and pained.

FRIDAY, NOVEMBER 1ST, 1872

Yesterday and today have proved exceptionally fine. We have succeeded in thrashing two stacks of barley, yielding 52 qr. each from machine. The stacks turn out in beautiful condition from ridge to floor, in perfect contrast to last year's grown and matted roofs.

The machine now stands in threatening attitude and contiguity by a large wheatstack in centre of the yard. On the morrow, if the day is fine, our curiosity about the yield will most likely be in a measure gratified. The foreman remarks that the barley is ten quarters per stack more abundant than last year, and finer in quality.

I will thank God and take courage. Farming with me is related to infinitely higher things. I am anxious to build up my own mind and character that my influence may increase in drawing people from sin to Christ. I am anxious to repair the financial state of the circuit. Market Rasen circuit literally groans under the burden of chapel debts. We have not yet succeeded in engaging a successor to Mr. Crombie. My friend Mr. Bond has engaged himself. Having placed himself at our disposal at a salary of £120 and our circuit committee not being in a position to offer more than the connectional minimum of £100, we failed in securing him.

I have spent the day in reading and study and crow shooting. Mabel has several times expressed a wish that Papa would shoot her a crow to cover a hat frame, and a very fine one of brilliant plumage, not a sombre dead black but strongly tinted with very dark purple, fell at the crack of my gun.

THURSDAY, NOVEMBER 7TH, 1872

My dearest wife,[172]

You will rejoice to hear that the children are very well though I am disappointed with the small progress Denison has made in his writing since my last inspection of the school. His comparison with Mabel is not favourable. The boy's physical sluggishness appears to retard his culture. His lack of organic energy and Mabel's superabundance of elasticity create a strong contrast. I trust his weak and incompitent liver will not weaken and jaundice his mind. I think the boy has a quick and observant eye. He is fond of physical activity when blended with the mental. He is fond of puzzles, pictures, and a little fancy for drawing with colours after his own fashion. As soon as I can get him into a laboratory and familiarise his mind with the various instruments of knowledge, into a muzeum and Zoological gardens, statuaries and Picture Galleries, and thus aquaint him with the objects of knowledge. I should like the boy's memory and imagination to be aroused early and receive while tender a large and more ineraceable seal than I ever had the priveledge to experience. I can never recover my loss of culture in early life. Books, society and business have composed the main instruments of my education.

When you received yesterday's abrupt and brief note, you will perhaps perceive that it was written in the Mechanics reading room, which I so frequently visit for the purpose of studying the numerous broad sheets, that I may more clearly understand the ways of Divine Providence. God can gather up the very crumbs of literature, the leaflets as well as the quarterly or more ponderous volume, and make them work together for the good of his Church and the advancement of His Kingdom.

I was not aware until last eve while in the Mechanics library, Mrs. Foster of Ludbro' and Miss Riggall of Tetford referred smilingly, expressive of surprise, to the children's (Denison and Mabel's) adventure alone to Dexthorpe last Monday. Miss Riggall informed me that Mrs. F. R. returned with them in the train.[173] It appears she had not the confidence in them that I had. Though defeated in my purpose the latter half of the journey, the former is an achievement which will make a mark upon their little faculties and upon their career. It forms part of the romantic element in their early biography. Such incidents in young life are highly beneficial in teaching observation, self-reliance, courage. They break the monotony of school routine.

The children have just returned from a romp at the straw stack in a fine gale of wind and under a clear sky. The month of November is redeeming its character by bursting forth into splendid gales, preparing the low wet lands for the wheat sowing.

Yesterday I sold 11 qr. barley at 41/-, 60 qr. wheat at 58/- to Mr. Newman to be delivered at Ludbro' Station. Yesterday I brought home [a book] on Charles Froude, the distinguished historian of the Elizabethan period.

BINBROOK, FRIDAY, NOVEMBER 8TH, 1872

My dearest wife,

I have labourers working in the garden this morning. James Drew, confined labourer, T. Smith and Bratby, daily men, the only daily men I intend to employ through the winter.[174] Have I informed you that Welsh Sen., formerly Mr. Farrows's, then Mr. Bingham's foreman, who has numbered my third daily labourer during the summer season, is paid off? I cannot afford to keep more labourers than I really require. Advancing rates, rents, Christmas bills, labour, forbid us keeping idle hands. We give more money per day and receive less work. We have ingratitude returned for kindness shown. I have told the men this morning to scatter themselves over the garden and allow me the priviledge of seeing an impression produced. Two of them were in yesterday and most to be seen is the disappearance of a few Autumn leaves. The men seem to have set their faces like flint against work. They combine to extort high wages, and reject work. As far as my own observation extends, the bulk of labourers have lost principle, enterprising activity, economy and thrift. They are advancing in intelligence and folding their arms simultaneously.

Unless industry keep pace with intellectual life and social accomplishments our progress is not sound and cannot last. Earnest, cheerful industry must ever lay at the roots of a permanent civilisation.

To change the subject, we have folded the rams and cut them a few turnips. The lambs cut their own. This is the second season that we hold back the turnip cutter. In conversing with Skelton I remarked that we had not so many deaths on this system, but he differed from me except one year when the mortality was very serious under the cutting system.

FRIDAY EVENING, NOVEMBER 8TH, 1872

My dearest wife,

Bratby has commenced cutting our most scraggy moss-grown garden hedge. Trimming makes very little impression upon it, and we are slashing it to the ground with the scotching knife; by placing some of the old layers in an horizontal position and partially covering them with earth in addition to cutting openings in the bark, we expect by this plan to renew the hedge with a multiplicity of young growth. The shoots from the Lodge garden hedge have in two summers sprung so numerously and branched so luxuriantly that we have removed the old nettle growing guard. This treatment of our home garden hedge is no new experiment.

As last winter we had such a felling of trees and reduction and baring of shrubs, I ordered T. Smith to trim them gently this year that a denser foliage may be produced, more pleasing to the eye than the long stragling branches bending here and there, presenting a formless and sluvenly appearence to the garden. A constant and more frequent application of the pruning knife is necessary to mentain neatness and order in shruberies. I trust it will prove a gratification when for the first time for several months you take a walk of survey. If my farming profits were such as admitted of a relaying out and replanting it on a more tasteful model, I should only delight in effecting so pleasing a transformation.

But our funds are too low to admit of much improvement in the furniture or the house or its surroundings. All that we are in a position to do at present is to observe sanitary laws and the strictest laws of economy. We had better furnish the children's minds than feast their eyes and perhaps vanity with gorgeous dresses and bright and expensive equipage or destroy their digestive organs by luxurious living. These wold farms under the present tenure are not productive enough in proportion to wear and expenditure to allow anything beyond necessary comforts and facilities for family living and education.[175] There is very little surplus in the bank at Spring when the income and expenditure are balanced. The general impression abroad among the smaller trade and labouring classes is that our profits are very handsome. There idea is that we have a bag of gold at command.

I suppose God willing we shall be safely housed in one completed family group under Dexthorpe roof [at Christmas].

I have sought out a home for Mr. Crombie at Binbrook.

The more attentively I study the 'English Independent' and 'Methodist Recorder' and compare them, the deeper my conviction grows in favour of the former.[176] The 'English Independent' contains a comprehensive, a faithful portrayal of the times and a clear view of the weighty responsibilities of the church, also her line of duty in relation to great questions to which the 'M.R.' cannot lay claim. The 'Wesleyan Methodist Connection' is simply a recorder of facts. She has no recognised standard of teaching. Her sons are left at sea in history, politics, ecclesiastical subjects, without a creed. She has no grand guiding organ of thought or opinion. Hence when a great practical question arises she has no defined, uniform principles upon which to take united action. Uncertainty, vacillation marks her career.

Yesterday Rose and Fanny were singed at the Mason's Arms.[177] Today I conducted Fanny to the blacksmith's shop to be shod. In returning home I mounted, and the beautiful creature carried me cheerfully as far as the stable door and with a little hesitation I rode her into the garden. The hesitation seemed a little on the increase and Denison led her out through the gate. I soon found her hesitancy had suddenly grown into obstinacy. Her obstinacy fired into fury. She commenced stamping and tearing the ground and rising on her haunches with forefeet in the air in perfect sulk and madness. When opportunity served (being dinner time and raining fast) I leapt to the ground and gave her a good caning, then mounted. That was not enough. I repeated the process and again climbed the saddle; she then carried me with a good grace back to the stable door.

I wish you could peep in while we are partaking our supper. Miss Dawson sits in her ordinary, invariably prim style, scarcely opening her lips for half an hour together, and not then unless some question is asked or some remark addressed to her and then her replies are few and brief.[178] You reccollect I used for many months to take bread and milk to supper, but now for sometime have changed to bread and butter and clear spring water which the groom draws from a spring at the village. Our supper table assumes no formal character. A common tray covered with a white cloth, a few plates, bread and pastry, but as a rule no animal food.

I wrote a letter this morning to Mr. Bond. I am afraid he will think me long in writing as he desired a letter last week. I responded to his criticism of Mr. Darwin.[179] These men of science are taking leave of their rational powers when applying them to questions of theology. Are mechanical instruments available for theological investigation? Are Divine truths to be tested by observation and experiment? Can the five senses find out the Divine Being and character? Can material instruments and methods of study unfold God's plan of redemption? Is it in the minds and purposes of men of science to bow God out of His Universe? Shall He be deprived of his personality and black and blank law be enthroned as an abstract Deity or Natural Selection or some other imaginary being or nonentity? Events must be ascribed to some cause either intelligent or otherwise. Mr. Bond referred to the flimsy character of the evidence he brought to the support of his favourite theory. Man's origin an ape with a tail. He confesses it forms no resemblance to the present species and that he cannot produce any geological specimens of the original from which he declares mankind to have sprung. There is not much sincerity or honesty of investigation or exposition of evidence.

BINBROOK, SATURDAY, NOVEMBER 9TH, 1872

Dearest wife,

We have witnessed finer weather during the last few days. Mr. Newman's delay in requesting delivery afforded us an opportunity of proceeding with our fallowing. Today we finish the 37 acre top of paddock and we proceed next to far 20 acre adjoining Binbrook lane. About 50 acre is now finished. It is cut in nice straight furrows. The ploughing is more generally workmanlike and creditable than it was twenty years ago. Our numerous ploughing matches lift up a standard of perfection before the eyes of the agricultural workman.[180] There is no department of human labour whether physical, intellectual or moral where excellence has not its prize awarded. Merit is the lever by which England exalts her sons in all labour connected with materialism. Talent and industry and economy forms the ladder of ascent to position and respect.

This morning I deserted my bed or mattress about five o'clock, an exceptional act for me to perform. Jane made me a fire in the drawing (now school) room, whither I retired to read Froude's 2nd vol. 'History of England'.

BINBROOK, THURSDAY, NOVEMBER 14TH, 1872

My dearest wife,

We have been delivering wheat and barley this week. The two barley stacks are now dressed once over in the barn and weighed up. There are 106 qr. best for market, and 3 qr. inferior for grinding. There are 63 qr. of wheat for market and 3½ qr. remaining at home for use.

I shall not soon forget my visit to Dexthorpe. Though we experienced many waking and watchful hours by night, we experienced many social pleasures by day.

Yesterday morning I drove Mrs. F. Riggall to Hackthorne to hear Mr. Simpson. He preached in the afternoon. In some respects I enjoyed his sermon. His subject was the copper penny. Show me a penny! He spoke of it as suggesting a number of duties and responsibilities. Our responsibilities to society, to the state and to God. All kinds of vices clustered around the heathen system of bartering, while many virtues were associated with paper and coin currency. It forms part and parcel of our complicated civilisation. Mr. Simpson said we ought to meddle with politics. He has been speaking upon politics but no one could tell what his politics were. He had given no party colouring. You don't know what my politics are. I don't know myself. Then, Mr. Simpson, do you intend to inform us your voting duty blindfold? If you have no clearly defined evils to correct nor reforms to accomplish? His mouth, like his tobacco pipe pours forth smoky politics.

FRIDAY EVENING, NOVEMBER 15TH, 1872

My dearest wife,

If I had no definite views upon political questions, Mr. Simpson would not clear my mind of the clouds of confusion. He does not refer to the sentiment of patriotism which forms the prompting impulse to render up the claims which the state has upon us. We are invited and urged to take part in the election of our legislative counsellors but we require political discrimination in the exercise of our choice. We should form some aquaintance with the legislative programme which the nation most needs to be carried during the coming session.

There are several reforms still needed to be effected before our national happiness is complete. The present system of assessment and taxation is a monstrous injustice. Manufacturers and tradespeople are paying a mere nominal contribution towards the highways and relief of the poor. Suppose Mr. Brainbridge is assessed at £80 per annum and perhaps his income amounts to from one to two thousand pounds, whilst a farmer like myself occupying 500 acres of land is assessed at over £600 per annum with an income of about £300, or a comfortable living on an average about as much loss as gain. It requires ample skill and experience and strict economy to keep everything in good repair, live respectably and comfortably and save two hundred pounds a year through a series of thirty or forty years. This is very small remuneration when we consider the capital employed. But how is it the country will not see the monstrous injustice of our diminutive income as compared with our assessment and the large overflowing incomes of tradesmen and manufacturers contrasted with their insignificant assessment. The income tax is proportionate, why not assessments. When the growth of a kind of wealth has become so enormous which formerly bore no relative proportion to the agricultural, there is created a gigantic necessity for the readjustment of taxation. Shall the land without a grumble or remonstrance bear the main burden of our national expenditure? A new mine of wealth has during the last half century been created and developed which has failed or refused to contribute its quota to the taxation of the country. How is the subject to be ventilated so as to raise the moral tone of public opinion? Ought not the question to form one of the leading features of our political Programme for the coming session?

Again, a large portion of that wealth belongs to Caesar which has now for some years been withheld. Christ's words cut at the root of all religious establishments. All endowed churches are state governed churches.[181] Shall Caesar usurp the throne of Christ? God above claims the sceptre over his church. Caesar has no right to conscience pennies. The pennies which belong to God have no legislative place in our national exchequer.

The last week has been unusually stormy, severely cold, with heavy rains and sleet. It is exceptional for the month of November to bring forth so many gales. It is mostly a heavy, stagnant month. Fogs come creeping over the ground and shut out all bright scenery. On the contrary, it is boisterously active. Wide breadths of the low lands cannot be sown with wheat until a great change takes place. Nature has assumed her skeleton aspect.

I have spoken to the foreman about the labourers getting us some more gravel for our yards from the old 9 acre hill, also cutting up our lane furze and grubbing up the roots; they harbour so many thistles and rubbish; also looking out for some Binbrook ashes.

We have finished delivering the first three stacks of our stackyard, and this evening led several of the widows' and labourers' and other neighbours' coals.

It has proved very unfavourable weather for the poor horses standing at Ludbro' station. How strange they don't build stables.

Mr. Gray and Mrs. Riggall and Frank came to Binbrook last Monday night. They had a very pleasant day's shooting on Tuesday. The two guns shot 28 head: 2 pheasants, 3 partridges, 1 woodcock, 8 hares, 12 rabbits.

I think I never felt more need of your help, my dearest wife. Everything seemed to drop out of my memory. My reccollective power was almost paralised. The house being cold when Miss Dawson and I arrived and everything to prepare for the company. I sent off for Mrs. C. Smith to assist in putting the house into habitable order. Well, Mrs. Smith appeared unequal to the task and so I was appealed to like a mistress, and was found wanting in household knowledge. I soon found that [in] the adjustment of a supper table I might never of witnessed the delicate arrangements which were required. It was evident at a glance Mrs. Smith was ignorant of the position the candles ought to occupy, also the glasses, the knives, forks, spoons, and even provisions' dishes. Each article must have a particular place assigned it before a table can present a tasteful appearence. The beauties in nature are the result of very careful adjustment. A beautiful table requires skilful adjustment. A sense of refinement is necessary to constitute a home beautiful. The table forms part of an ornamental home.

By means of glass vases flowers have become our table and mantlepiece companions. This is a new feature in modern farmhouses.[182] Floral decoration gives a more beautiful appearence to a room than mere works of art. It will soon become the rule in farmhouses to see the dining and drawing room walls decorated with chromos or engravings or even paintings, and the carpets blazing with floral representations, and the furniture lustred with French polish and carved into beauteous forms, and the windows corniced and fringed and draperied with richly embroidered drapery.

The orderly and adjusting mind of a clever housewife is needful to give to furniture its tasteful relationships.

SATURDAY EVENING, NOVEMBER 16TH, 1872

My dearest wife,

You and I have often remarked how fond Mabel is of flowers. We have sometimes regretted that we have given so little attention to their cultivation. I am ignorant myself of a tasteful plan upon which to construct a garden. I feel unbounded admiration when my eye catches any kind of floral display especially in a garden setting. Some persons might judge me insincere in such a statement, as my own has suffered such neglect. It is an incident worth noting that yesterday I was conversing with the foreman upon a scheme for providing a new house for the poultry in the stackyard, thus dispensing with their present habitation adjoining the house, and ridding the garden entirely of their assistance in raking the beds. They seem to possess a propensity to destroy the rarest and most delicate plants or flowers we wished to raise. Their gardening is both obstructive and destructive and sets at defiance our most careful work. Hence we intend to banish them from their present haunts and tracks.

After yesterday's expression of our intentions to remove the fowls from their present domain and secure fresh soil to elevate our little bed-mounds to improve their appearence and render them more fertile and fruitful, I met this afternoon with a laudatory little review of a work entitled 'Mary's Garden', pub. by Seeley, Jackson and Haliday. It has given a fresh impetus to my intentions. It has struck a new idea which has not struck me in the same light before. I had not realised a flower garden as constituting a play ground for children. And yet there is room for the full swing of their physical and some of their mental powers. I suppose it will teach the little gardeners to play their task and create a little paradise of flowers by their own hands. With your permission I will secure the book and we can study its contents together these winter evenings and thus furnish the children's minds upon this subject, and, with God's blessing in the opening Spring, fill up the brown barren waste with a new series of beauties while we fill up many vacant hours of the dear children's time which might otherwise be void and irksome. They are already brimful of anticipations concerning the social Christmas tree and what toys and fruits and other decorations are to be hung upon it. Are not children's minds greatly educated by these things?

THURSDAY, NOVEMBER 21ST, 1872

My dearest wife,

The dates of the numerous letters I have written you during your long sojourn at Dexthorpe would enable a person to form an approximate idea of its duration. During your much observed absence, business both indoors and out continues to progress. The newly tired and varnished waggonette returned home yesterday. A waggon, I think the second or number 2, is now in Parker's shop court, to whom I have given directions to rim and tire the far hind wheels. I found fault with the old tire and nails. The strokes were too short and the nails did not fit in a workmanlike manner. Was there not remark made about last Friday night's rainpour? I suppose it did not come in drops but sheets. The year 1872 will be memorable as the year 1860. The rainpours have been more copious.[183]

Did I inform you of our pig killings? We slaughtered three, being one half the number we are feeding this season. I do not reccollect us commencing so early before. They are ripe earlier in consequence of confinement in the crews through the summer, and gradually improved. We discarded the old method of running off their flesh at grass and stubbles and stying them poor in the month of October.[184] This was the system of our fathers.

Yesterday I purchased 8 young pigs of C. Fletcher in the pig market, £8/0/0 the lot and 4/- for luck.

In looking through the window into [the] front garden my eye catches a dahlia, about the last relic of our few summer flowers. They were planted late and grown slowly and we have experienced very few frosts, being favourable for late flowering. It is favourable, too, for late turnip bubbing.

You will perceive by the numerous repairs going on through this year our Christmas bills cannot be very light. Repair of buildings, cistern cementing, tools and implements, forms a considerable total. The great difficulty in the farming business is to keep down the expenditure within the income.[185]

The coming Christmas, too, will be exceptional in the heavy drain upon our Chapel Trust funds.[186] The renovation of our Free Methodist Chapel and vestries by white and colour washing walls and ceiling, staining and varnishing of pews and partition, painting of pulpit, windows, doors, etc. inside and out, cocoanut matting of aisles, renewing of warming apparatus piping, also of outer wall and front steps, and lastly new lamps, being the third change in this particular. You will not be surprised then, dearest, if I, as treasurer, have to turn out a heavy bag of cash over into tradesmen's hands. I ought to thank God for a good harvest to enable me to meet the demands. I had better pay a good round sum in hard cash for my country's freedom than have to spill my blood. Our forefathers gave their bodies to be burned. They responded to the call of God's Providence. Shall we refuse to untie the strings of our purses? This is our call in the material department of giving. Money is required to free our chapels of the incubus of debt. While cash has been created so abundantly by Divine Providence and our Trust exchequers are so empty a coin, whether copper, silver or gold, dropt in creates a terribly hollow sound.

I think I neglected to inform you that Mr. Lawton is holding special services this week and next.

The pigs were distributed among our three labourers,[187] C. Smith, foreman, Coney and Skelton. C. Smith's weighed 29st. 9 lbs., Coney's 29st. 9 lbs., Skelton's 32st. 8 lbs. I expect the machine coming today for a second thrashing this season.

SATURDAY EVENING, NOVEMBER 23RD, 1872

My dearest wife,

Today I met your dear Father at Louth Martimus Fair. We also came in contact with George and his son Harley. The uppermost topic of conversation was the recent and sudden death of Mrs. J. West of Dunholme Lodge. What a Providential stroke of chastisement to him, which I understand he feels most acutely. They were a perfectly happy couple. As far as we can judge they were made for each other. It is generally thought they were a perfect exemplification of matrimonial bliss. She was indeed a fruitful vine by the sides of his house, and her nine children were like olive branches round her table. She was prematurely confined, though that was not the cause of her death. It was discovered when death seized her frame that the lungs were gone. The doctor and her husband were not aware of this. One hour before the dread event happened they had concluded her recovering. What a dark cloud of mystery hangs over that house as contemplated by a distant observer. Apparently the most valuable parent of nine children suddenly struck down. Oh, think of the appalling fact, nine children bereft of their mother at the period when most needed! My dear Father-in-law was intensely puzzled by the insoluble mystery. Here we have a Christian family under the sharp rod of correction. The mother is taken and the wisest philosopher and most mature Christian cannot tell why. The strongest intellect must bow before the awful mystery. It is only another addition to a myriad other confirmations of God's word. His ways are past finding out. We are certain that He is 'too wise to err and too good to be unkind'.[188] There is no doubt when the light of eternity falls upon these constantly repeated tragedies we shall clearly see the meaning and they will no longer wear their tragical disguise.

However, dearest, I can thank God that you are still spared to me while the strongest are taken. The doctors failed to sound your complaint, and God directed you to Matlock. You are a living monument to the power of God in answer to prayer exercised in connection with the Matlock treatment. While we rejoice together, let us sympathise and pray for the consolation of J. West in the darkest hour of his life. No mere natural causes are sufficient to account for your surviving so many of your friends. It is of God. We cannot spell out the 'why' until we ford the river of death and climb the opposite banks all 'dressed in living green'.

THURSDAY, NOVEMBER 28TH, 1872

My dearest Mama,[189]

In writing to you yesterday my time was too limited to impart more than glances of events transpiring around me. Oh, I wish my gratitude were more kindled up! Lizzie and baby came home last Monday in capital spirits after enjoying nearly a month of parental hospitality at Dexthorpe. After dining at Mr. Riggall's of Grimsby, we attended the Wesleyan Missionary meeting. At the close Mr. Kirby and I walked to Freeman Street Free Methodist tea meeting. After tea a public meeting was held, addressed by Mr. Colam of Louth. A. Sharpley in the chair. I assure you we had a very enthusiastic meeting.

Miss Dawson of Louth continues to instruct the children. My dear Lizzie is quite a marvel. She will scarcely allow the baby to be taken out of her sight. She is a true mother in affection and watchful care. I said to her last night how wonderful it was to see her so active after being a prisoner so long.

We are thrashing four stacks of barley and one of oats; commenced the third of barley this morning. 58 and 60 qrs. came from the former two, roughly measured from the machine. We continue fallowing with three ploughs. In addition to the boom of the thrashing machine, a shrill halloo after dogs and rats comes into my window. They have not much chance of escape from my premises. This is an unprecedented year for rats and vermin of all kinds. A wet season appears favourable to their increase.

We have two or three fine days for thrashing, thus forming an exception to the rule. Praise God for another fine thrashing morning! The wheat plant has struggled its way out and can be seen in lines across the fields.

NOTES

1 Frank Riggall, who lived at Hackthorne. Brother of his wife, Elizabeth.
2 His elder brother, George, who left Binbrook Hall Farm in 1854, at the time of his marriage: see Appendix III. George at this time was tenant of a farm at Sotby, near Wragby.
3 One of a series of lectures given by Rev. W. Morley Punshon delivered to the Y.M.C.A. in London in 1856 and collected with others for publication by James Nisbet and Co., price 3d.

4 A 'double-furrow digging plough', supplied by R. Hornsby & Sons of Grantham.
5 Husband of his younger sister, Maria, who farmed at Grainthorpe: see Appendix III.
6 Probably Wragby Fair, which he would have visited before going on to Sotby. The fairs he more usually attended were those at Partney, Louth, Caistor, Horncastle and Lincoln.
7 The Glossary contains a list of agricultural terms used throughout the Journals.
8 Benjamin Disraeli (1804-81). 'Lothair' was one of his last two novels, published in 1870.
9 See Glossary.
10 His eldest son, Cornelius Denison, then aged eight: see Appendix III. The name 'Denison' was added at the request of Cornelius Stovin's landlord, Mr. Edmund Denison, later named Sir Edmund Beckett. See Introduction, pp. 11-12 and Appendix IV.
11 A Liberal paper, started under Charles Dickens's editorship in 1846. Development of branch railway networks had enabled newspapers to be distributed to the most remote rural areas. Papers were delivered by the Binbrook mail cart from the post office, or fetched by Cornelius Stovin (hereinafter C.S.)
12 Cousin of his mother (née Sarah Sharpley). One of many references to members of the Sharpley family with whom he associated closely both in farming and Methodism. See Introduction, p. 4.
13 The second daily paper which was delivered to the farm. A Conservative newspaper, with both morning and evening editions, it had one of the largest circulations at this date. Like other penny dailies, it catered distinctively for the upper and middle classes, and almost exclusively for the male reader.
14 Farm tenanted by his wife's parents, Francis and Elizabeth Riggall. It was situated near Spilsby. See also Introduction, p. 3.
15 His mother-in-law, Mrs. Francis Riggall.
16 William and John Riggall, two more of his wife's brothers. These two brothers took over a woollen mill in the West Riding for a few years, but the venture did not prove a success. The West Riding was one of the main markets for the wool of Lincolnshire sheep at this period.
17 Son of sister, Maria, and brother-in-law, J. B. Atkinson.
18 C.S. was a class leader at Binbrook Free Methodist chapel. Class leaders were important lay officials in Methodism, having a pastoral oversight and responsibility for their members. Regular attendance at weekly class meetings was a test of membership, as important as attendance at Sunday services.
19 See Introduction, p. 7.
20 Farm near Lincoln tenanted by Frank Riggall.
21 Free Methodist minister, Market Rasen circuit.
22 Franco-Prussian war, 1870.

23 An instance of his use of his journals to explore thoughts and ideas later incorporated into sermons and addresses. See Introduction, pp. 3 and 14-15.
24 Louth Mechanics Institute, founded in 1834. In 1854 it was moved to the Mansion House in Upgate, which accommodated a library of 2,500 books, and a museum and reading room for 400 members. Classes and lectures were held on a wide variety of subjects. The reading room was a favourite haunt of the writer on his visits to Louth for the weekly market, business or shopping (David N. Robinson, 'The Book of Louth', Barracuda Books Ltd., 1979).
25 Issued by the Religious Tract Society.
26 Cartoon published in 'Punch', July 29th.
27 Migrant labourers travelled from south to north during the harvest period, but when corn ripened evenly over the whole country, extra labour was not available at the critical time in each region.
28 Contradictory traditional weather signs - smoke falling indicated changeable weather, swallows soaring high, fine weather.
29 See note 122 below.
30 Annie Riggall, his wife's younger sister.
31 The article in the September 1871 issue of the magazine on 'Technical Education in England' deplored the lack of progress since the 'industrial triumph' illustrated by the 1851 Exhibition. The author of the article, W. T. Thornton, commented that the cause was the lack of adequate general education in England, which had given rise to the lack of demand for technical education. He compared this with the growing network of institutions in France and Germany.
32 A monthly religious periodical which specialised in material for use in sermons - expositions of passages from the Bible, biographical sketches of preachers, etc. C.S.'s journal entries showed his considerable dependence on suggestions made in issues of the 'Lantern' for his own sermons. A note in 'The Congregationalist', another favourite periodical of the writer, publicising the 'Lantern', commented: 'Why is this bright magazine called "a lantern"? Some more cheerful name might have been found for it. It is full of excellent suggestions and advice, and we think it very likely that congregations have had better sermons because their ministers have tried to walk in its light.'
33 His two eldest children. See Appendix III and comments in Introduction, pp. 8-9.
34 See Glossary.
35 His interest and concern arose out of his work as Parish Overseer from 1854, and his recent appointment on the Louth Union Board of Guardians. Parishes, governed by the vestries, were still left duties and responsibilities after the establishment of the Poor Law Unions in 1834 (Lincoln Archives Office, Binbrook Vestry Minutes).

36 The Religious organisation of Mormons or Latter Day Saints was founded by Joseph Smith (1805-44).
37 In Louth.
38 The home, situated on the outskirts of Oxford, of his cousin and brother-in-law (his sister Elizabeth's husband), Dr. Cornelius Frederick Stovin: see Appendix III.
39 According to the editorial, this new periodical contained 'good practical sermons by ministers of the several divisions of the Church of Christ', and articles and meditations 'of a devotional and instructive character'. 25,000 copies of the first issues were printed, and 'demand continued brisk'. Through it C.S. was brought into contact with the foremost Church of England divines, as well as all branches of Dissenting churches. His reading included works by the higher clergy which may well have been advertised in this or other periodicals which he read regularly.
40 A chapter in R. Thomas's 'Ecclesiastical History', Hamilton, London, 1871.
41 Between 1850 and 1860 private companies had opened telegraph lines. These were taken over by the Post Office in 1868.
42 Elizabeth Stovin: see Appendix III.
43 Anthony Sharpley of Torrington, another cousin of C.S. with whom he frequently associated, also a leading member of the Free Methodists in the district.
44 It was in Rochdale in 1833 that many devout Methodists, who were all concerned with protests against an increasing tendency to clerical government, and a departure from simplicity of worship, met and made specific demands of the Methodist Conference. Again, in 1855, it was in Rochdale that 87 trustees and other officers petitioned the conference with a summary of their grievances, and declared that the sole remedy was the immediate admission of the people to 'such a share of power as should make their concurrence necessary in all matters of legislation, finance and discipline' (W. J. Townsend (ed.), 'A New History of Methodism', Hodder and Stoughton, 1909).
45 The revolt in 1835 had been sparked off by the establishment of a Theological Institute in 1834 by the Wesleyan Methodist Conference for the training of its young preachers. It was felt that young preachers trained together in one system might lack the variety, force and originality of earlier preachers. In 1849 further revolts were caused by the expulsion of ministers and local preachers because of criticisms voiced in four pamphlets styled, 'Fly sheets from the Private Correspondents'. They criticised the desire by leaders of the time to conserve all ultimate authority in the ministers (Townsend, 'A New History of Methodism').
46 John Petrie (1791-1883). One of the signatories of the Rochdale Petition. He was a distinguished Methodist and civil leader, close friend of Cobden and Bright in the Corn Law

and Church/State agitations. Bright referred to Petrie's life as a guarantee of the reality of religion (Townsend, 'A New History of Methodism').

47 Rochdale enshrined for C.S. the principles of democracy and freedom in religious and civic affairs. From the 1840s until the 1870s, the result of national legislation accompanied by local legislative self-help, Victorian towns and cities began to take new pride in themselves, as 'growing points of a new world order, where the expansive power of trade could be allied to traditional cultural standards of amenity and style'. This was reflected in new civic buildings such as the Rochdale Town Hall, described effusively and at great length by C.S. as built 'in the very spirit of Protestantism'.

48 Service of Renewal held at midnight on New Year's Eve in Methodist chapels.

49 New methods to control pests and diseases in crops and farm animals were being developed throughout his lifetime, and he was always eager to try out new methods - not always successfully, as he showed in this case.

50 John Angerstein owned some important concentrations of land in Lincolnshire, including the parish of Stainton-le-Vale, neighbouring parish to Binbrook. He resided in Norfolk. He and E. B. Denison owned some 3,000 acres of the tracts of wold land surrounding Binbrook village (R. J. Olney, 'Binbrook in the mid-nineteenth century', Occasional papers in Lincolnshire History and Archaeology).

51 By a Lincolnshire custom, which was to be the basis of the 1875 and 1883 Agricultural Holdings Acts, outgoing tenants-at-will (those on annual tenancies) were compensated by landlords for work done on the farm, improvements made, etc. By the 1840s there had developed a uniformity in tenant-right awards which had spread to other parts of the country. The incident which C.S. related here showed a flagrant disregard by this landlord of a common custom which was intended to encourage farmers to cultivate and develop their land with confidence in getting a fair return.

52 Agricultural Trades Unions had become established by 1872 in many parts of the country and were alarming farmers. From January onwards throughout 1872, local Lincolnshire newspapers carried articles, notices and letters concerning public meetings and the formation of local associations of agricultural workers - separate trades unions, with their own rules, aims, subscriptions, titles, etc., as no single overall union yet existed in Lincs. They were all pressing for an increased wage and a nine-hour working day, and processions and spasmodic short-lived strikes were already in evidence (Rex Russell, 'Revolt of the Field in Lincolnshire', 1957).

53 One of the few chapel duties which his wife undertook and which she soon gave up because of her ill-health and child-bearing.

54 Although veterinary surgeons were advertising their services in the Lincolnshire White's Directory in 1872, farmers still relied on the local farrier and his traditional remedies, in this case, Joseph Kime, Binbrook farrier.

55 Local unions were asking for 2s.9d. a day. 'To judge from the common conversation among farming men a general strike on the question of wages seems imminent. Many of them have already taken the initiative, and express a determination to stand out for 2s.9d. the day... it is decidedly ominous for the maintenance of past wages that the men have begun to hold regular meetings for discussion and to organise their strength.' (Report from the Caistor district, in the 'Lincoln Rutland and Stamford Mercury', 2nd Feb. 1872, quoted by Rex Russell in 'Revolt of the Field'.)

56 His landlord, Sir Edmund Beckett.

57 Water supply was always a difficulty on the chalky wold land, and farmers were experimenting with wells and water towers. There are examples of water towers built in the 1850s, but Binbrook Hall Farm depended on two ponds for farm use, and water carried from the village for drinking, until the building of a water mill in 1907, after the Denison family sold the farm.

58 New style farmers in mid-Victorian England employed governesses for their young children rather than sending them to the village school. They relied on the almost limitless supply of untrained young ladies, portrayed so often in fiction of the period. C.S. gave clear glimpses of their uneasy position, the shortness of their stay, and the dullness of their instruction - which he tried to enliven with his own contributions.

59 News of local action was carried to isolated farm workers by men employed by firms contracted by farmers to do their threshing.

60 Charles Haddon Spurgeon (1834-92) was a Fundamentalist Baptist minister and celebrated preacher, famous for his humorous sayings, who had an immense following, and whose sermons, published weekly, sold extremely well.

61 A 'basket phaeton'. This was a low pony phaeton in use about 1870, with the body composed of wickerwork, easy to get in and out of, and useful for carrying children. It was not often seen after 1900 when the safer Governess cart was invented. (Marylian Watney, 'The Elegant Carriage: Illustrated Record of Horse-drawn Vehicles', J. A. Allen & Co. Ltd, 1961).

62 When C.S. first commented on the 1870 Education Act in his Oxford Journal of that same year, he was more hopeful of its influence and action. As he read and thought more about it (his views strengthened by articles in 'The Congregationalist' which strongly denounced the Act for the ties it effected between the state and the established church), he became particularly critical of the discretion given to School Boards to determine what religious instruction should be given in

schools founded or maintained by ratepayers. 'In a large number of schools, the managers represent no one but themselves' ('The Congregationalist').

63 Books of school subjects for young children in question and answer form, written by Henry Frowde (Hodder and Stoughton).

64 Both C.S. and his wife were devotees of the then fashionable spa treatment for all kinds of ills. They patronised Smedley's Hydro, founded by John Smedley, a mill owner, who founded his own hydropathic centre at Matlock early in the 1850s after undergoing a spiritual conversion when undertaking a cure for a fever at another centre. The small house at Matlock, where they charged patients 3s. a day, was soon enlarged to take 100 patients. It continued as a hydropathic centre until the 1950s - when C.S.'s youngest son, Walter, then in his seventies, stayed there for a month. Caroline Smedley, John Smedley's wife, published in 1861 a 'Ladies' Manual of Practical Hydropathy for Female Patients', and a nurse from the Hydro, Mrs. Beswick, attended at the farm for Lizzie's confinement in September 1872. C.S. in the Second Journal refers to the drastic use of cold sponges, mustard plasters, etc. recommended by the Smedleys for the treatment of colds and fevers (E. S. Turner, 'Taking the Cure', Michael Joseph, 1967, pp. 184-91).

65 See Glossary.

66 'Confined men' were hired annually at hiring fairs held in the wolds districts at Caistor, Binbrook, Louth and Market Rasen. They usually included the foreman, shepherd, garth - or stock man - and waggoners. 'Day workers' were paid weekly or fortnightly according to days and hours actually worked.

67 The 1851 census seems to show that the unmarried waggoners lived in the farm house, the common practice earlier in the century. After the foreman's cottage was built in 1856, they boarded with him. The cottage was built with a large bedroom in which five or six young farm servants could sleep in truckle beds. (Information from Mr. Michael Sleight, present owner of Binbrook Hall.)

68 In October 1871 the Prince had become ill with typhoid fever, infected by foul drains while on a visit to Lady Londesborough, near Scarborough.

69 In 1865 a man claimed to be Roger Charles Tichborne, heir to a large estate in Hampshire, who had been missing at sea since 1854. After two marathon trials (1871 and 1874) which attracted wide publicity and during which the claimant won a large following among the British public, he was declared to be an imposter, a certain Arthur Orton, a butcher's son from Wapping.

70 The thin chalky wold soil needed considerable investment in fertilisers to support regular cropping, and records exist to show the use of ashes, alongside boning, soot, town and cake manure, and claying and marling. Thomas More recorded

in 1847, 'The turnips were decidedly the best on the side manured and ashed, and it is much the poorest side of the field and always has been' (T. H. Beastall, 'The Agricultural Revolution in Lincolnshire', History of Lincolnshire, Lincolnshire Local History Society (1979).

71 Before the Binbrook Enclosure Award in 1740, much of the wolds had been sheep walks and rabbit warrens (R. J. Olney, 'Labouring Life in the Lincolnshire Wolds'). Throughout the Journals, C.S. illustrates the constant battle of the farmers on these uplands against the inroads of vermin.

72 The contrast C.S. made between the role played on the farm by his mother and his wife clearly illustrates the changes in the life style of the 'new' farmers' wives in the second half of the nineteenth century, which went along with the rising standard of living and expectations of the farmers. 'Farmers' wives abandoned the dairy [and the poultry yard] for the parlour, now adorned with a piano' (James Obelkevich, 'Religion and Rural Society, South Lindsey, 1825-1875', Clarendon Press, 1976).

73 See Introduction, p. 3.

74 The landlord's agent, who took over the supervision of the farms in the landlord's last years. The comments on the distancing of tenant from landlord illustrate a general trend which developed during the middle and later years of the nineteenth century. In a letter to his landlord dated August 16th, 1871, the day before the First Journal starts, C.S. so describes the agent: 'If I may be allowed to speak to you in confidence in relation to the man appointed to be your agent, I should say he is a gentlemanly man in his manners, affable and fluent in conversation, highly intelligent in general business information. The all absorbing object of his life is the acquisition of wealth. He seems to have most respect for the man of property... He has behaved anything but politely to me...'

75 In a Journal entry made on Jan. 4th, 1893, he gave a fuller account of his early conversion during a revival service when he was eighteen years old.

76 Mr. J. B. Sharpley, his mother's cousin, and prominent Louth citizen. See Introduction, p. 4.

77 Louth Union Board of Guardians, set up in 1837. For some years previous to 1871, he had been one of the Overseers of the Poor for St. Gabriel's Parish, Binbrook, and he served in both capacities for a time (Binbrook Vestry and L.U.B.G. Minutes, Lincoln Archives). See Introduction, p. 14.

78 A settlement was made in 1872 of the claim by the United States for compensation of losses inflicted from a long and destructive warfare on their commerce by a disguised privateer which had been allowed to escape from Liverpool Docks in 1862, and which, when once at sea, hoisted the Southern colours. It was claimed that the 'Alabama' and her consorts prolonged the civil war by two years. The settlement, made

before the Geneva Tribunal, was one of the landmarks in the history of international arbitration, and put an end to the period of strained relations between England and the U.S.A.

79 Samuel Wilberforce (1805-73). Referred to in later journal entries in connection with his opposition to Darwin's 'Origin of Species'.

80 The views expressed in articles in this new periodical fitted in with those of C.S. on democratic organisation in churches and the independence of each chapel; also the outspoken comments on the 'unspiritual temper' of the age. He found the periodicals published by the Congregationalists less narrowly religious than the 'Methodist Recorder', and more concerned with social and political affairs.

81 See Introduction, pp. 12-13 for background to this incident.

82 See Introduction, pp. 13-14 re his own position as one of the few Methodist farmers on the wolds.

83 Free Methodist minister, Market Rasen circuit.

84 The price of wool was driven over-high by the cotton famine and also the trade boom of the early seventies (Beastall, 'The Agricultural Revolution in Lincolnshire').

85 See Rex Russell's 'Revolt of the Field' for details of meetings, strikes, etc. of farmworkers in north Lincolnshire in 1872.

86 Another illustration of the separation of rural social classes in the mid- and later nineteenth century.

87 James Anthony Froude (1818-94). Articles originally published in 'Radical Reviews' were collected in four volumes entitled 'Some Short Studies on Great Subjects'. Although Froude went back to manuscript sources in his historical studies, his writing was often imaginative and emotive. He became a disciple of Carlyle. Both writers had great appeal for C.S.

88 An annual circuit rally with special services on Sunday and Monday when it was traditional for the President or some particularly noted Methodist to preach. The Monday service was always followed by a lavish tea for those who attended. The Free Methodists followed the Wesleyan practice in their Aggregates. (See Robinson, 'The Book of Louth').

89 Henry Thomas Buckle (1821-62). Left uncompleted his great work, 'History of Civilisation in England'. He held that just as individual actions, so the destiny of peoples and the growth of civilisations, come under the scope of natural causality, the laws of which can be discovered. He established the closest and most direct contact between history and philosophic rationalism. (Emile Legouis and Louis Cazamian, 'History of English Literature', J. M. Dent and Sons, 1951).

90 See note 68 above. In spite of his views on the monarchy and the establishment, C.S. had considerable regard for the Royal family in his own time and joined, with some reservations, in the national celebration.

91 Rents to landlords increased by a quarter between 1850 and

the late 1870s. (J. H. Clapham, 'Economic History of Modern Britain, 1850-1886, C.U.P., 1930).

92 The Market Rasen United Methodist Free Church Circuit Accounts show that the growth of Free Methodism in north Lincs. continued during the 1860s and early 1870s. Income came solely from the 24 village chapels, surpluses from circuit teas, bazaars, etc. Chapels were still being built, or taken over from Wesleyan Methodists in the mid-1870s (see C.S.'s reference to laying of foundation stones), but the circuit accounts show a gradual decline in numbers and a fall in village contributions. Villagers often attended more than one chapel, and during the later 1870s and 1880s villages were unable to support the two or three Methodist denominational chapels which had been built during the century. The agricultural depression which affected labourers, craftsmen, and farmers alike, contributed to the decline. The Second Journal reflects the writer's increasing anxiety about the financial situation (Market Rasen U.M.F.C. Circuit Accounts, 1867-1891, Lincoln Archives).

93 C.S. here succinctly expressed the principles on which Free Methodism developed, and which divided the early Reformers from Wesleyan Methodism, in which the National Conference was the ruling body.

94 White's Directory (1872) names George Smith as the Binbrook wheelwright. The Free Methodist congregations had a predominance of craft and labouring classes: see Introduction, p. 12.

95 Occupier of the neighbouring farm of Kirmond-le-Mire.

96 Dobbs was one of the four Binbrook carriers (White's Directory, 1871).

97 An early novel of Disraeli's, published in 1832.

98 Thomas de Quincey (1785-1859), a contemporary, friend, but also critic of the Romantic poets. His 'Lake Reminiscences' were first published in magazine form, and offended Wordsworth and the other Lake poets. Earlier he had been one of the first to appreciate the revolutionary importance of the 'Lyrical Ballads' (1807).

99 Binbrook Free Methodist chapel had only been built sixteen years before this date, in 1855. The rebuilt chapel still stands, and is now used as a youth club.

100 See note 64 above.

101 During the first ten years of marriage, his wife had three miscarriages, had borne two children, and was again pregnant. For comment on her problems and her husband's attitude, see Introduction, p. 7.

102 This passage, among many others in the Journals, illustrates his philosophy of the effectiveness of human and divine cooperation.

103 Long gaps in the journal writing were usually caused by untoward events in the family and on the farm, but see Introduction, p. 2.

104 The sense of obligation to carry the Gospel to all nations did not arise until the end of the eighteenth century, and accompanied colonial expansion. The Methodist Missionary Society was one of the last of the Protestant churches to found a society. (Alec R. Vidler, 'The Church in an Age of Revolution', vol. 5 of the Pelican History of the Church, Penguin Books, 1971).

105 Resentment at the payment of tithes had not been reduced by the Commutation of Tithes, 1836, and the burden was still resented by farmers. C.S. felt the more strongly because of his general attitude towards the appropriation of such funds to support the established church.

106 A judgement made by the Judicial Committee of the Privy Council on 8th June, 1872, after an action brought by a Mr. Sheppard against the Rev. W. J. E. Bennett of Frome, who in certain writings on the Sacrament of the Lord's Supper had offended against the Articles of the United Church of England and Ireland. The issue was fully reported in 'The Times' (June 10th) and the weekly 'Church Times' (June 14th). The decision to acquit Mr. Bennett seemed (from the tenor of letters in the 'Church Times') to be regarded as a gain for Roman Catholicism and indicated a swing to a more liberal view and regard to that branch of the Christian faith.

107 See Appendix VII for record of contemporary prices of wheat.

108 See notes 52 and 85 above, and Introduction, pp. 12-13.

109 See Appendix VII for contemporary weather records.

110 The numerous references to his purchase, sale and attention to his horses shows their importance as his second 'work force'. Indeed, he often seems to express more concern, in his journals, for his animals than for his human labour force.

111 The separation of church and state in America, the freer methods of evangelism and more flexible attitudes of the Methodist, Baptist, westward-moving pioneers and their simple emotional preaching of the Gospel with a view to securing sudden conversions would particularly appeal to C.S. Works by famous American preachers were advertised in the 'Preacher's Manual'; especially prominent was the Rev. de Witt Talmage of Brooklyn, New York, who in 'The Abominations of Modern Society', was 'vehemently earnest in his denunciations'. Henry Ward Beecher (1813-81) was an American liberal Congregationalist minister, renowned nationally and internationally for his oratorical skill and social concern. He lectured in England in 1863, and both wrote for and edited 'The Independent', a Congregationalist journal on which C.S. commented with approval.

112 Anthony Sharpley of Torrington. A leading Free Methodist, and another cousin of C.S. They frequently associated on platforms, at openings of chapels, anniversary and mission meetings, etc. C.S. expressed his familiarity with the

character and style of his Methodist and farming neighbours with dry and genial humour.

113 A nurse from Smedley's Hydro, Matlock. She was later found wanting 'as an experienced nurse for a confinement'.

114 The writer's preaching engagements were largely within the Market Rasen circuit, but contemporary preaching plans (now in Lincoln Archives) show that he also preached in chapels in the Louth circuit. See Appendix VI for sketch map showing the considerable area he covered on foot, riding his horse, or driving in gig or cart.

115 See note 45 above.

116 See Introduction, p. 10 for comment on his particular financial difficulties.

117 In a journal entry of July 1869 (an addition to the Irish Journal), C.S. described a visit to the Leeds National Exhibition of Art which opened in the Infirmary, designed by Gilbert Scott (1868). Eight paintings by Rosa Bonheur (1822-99), friend of Landseer, were shown at this exhibition. None of these were, in fact, 'harvest scenes', but C.S. may well have remembered a painting of cattle and sheep being brought home from pasture in the setting sun, which irradiates the whole painting. (Illustration of a painting, dated 1862, can be seen in a file of Rosa Bonheur's work in the de Witt Gallery, Courtauld Institute.)

118 The famous meeting of the two men had taken place at Ujiji on November 3rd, 1871, and in August 1872 Stanley extolled the exploits of Livingstone when he was entertained at the Garrick Club, so enhancing his own reputation ('Illustrated London News', 1872).

119 More descendants of Roger Sharpley of Wakefield, who had driven his flocks and herds down to Lincolnshire in the mid-eighteenth century. A century later, members of the family owned or tenanted a number of farms on the north Lincolnshire wolds, while others had professional positions - solicitor, doctor - in the market town of Louth.

120 After the Act of 1871 which created the Local Government Board, sanitary power was concentrated in the board's hands. It was then obliged to appoint medical officers, but usually, because of economy, these were part-timers with small salaries (Clapham, 'Economic History'). It was often difficult to find local doctors willing to take on the work. In the Louth Union Board of Guardians' Minutes for 1871-2 it was reported at a meeting of 26th June, 1871, that 'as there was no medical practitioner in the district, Mr. Bogg, surgeon of Louth, is hereby appointed to act in the Welton-le-Wold district at a salary of £40' (Lincoln Archives).

121 See note 61 above.

122 The gate on the far side of the courtyard outside the back-door of the farmhouse, leading to the farmyard. Local agreements were made by farmers for harvest work taken on by day labourers, who included many Irishmen who travelled

from south to north as the corn ripened for cutting. The Irish lived rough in the farm buildings, and some years later than this journal entry there was a bad fire in one of the buildings in which some of the men were burnt to death.

123 'The Peep of Day', published by Ward, Lock & Co., was a book of simple religious instruction, by question and answer. 'Stepping Stones to Knowledge' consisted of school subjects for young children, using a similar method.

124 See note 111 above.

125 See note 76 above.

126 Farmers on the wolds often rented grassland on the marshes near the north Lincolnshire coast on which to fatten their cattle and sheep, as the light soil on the wolds did not provide enough rich pasture unless the growing season was unusually wet.

127 See note 92 above, on growth of Free Methodism, and building of new chapels into the mid-1870s.

128 C.S.'s use of 'suburban' here and on other occasions expressed appreciation of the new developments in building on the edges of towns and villages, which were a feature of the nineteenth century, and made possible by the railways which brought an influx of town and city dwellers to more rural areas. (W. J. Reader, 'Life in Victorian England', Batsford, 1964). C.S. sometimes used the word more vaguely as expressive of the blending of buildings in a landscape.

129 See Introduction, p. 4.

130 A rather obsessive concern with his own and his family's health led him to try out a number of devices or practices which he saw advertised or which were suggested as beneficial to cure minor ills. His wife commented on his inclination for 'new things'.

131 'The Higher Ministry of Nature reviewed in the light of modern science and as an aid to advanced Christian Philosophy', published in 1872.

132 Gladstone's government's popularity was decreasing by this time, and the bill for reform of local government and taxation was withdrawn, like a number of other bills.

133 The Rev. John Thomas Huntley, M.A., J.P., Rector of Binbrook.

134 Before the Burial Act of 1880, Dissenters could not be buried in church graveyards.

135 An example of the control exercised even by absentee owners of large estates within a parish, who contributed to parish expenses. The new parish church of St. Mary and St. Gabriel was built in 1869 after the amalgamation of two Binbrook parishes (Olney, 'Labouring Life').

136 Alessandro Gavazzi (1809-99). Reformer in church and politics during the Risorgimento, the unification of Italy. He inveighed against the neglect of social problems and Italian unity by the Papacy, and was considered a heretic by the Pope. He left his religious order, and after arousing English

interest in the Italian revolution, he served as chaplain in Garibaldi's army and shared in the formation of the Italian Free Church (1870).

137 Flour was ground at the water mill in Binbrook village.

138 Seasonal day labourers.

139 Diarrhoea was a common complaint, one cause of which would have been a contaminated water supply, dependent as the household was on a limited supply of drinking water brought in a cart from the village.

140 In the Second Journal (1874-5), C.S. entered details of his fortnightly wage payments more frequently. His confined men, paid at an annually agreed rate, sometimes 'drew' additional fractions of their wage at Christmas, or for some special occasions.

141 As a leading member and circuit representative of the Market Rasen circuit, C.S. felt a special responsibility for the ministers, and rehearsed in the pages of his journal his speech of welcome to the new young minister.

142 See note 117 above.

143 Public Health Act of 1871. The Public Health Act of 1848 had encouraged local authorities to devise and enforce building codes and institute sanitation measures. The Act of 1866 compelled local authorities to provide sanitary inspectors and allowed the central government to insist upon the removal of nuisances, the provision of sewers and a good water supply. In 1871 the Poor Law Board was handed over to the Local Government Board, a new government department which controlled both poor relief and public health.

144 Binbrook doctor, and part-time medical officer appointed by the Louth Union Board of Guardians. See note 120 above.

145 See note 18 above. Thomas Surfleet was a tailor and draper in Binbrook (1871 census).

146 Charles Darwin's 'Origin of Species' was published in 1859. A. R. Wallace's theory of evolution was similar to Darwin's, except that he left a loophole for direct divine intervention. See Introduction, pp. 16-17 for comment on C.S.'s conflict between his firm religious belief and the 'new' science, the more bitter because of his previous enthusiasm for earlier scientific discoveries and their application in his world.

147 Thomas Reid (1710-96). A philosopher who espoused a philosophy of 'common sense' as against Hume's scepticism. The two works which C.S. read were his 'Essays on the Intellectual Powers of man' (1785) and 'Essays of the Active Powers of Man' (1788).

148 C.S. took his standard of a comfortable 'middle class home' rather from his wife's expectations than his own inclination. The detailed account of the rebuilding of the farmhouse which he gives in the Second Journal shows clearly what was considered desirable for a 'respectable' farming family. For Skallows Hall see Appendix VIII, Farm Plan.

149 This may be a description of foot and mouth disease which

was endemic in flocks and herds at this period. It is another example of his sensitivity to the suffering of animals which, in one way or another, is caused by man. It is part of his wider belief in the responsibility of man as tenant of God for all forms of created life on the farm, animate and inanimate.

150 Horace Bushnell (1802-76). American Congregational minister and controversial theologian. His essay on 'Science and Religion' (1869) shows his resistance to Darwin's evolutionary theory.

151 Richard Chevenix Trench, Archbishop of Dublin. 'On the Study of Words, Five Lectures', had its first edition in 1851. There were 19 editions up to 1886. A. P. Stanley, Dean of Westminster. 'Lectures on the History of the Jewish Church', 4th edition, 1866-77. John Stuart Mill (1806-73). Philosopher, economist and exponent of Utilitarianism (inherited from Jeremy Bentham).

152 The Ballot Act of 1872 introduced the secret ballot and made old electioneering practices impossible.

153 Took over the tenancy of Parsonage and Binbrook Hill Farms from his father, John Iles, a long-time neighbour of the writer, and former Chairman of the Board of Guardians (see Appendix V).

154 It was normally the landlord's responsibility to help to keep farm buildings and fencing in repair. Sometimes, as in this instance, the landlord provided the materials and the tenants all or half the labour (F. M. L. Thompson, 'English Landed Society in the Nineteenth Century', Routledge, 1963).

155 James Obelkevich in 'Religion and Rural Society, South Lindsey, 1825-75', comments on the break-up of the rural community and the growing separation of the interests of its members, which increased during the nineteenth century: 'The farmers lack of supervision of their servants may well have reflected their general unwillingness to involve themselves in the lives of their inferiors.' C.S. does not seem untypical of farmers' attitudes in this respect, although his wife's repeated illnesses may have contributed to the lack of supervision, and his own rather narrow moral outlook separated him still further from the young men and women who showed in their outbursts a need of respite from isolation and their long hours of hard physical labour.

156 Frank Riggall Stovin: see Appendix III.

157 See Appendix VII.

158 Perhaps foot and mouth disease (see note 149, or pleuropneumonia (see Appendix VII).

159 Isaac Sharpley.

160 Like 'The Cornhill', a 'middle-brow' magazine with a mixture of serialised novels, poetry and general articles.

161 Mr. Paget was the son-in-law of the landlord, Sir Edmund Beckett, and a regular member of the shooting parties on the farm. In a letter to his youngest daughter written in 1904, C.S. remembers Rev. Paget as a poor shot: 'He managed to

shoot one rabbit. Was it not a sublime feat...' His resentment at the landlord's use of the farm for game preservation is echoed by many tenant farmers, although those with rising expectations of acceptance in the gentry class were more muted in their criticisms.

162 Septimus Sharpley farmed at Torrington, near Wragby, some twelve miles from Binbrook. The drover would need to set out the day before the fair to arrive before the start.

163 Later in his journals C.S. styled himself an 'eccentric agriculturalist', and in contemporary farming circles he was often looked on as bookish and impractical, so that he took particular pride in his successes.

164 In White's Directory for Lincs. 1872, Woodhall is commended as 'rising rapidly in estimation for its medicinal virtues'. It was especially known for the cure of rheumatism, chronic diseases of the joints, epilepsy and congestive disease of the brain - one of the very few spas which contained in any medicinal quantity bromide and iodine.

165 John Henry Newman (1801-90). Played an important part from the beginning of the Oxford Movement, and in 1845 became a convert to Roman Catholicism. C.S. admired his oratory while abhorring his doctrine. In his Oxford Journal (1870) he fulminated against the Oxford Movement and its emphasis on ritualism in the Church of England.

166 The expansion of the market in engravings in the middle of the nineteenth century took art out to the widest public it had yet reached. In 1860 chromolithographs, pictures printed in colours from stone, were developed. The colloquialism 'chromo' was used from 1868 ('Notes to the Exhibition of Victorian Art', Royal Academy, 1978).

167 See note 143 above.

168 For comment on his farming practice see Introduction, p. 10.

169 See Introduction, p. 15 for comment on his pride in being a part of a long tradition of Dissent.

170 Anthony Sharpley.

171 His friend in Oxford (see p. 40). He finally accepted a position as minister in the Market Rasen circuit in 1876, as C.S. related in the 1876 Journal.

172 For comment on letters to his wife, see Introduction, pp. 7-8.

173 His mother-in-law, Mrs. Francis Riggall. The distance to Dexthorpe from Binbrook was about 20 miles. At this time Denison was eight years old, and Mabel seven. See C.S.'s ideas on education, Introduction, pp. 8-9.

174 See note 66 above.

175 Although the 'golden age' of farming had not quite ended in 1872, C.S. had never reaped full benefit from the generally buoyant period of high farming between 1850 and this date because of his father's illness and the consequent ill-management of Binbrook Hall Farm. While in 1872 he just 'kept expenditure within income', the Second Journal, written as the farming situation generally worsened, reflects his particularly serious financial situation.

176 See Introduction, p. 15, and note 80 above. The 'English Independent' was another periodical published under the auspices of the Congregational church.
177 The Mason's Arms was a coaching inn, Louth.
178 See note 58 above, on change of governesses and their position in the household.
179 See Introduction, p. 17.
180 The North Lincs. Agricultural Society founded by the Earl of Yarborough in 1846 confined itself to stock and machinery and ploughing competitions, which were delegated to local societies in the market towns of Lindsey. Ploughing meetings were held in the autumn after harvest and before the autumn sowing (Olney, 'Lincolnshire Politics, 1832-85', Oxford, 1973). The Vicar of Barton-on-Humber observed in 1873 that 'the ploughing competitions [tended] to counteract the efforts which have been made in this county and throughout England to set class against class' - a reference to the strains put upon rural and social harmony by the growth of Trade Unionism (Beastall, 'The Agricultural Revolution in Lincolnshire').
181 It was C.S.'s cousin, J. B. Sharpley (see Introduction). who led the opposition in Louth to rates for the upkeep of the parish, and C.S. was within the family tradition of criticising both local and national expenditure directed towards the upkeep of the established church.
182 See Introduction, pp. 16-17, and note 72 above.
183 See Appendix VII.
184 See Introduction, p. 10, for comment on C.S.'s interest in trying out new methods in farming.
185 See Introduction, p. 10.
186 See note 92 above. The clash of priorities between C.S. and his wife gave rise to increasingly serious disagreements in the harsher years to come. See Introduction, p. 7.
187 A pig was given to each 'confined' labourer as part of his annual wage 'in kind'.
188 See J. C. Hare in 'The Years with Mother', ed. M. Barnes, 1952: 'On religious grounds it was thought wrong to contend against the wonderful leadings of God's Providence... pain was sent to be endured and sickness as a tractor to draw its victims to heaven.'
189 The last letters which end the First Journal are written to his mother-in-law, Mrs. F. R. Riggall. Two letters follow this one on the work of the Board of Guardians and are commented on in the Foreword, p. x.

SECOND JOURNAL

BINBROOK HALL FARM

September 7th, 1874 to June 7th, 1875

MONDAY MORNING, 8 O'CLOCK, SEPTEMBER 7TH, 1874.
BURTON'S SHOP, BOOKSELLER, LOUTH

Sydney Sharpley and Denison have returned with me this morning back to school after spending Sunday at Binbrook.[1] I find these Grammar Schools are too exclusively classical.[2] It appears they only learn English Grammar once a week while Latin comes on every day. Cannot the classics be mastered simultaneously with the English? The faculties would be more harmoniously developed by combining the classical, commercial, scientific. The significance of dry elementary education would at an earlier period become manifest to the youthful mind. The classics unlock ancient history, poetry, philosophy, art, eloquence, but they give only a pagan representation of Divine Providence and religion. The classical ideas of God and man, religion and virtue, are narrow and defective and awfully adulterated with error. Why do not our schoolmasters supplement the ancient learning with modern ideas. This must be the proper plan of wide culture. We want a catholic system of education. We require eclectic schools for boys as well as eclectic philosophy for scholars and philosophers. Boys ought to be schooled in picture galleries, in scientific laboratories and observatories. It is a most astonishing fact that with the growing wealth of our country and even the endowments of existing schools we are so weak and poverty-stricken in educational machinery. Our schoolhouses are miserable specimens of architecture miserable in their sites and arrangement for physical health and development as well as mental stimulus.[3]

Louth Mechanics Reading Room,[4] 9.25 a.m.
Denison and Mabel were home in time on Saturday for seeing the last harvest load come in. Denison and Sydney climbed up the waggon to join the group of shouters.[5] It was a little reluctance I felt at having to leave them so early yesterday morning. I was planned to preach at Torrington morning and evening. I took for my texts the expediency of Christ's departure and the sin which the Comforter should convince, John 16ch. 9v., and at night 'The fashion of this world passeth away', 1Cor. 7ch. 31v. The congregations were not large.

In looking through the list of advertisements I see this morning an announcement of a grand volume on trees and what ancient and modern poets have said and sung about trees and woodland, having for its object the awakening a new interest and more enlightened understanding and appreciation of our English Landscapes. There are several chromo drawings of historical trees. The price to original subscribers is £4 or £5 to general purchasers.

It is exceptional for us to be turning four skarifiers [scarifiers] into our turnip fields after harvest.

Our orchard is more fruitful both in plums and apples than for some years past.

We have eleven wheat stacks from 130 acre, five barley stacks from 70 acre and one long oatstack from 20 acre, total being 220 acre in 17 stacks. I have been able to give a personal supervision to stack building, the middle well filling up in the roof, etc.

I have lately felt drawn out in prayer for my fellow men. I feel a grave responsibility resting upon me in relation to my children. The evil influences are so terribly strong into which they are constantly plunged in order to secure intellectual education that fear, causing sadness, sometimes possesses me. Must the intellectual be obtained at the expense of the moral and religious? But I must not neglect to note the painful calamities which have in quick succession overtaken dear little Frank during the last week. From Saturday to Saturday last he has fallen four times, first from the top step into the courtyard while looking at his mother, then off the donkey, also out of his perambulator, and finally on the lawn-mower while with me in the garden. The last fall being most serious having cut his forehead over his eye. We brought him to the doctor that it might be properly closed up, avoiding a scar as much as possible. Dr. Sharpley plaistered it up.

I had to find a few ideas as best I could for last night's sermon. I took the text for the first time and knew not in the morning what I should have to say. However, the first service was concluded soon after seven and I arrived about 9.10, well nigh as early as our household returned from Binbrook.

I found my wife's authority had not proved strong enough to hold the youngsters in order. They had not much reverence for God's day. It excited melancholy sentiments and forebodings in regard to Denison's moral future. I am afraid he is not being taught to build up a character for eternity. Is it presumptious to pray that God will preserve him. On Sunday he attends church in the morning and the Free Methodist chapel at night.[6] Before walking up to the Board[7] I have been able to improve my leisure (created by bringing the boys to their 7.30 school hour) in sketching a small fragment of my farming life. I should like faithfully to unfold my private personal domestic, social and public life in a literary drama if a single life can be said to form a drama. It may never assume any importance in other eyes. It may prove valuable to myself at some future time. It assists reflection and reccollection. It enables me to understand better my own life and character; where to mould and correct, to kindle aspiration and lawful ambition, to form and consolidate resolution and translate them into nobler action, more skilful accomplishment.

TUESDAY, SEPTEMBER 8TH, 1874

The influences surrounding Denison's character at school are anything but salutory [salutary]. He says that Mr. Page swears at the boys and in fits of passion boxes some of their ears.[8] I am afraid lest Denison's moral character should receive injury. I had hoped that the roughness and uncouthness of his pronunciation and general manners would be corrected, that his habits of orderliness and cleanliness in his person and dress would be promoted. However, it seems the defects are being aggravated instead of removed. As far as opportunity allows me to judge there is but little sunny discipline pervades the household. The physical characteristics of Mr. Page's house are by no means attractive. The exterior is gloomy and prison-like in appearence. There is no open landscape and playground in the centre. The little contracted playground, more like the ward of a common gaol, does not strike me as tending to make the hours of the boy's relaxation playful and gay. The sun must climb loftily the heavens before the dark shadows of the premises are dispersed. It is almost noon before the relicts of twilight depart. The front of the dwelling, though neatly constructed, faces north and east, stands shivering with its back to the sun. It gives one the chill to gaze at the shades hanging over it. If it be a symbol of the household life enshrouded within it is not calculated to conserve and promote moral, intellectual, physical refinement and gentlemanly aspiration and sensibility. It cannot be illuminated by cheery animation. Youthful energy when cramped, darkened and soured bursts forth with mischief. It is a nursery for imperfection and vices. Human nature is so constructed in depravity that depraving influences are more readily imbibed. It yields more easily to depraving circumstances. It is more impressible to evil than good. The stamp of evil leaves a strong seal and deeper impress. This is one reason of evil's perpetuation.

This afternoon my wife and I, Frank and William Norman, rode together with Ted and waggonette to Binbrook Post. We met Mrs. C. Fieldsend and her daughter. They intended calling to see Lizzie. A servant named Westermond, their cook, is about to be married and they have entered five Registers' Offices, two at Lincoln, two at Louth and one at Rasen.

I have read a sermon by Dean Stanley upon the letter and the spirit, original in its structure and language but almost void of supernatural and evangelical sentiment. Very beautiful, but of the earth earthy.

We have had a fine sunshiny breezy and happy day. I have enjoyed a walk over the farm amongst the skarrifiers [scarifiers], in seeing the turnips much improved, even beyond expectation. In strolling through the old pleasure ground the spirit of heavenly poesy inspired me. How differently the home, the garden, the farm, appears according to the state of our own hearts. The poet says 'All things are dark to sorrow', etc. When there is light within, when the spirit of admiration is alive of all God's works, it transfigures nature and human life, the church and temple, and illumines them with the glory of the Shekinah. An experience like today is worth recording in letters of gold though it could not be purchased by the wealth of a nation. 'I'll praise my Maker while I have breath.'

Frank's birthday, the second of his new existence, is fast approaching. Next Friday, the 11th of September, Frank concludes the second year of his life.

WEDNESDAY, SEPTEMBER 9TH, 1874

To my new Landlord.
Dear Sir,

Will you allow me to speak to you as freely and confidentially as I have been accustomed with your Father. I should like to have attended his funeral but did not know what day he was buried nor whether it was agreeable for his tenantry to attend.[9]

In relation to the deceased I can note with sincerity that as a landlord my respect for him has always been permanent and unwavering. His visits in former years have formed a pleasing retrospect. He always treated me with such extraordinary geniality. He was so royally liberal in his expressions of satisfaction with my system of farming. He was in full sympathy with agricultural progress. His business qualifications were such that no improvements made on the farm escaped his notice. It is a great question whether my brother and I would ever have succeeded to the same extent had he not come over and demanded from us a revision of our system of farming.

The farm was poor and in a rubbishy condition and Father was unable in consequence of fits, partially destroying his business faculties. I shall never forget the excitement in the family when Mr. Denison (since Sir Edmond Beckett) came over and conversed with Mother, advising her to push her sons out into business. I often wonder at the confidence reposed in me, having the banking book in my possession before twenty years of age. However, we set to work and improvements commenced in every part of the farm, the fences, the land, the stock, etc. Trees and hedges were taken up, a portion of the farmstead newly built, and two new cottages.[10] There is not a farm in Lincolnshire where more capital, energy and enterprize have been expended towards rendering it productive and profitable.

You will perhaps excuse this brief reference to the past, also asking for some communication from yourself. You are perhaps not aware that the deceased has not visited us now for several years, that is since the appointment of Mr. Vesey as his agent.[11] Now, speaking in confidence, during the whole of that period I have received no expressions of approval or disapproval. Any request I might make has been heard in a gentlemanly manner with a promise to come over but with no performance. I have been quietly ignored in every shape except when the rents were due, and then I am recognised as a tenant. It seems a great contrast to be left out in the cold after enjoying the sunshine of my landlord's approbation. When Sir Edmond gave the estate his personal supervision I could almost ask and receive but since that time the smallest favour has been silently denied. Now I have avoided disturbing the peace of the late Sir Edmond, thinking he must be drawing near his departure. I have borne the annoyance silently and, I trust, patiently. When the labour difficulty arose last summer, Mr. Vesey promised some new cottages. I entered rather prominently into the struggle and helped to carry it on to a successful issue.[12] In the meantime Mr. Denison's death transpired. Of course in consequence we declined to trouble the late Sir Edmond about it. Since his death Mr. Vesey said you were coming over and I must see you respecting them. As we are not honoured by a visit my alternative is to write. Being authorised to state my case, I will candidly express to you my desire. While the farm has undergone a complete transformation to the absorbtion of the principal portion of the profits,[13] the house has remained.

Here begins my list of complaints. The house is damp and unhealthy.[14] It has harboured sickness now for half a century. No doubt my mother and eldest sister's days were shortened after many years of suffering.[15] My wife has experienced an inquisitorial torture through most of the period of our married life. If you will allow me to put the questions in as few words as possible:
Will you build me a new house or improve the present one?
Will you build two more double cottage tenements?
Will you allow me to stubb up two or three more old useless hedges?
Will you open out the farm and render it more airy and healthy for the cropping and sheep; by cutting down a large number of the hedgerow trees which become so overgrown, destroying the productive power of the headlands.[16]

Yours etc. C. Stovin

It is raining freely and continuously to the full satisfaction of the turnips if not to the gratification of Mr. Paget and his sporting friends.[17] I expected him over my farm today but I think this pouring rain will destroy their sport.

THURSDAY, SEPTEMBER 24TH, 1874

Am I only to wake fully up to a consciousness of life's responsibility when more than half its period has elapsed? Oh that from this instant I might candidly read the indications of Divine Providence in relation to my own future course of life that I may lay aside every weight. I trust a new era is about to open upon me of new experiences and increased usefulness. I desire to attend diligently to my business, to make farming a success and simultaneously the cause of Christ in this circuit and neighbouring districts a success. My heart is drawn out in prayer for the financial prosperity of our circuit and also Grimsby.[18] May the living Christ of our beloved Gospel lift from off our shoulders the nightmare of debt that we may become tenfold more hopeful and confident in our work of saving souls.

On Monday last I attended the Grimsby Chapel Anniversary. Mr. Smart, the Babtist Minister, remarked at the close that it was the most interesting meeting ever held in that chapel. I met Mr. Garside (President of our Annual Assembly) for the first time on the platform, also Mr. Lauderdale, Babtist Minister, Spurgeonite Jack, Wesleyan Minister, Mr. Travis, Free Methodist Ministers Mr. Colam, Mr. North, a batch or band of five earnest men. May Heaven help us out of debt at Grimsby and may the people flock like doves to the temple.

At Partney Fair on Saturday last I purchased 12 beasts a year and a half old at £14 each of Mr. Lill, also 6 heifers at £18/10/0 each of Edward Mackinder, and 3 of Longstaff at £16/5/0. I also took a ram off Frank's hands he bought of Mr. Mackinder at £8/8/0.

Yesterday I bought an Irish mare for £30 of Ash.

We are now emptying our crews; we only managed to clear one before harvest.

We have ploughed 30 acres of seeds for wheat, the rest must lay down until Christmas in consequence of the deficient turnip crop. At present the weather here is all we can desire to promote the bulbing; where there is plant on my farm it is scarce.

We have just finished thatching.

We have thrashed two stacks of barley and two of wheat. Sold the barley for 42/6.

We had a glorious dew last night, still no very abundant rains to saturate the land.

Yesterday wheat made 44/-. I feel almost inclined to speculate on my wheat.

A week last Saturday, September 12th, I gave Mr. Page and his Grammar School boarders a treat of dinner, tea and afternoon entertainment which they appeared much to enjoy. They gave us three cheers on the lawn before leaving.

We are tired of George Taylor as houseboy and have sent him into the green lanes to tend cattle.

It is a fortnight last Saturday, September 5th, since our dear little Frank fell on the lawn mower and cut his forehead. The Dr. S. plaistered him and it still adheres to disfigure his little brow.

Poor old Smart is sold for a five pound note. She got entangled in the stable and poll evil ensued.

Thursday Evening, September 24th, 1874

We have received a delightful thundershower this noon which has only obscured the sun for a short period. It is one of the most brilliant turnip growing days of the season.

My Autumn purchases have consisted today in horses; one three year old brown mare price £30, one do. black horse three years old, one bay horse two years old, £26 each; one light bay pony two years old £19. Ash says that if a horse's tail touches the ground it is safely two years old. Sometimes a yearling can scarcely be distinguished from a two years old.

My dear little William Norman is much beloved in the family.[19] He bears upon the whole the best character as a baby of any yet presented to us by Divine Providence. Though an intensely pale looking child (unlike the others) he has suffered from no serious illness. I think the Dr. was specially called to the other three.

On Tuesday last, September 22nd, I attended the first meeting of shareholders for the purpose of re-electing the Directors and declaring and confirming the dividend, which is eight per cent to be paid upon the amount paid up. The foreman showed us over the mill and all appeared satisfactory.[20] The warehouses were very full of seed and it appears the speculation has proved very unprofitable as the same quality of linseed can now be purchased at considerably less money.

I am now reading Dr. Farrar's 'Life of Christ'.[21] I think it is already forming a new and most important epoch in my own Christian life. The author opens the great life before the reader's mind in a new and most enchanting light. I feel it deepens my Christian experience. It strengthens and confirms my habit of prayer. Transforming virtue comes forth from the Saviour to my soul as the author leads me into his presence. I enjoy such intense relish that I yearn for leisure to give it a tenth reading. And yet I have fallen short of discerning its mighty efficacy and opened my passive and receptive powers to realise all I might. Oh that God the Spirit would mercifully continue his soultransforming and truth-revealing work that I might become more nobly useful to His church.

THURSDAY, OCTOBER 8TH, 1874

I have just finished copying the chapel accounts. It is now nearly ten o'clock p.m.

Yesterday Lizzie, Denison and William Norman went with Pink and phaeton to Hackthorne. Lizzie will be very much surprised to find on her return tomorrow that Sir Edmond Beckett has written a very polite note stating his willingness to build me a new house on condition that I will pay five percent upon the outlay. I have written by return also, stating that according to his wish and request I will see Mr. Vesey at once respecting it.

We have been leading manure today and spreading on new seeds. Having only ploughed thirty acres up for wheat, time has been afforded for Autumn manuring. In two or three more fine days my new clovers will the greater part be covered and protected for the winter.

We have steam-dragged fifty acres of wheat stubble, and if tomorrow be fine, forty of the same will be run over with the new light drag or steam harrow as the men call it. For the heavy and light dragging, the cost is 12/6 per acre, exclusive of coal, water leading, etc.

FRIDAY, OCTOBER 9TH, 1874

Another very rainy morning and of course no more steam-dragging for the present.

I will now write out a copy of Sir Edmond Beckett's first letter to me.

Wyebrook House Buxton
7th Oct. 1874

Dear Sir

Mr. Paget has written to me about your house, saying that you are willing to pay 5 per cent on the cost of a new one in a better situation.

It is rather a large undertaking, but still I am willing to do it for you on these terms. As I know practically nothing of Binbrook and cannot go there at present (though I hope to do so before long) I must ask you to consider this matter with Mr. Vesey, and you had better ascertain as well as you can beforehand what it is likely to cost.

If it is to be done I should like it to be well done, and I shall take some interest in the plans myself; but you must settle for yourself what sort of rooms and general accommodation you will want. I am here for the next fortnight certainly.

Yours truly,
Edm. Beckett.

Yesterday I wrote an answer to his letter stating that I would see Mr. Vesey at once.

WEDNESDAY, OCTOBER 14TH, 1874

Today I have attended Partney Fair for sheep. Best lambs from 30/- to 41/-. The ram I bought of Frank from Mr. Mackinder broke his neck and I have bought another today of him (Mr. Mackinder) for £10/10/-, a grand sheep he is. My waggon and four horses have been to Louth to fetch 15 qr. of old oats at 32/-, 11st. per sack, from Mr. Roberts' warehouse. A week today I paid Mr. Roberts the balance due to him on account of some wheat being thrown up last summer which was kept too long owing to my labourers being on strike. It has cost me about £60.

Mr. Roberts paid me for 140 qr. barley at 42/6.

I called upon Mr. Vesey to consult him about building. He said he was coming over to shoot with Paget on the 20th and he will look over the house.

A week last Sunday was the first day when the freewill offering boxes were brought into use.[22] 7/- was realised. These boxes are intended to supplant our usual quarterly collections.

My dear Sir,

If I must have fifty pounds a year added to my rent in consequence of the new house being built, I feel bound to make a very urgent request that you will allow a large proportion of hedgerow timber to be cut down as my farm is choked up with trees. Almost every field has a large border cut off.

Mr. Bryant has sent me George Steward's book on the 'Mediatorial Sovereignty'.[23]

THURSDAY, OCTOBER 15TH, 1874

It was very kind of Frank and Mrs. Riggall to come over from Hackthorne late last night for the purpose of giving us some suggestions as to the situation of a new house if we build one, also some suggestions respecting the improvement of the old house.

Mrs. Riggall advises us to improve the old house if the landlord will build us three new cottages. As Sir Edmond remarks, the new house will incurr [incur] a serious outlay and prove a rather great undertaking. It is a great matter to have a house where respectable servants will like to live, and good stabling that a groom would take some pride in keeping in order.[24] Mrs. R., Frank,[25] Lizzie and myself drove the phaeton into three fields to find a site and we decided the corner 16 acre, the last field at the right of the Bin[brook] road. We thought it would be sheltered all round by plantation and pleasantly near the road and considerably nearer the village.[26] It seems altogether a pleasant nook. We had a beautiful shower again last night; the air today has been balmy and forcing to grass and roots. The weather is all we could desire for our late sown turnips. (Wages drawn.)

SATURDAY, OCTOBER 17TH, 1874

Another Michaelmus Caistor is over. Today I have bought 5 beasts; 3 maiden heifers with long horns and two young steers at £13/17/6 each.

My waggoner [drew] £2/10/0 upon his wage. One sovereign when they went down to Cleethorpes and thirty shillings on Thursday night last, professedly to pay for breaking the Ludbro' guide post.[27]
Dec. 18th. My waggoner drawn £1/0/0/
Jan. 22nd. Waggoner drawn for candles 14.
Feb. 6. Waggoner drawn 20/-, also March 19th do. 20/-.

It is now six weeks last Wednesday since Hannah came.[28]

George Taylor, the houseboy, has left today.

On Wednesday last we fetched with waggon and four horses 15 qr. old white oats, 11stone per sack, price 32/- per qr. also ½ ton linseed cake.

It has been raining most of the day. I rode Charlie to Caistor and Mr. Hewson bid me £32 for him.

We have received a letter from Ma stating that she thinks we shall save half the expense by improving the old house instead of building a new one.

WEDNESDAY, OCTOBER 21ST, 1874

Dear Sir,

Yesterday Mr. Vesey looked over our house. He thinks the

present one may be made comfortable by putting out new bay windows in front and side, turning kitchen into a dining room and building more kitchens and bedrooms at the back. I suppose the cost would be about £500. Mr. Vesey observed the house was damp and badly built but thinks the cost of a new one would be very serious for us in that it leaves us entirely in your hands. Of course this will raise my rent £25 per annum. When I agreed with Mr. Paget to pay five per cent it was for the cost of improving this. Mr. Vesey has built himself a new house and he warns us very strongly, having found by experience the serious character of the expense. When the house is built on a new site there is so much outlay in furnishing, in planting and fencing and levelling.

If the farm were more profitable a new house is just what my wife and family would like. Perhaps you are not aware my farm is more densely enclosed than Mr. Iles's or any other in the parish.[29] The shadows created are deep drawn over the fields by such long and lofty belts of foliage. Those trees are many an hour luxuriating in sunshine which ought to be quickening and ripening my grain crops. Hence in the neighbourhood of plantations and hedgerow trees the crop is poor and scarcely worth reaping. By the morning sun being excluded the foggy rhymes [rimes] linger and the general climate of the farm is rendered less genial and healthy. Various diseases almost annually visit our flocks, which take my profits so that we can only just comfortably live and I do not realise interest for my capital. Notwithstanding all drawbacks, from domestic associations I naturally cling to the place, my son Denison being the fourth generation on the farm.[30]

I give you a frank and true statement and leave myself in your generosity as I have always done with the late Sir Edmond, just stating that we need cottages which were promised to us last Spring in consequence of the labour struggle.[31] We also need a better house but cannot afford to pay interest upon the cost of a new one.

BINBROOK, THURSDAY, OCTOBER 22ND, 1874

Rev. S. B. Paget and Mr. Vesey dined with us last Tuesday. They were very pleased with their day's shooting. 88 head of game was a very gratifying exhibition; the most numerous that our courtyard green has had spread upon it.

Yesterday I drove to Louth Market and sold 20 couple fowls at 4/9. I posted our letter (for my wife assisted me to write it) to Sir Edmond Beckett. It was after three when I reached home for dinner, then drove Charlie to Rasen Aggregate circuit tea.[32] The meeting was cheerful and eddifying. Several representatives from the rural societies gave addresses of about 5 or 10 minutes in length.

Today I have occupied my morning in farming. The new seeds improve with sheep on them, which is unusual with us. Of course the weather is still what we desire. It has been extremely forcing to vegetation. The turnips are somewhat deceptive from the road. The tops are larger than the bottoms being late sown. It will require a month or six weeks more open weather before the bulbs can be fully grown.

Lizzie bought Denison a pair of white kidd [kid] gloves today for a birthday party at Mr. Page's. It is pleasing to hear that he is at the top of his class.

We have had two or three windy drying days and the four horse harrows were working the steam cultivated 20 acre.[33] Mr. Parr's old shepherd French has seen the ram I bought of Mr. Mackinder for £10/0/0, and pronounces it one of the best in the neighbourhood. We have given him 80 ewes. My ewes run tupping very fast.

Copy of Sir Edmond Beckett's letter.

Buxton but going to Doncaster.
22nd October, 1874

Dear Sir,

I am not surprised at your finding that building a new house would be a very serious undertaking, especially on a different [site] so that everything would have to be new. If you are satisfied that the present house can be made fairly good and healthy by such alterations as you mention, I will do it for you on the terms before stated.

I will do the same also for cottages which you say are wanted.[34] Perhaps it is worth considering whether the cost of altering the house and building the cottages would amount to much less than building a new house and turning the present one into cottages. But I should guess that it would.

If you come to the conclusion to do this, you had better arrange for it yourself, subject to my approval of the plans, of course. But you had better not make any contract with a builder in a hurry, and if you consult an architect take care that you are not bound to employ him further than you like. If you have a good builder who could be trusted, an architect ought not to be required at all for such work as that. The builder ought to be able to give you a plan and estimate and engage to do the work to your satisfaction.

Mr. Stovin.

Yours truly,
Edm. Beckett.

BINBROOK, THURSDAY EVENING, OCTOBER 29TH, 1874

Today three ploughs turned up the headlands after steam cultivator. One horse and cart also leading heaps of twitch dug out of the 90 acre fallows, also 3 labourers, viz: Brumpton, Rook and Branwick, digging or forking twitch out of Black Pond field fallow.

I gave notice to my labourers on last Saturday to reduce wages from 3/- to 2/9.

The whole of our manure is spread out on new seeds and sainfoin field, an unique event so early in the Autumn. Of course this could not have been done except that we have only sown about 30 acre of wheat. We find 60 acre of pasture, though exceptional, extremely useful as the season continues so moist and mild.

BINBROOK, FRIDAY, OCTOBER 30TH, 1874

Received from Mr. Crombie a letter stating that he would visit us on the 8th of November next and conduct a week's special services on condition that we held a series of prayer meetings through the week prior to his coming. Mr. Travis has written a very kind note acknowledging the hare and enclosing his carte asking Mrs. Stovin a place for it in her album.[35] It is a priviledge to entertain such men of God and sit under their ministry. We very much enjoyed his company. He and I had a most interesting conversation and walk together through the farm on Monday morning.

Today has been cooler and more bracing, the two previous days being foggy, close and relaxing. November weather in October. The Autumn leaves already thickly strew the ground though the weather is unusually forcing to vegitation such as grass and turnips. Lambs are much higher in price than in August, running from 20/- to 40/- and even more for the very first class.

Miss Kenedy appears to be very successful in increasing our Free Methodist Day school.[36] The numbers are almost weekly increasing amounting to about a hundred on the books. I am afraid it will militate against our being recognised as a Government school.

Sir Edmond Beckett's last letter is dissappointing and discouraging. It contains no response to my request respecting the cutting down of hedgerow timber and remodelling of the farm's general enclosure.

I am more disposed to recognise the Divine Government as extending over my farm, my household, family as well as church, or our society, or circuit, and indeed my own person. I pray more earnestly for guidance in business as well as wisdom and unction in ecclesiastical and spiritual work. We need to pray for more financial power. Chapel debts are depressing to our churches. These debts have been heavily on my heart.

BINBROOK, NOVEMBER 2ND, 1874. MONDAY MORNING, CANDLE-LIGHT

On Saturday last Mr. Dixon came to take my thrashing by the lump.[37] I agreed to give £35 fast for 17 stacks.

Commenced fallowing last week. Labourers digging twitch before the ploughs.

Yesterday Mr. Cash from Ohio took my appointment at Market Rasen. He is a cloudy, monotonous preacher. Not a gleam of heavenly sunshine ever flashed from his eye. There was very little of Tabor radiance shone upon his brow. A heavy manner and monotonous tone of voice specially characterises his delivery. He never smiled even while portraying the reception of the prodigal. He failed to make the ring sparkle with diamonds or to unfold the embroidery of the garment or the joyous character of the feast. Religion is resplendent with jewellry. It robes a man in beauty. It feasts man's nature with the richest joys.

This is a damp mild cloudy morning.

BINBROOK, MONDAY EVENING, NOVEMBER 2ND, 7 O'CLOCK

On Saturday night last I called upon Mr. Vesey and we decided for the builder to come and look over the old house that he may draw plan and give estimate for the improvement. We require new staircase, 5 bay windows, water closet and dressing room, a more commodious dining room. We think of transforming the present kitchen into one and building new kitchens at the back. The old back kitchen and saddle house which stands as a detatched building is marked to fall. In considering the site for the new portion of the house we must bear in mind the cistern and sesspool [cesspool].

BINBROOK, THURSDAY, NOVEMBER 5TH, 1874

Another brilliant day though a little foggy at early morn. I have been to Binbrook today and bought 4 beasts (steers) of Robinson at £14 each and 50/- for luck.

Thrashing wheat yesterday and today. The stacks yesterday contained 48 qrs. as measured from the machine.

I saw my brother at Louth yesterday and he says I was to see the landlord and ask him to let me have the Hall as it belongs to the farm.[38] For some years it was unoccupied and in my possession for cottages.

We are dragging with 4 horses in the sainfoin 20 acre. Baby enjoys his mother's breast more than bottle. He is now 7 months old and no teeth yet appeared. Frank had two visible at that age. All the others had the bottle considerably earlier.

I bought a furnace of Robinson for 30/-.

We are holding special prayer meetings preparatory to Mr. Crombie's visit next Tuesday and 4 following nights. I attended the last two nights. The schoolroom was well attended.

Thursday Evening, 9 p.m.
Just returned on Charlie from prayer meeting.[39] Though this is an eve of bonfire demonstration and excitement and also a public sale, we have had a happy season, about 14 in number. God is endowing his people with the supplicating grace. As old friend Giles said in his prayer, 'We have heaven here and heaven yonder, heaven below and heaven above.' I am now reading George Steward's 'Mediatorial Sovereignty' and Dr. Alexander Raleigh's 'Quiet Resting Places',[40] also Dr. Bushnell's 'Forgiveness and Law'.[41] Oh, what rich enjoyment I have in communion with God and his church, in my family, in business, in private prayer. I cannot

agree with J. S. Mill that this world is clumsily constructed and unbenignly governed.

We folded our lambs on the turnips last Monday, almost a month later than previous years, the 11th of October being the rule.

On Monday last Rev. Smith, the Stewton clergyman, was exceedingly communicative upon the planting of apples and strawberries.

NOVEMBER 8TH, 1874. ANOTHER BRILLIANT NOV. SUNDAY MORN.

This almost cloudless Sabbath helps to brighten up my evidence. The evidences of Christian experience seem clear and strong. All glory and praise to Jesus for his redeeming grace. How His grace intensifies and develops home life and blessedness. The tide of domestic joys rise with the increase of family. While I write in the dining room, William Norman (now in his eighth month) lies in his cradle asleep. Frank has gone with his Mama and Rev. A. Crombie to chapel. I feel the religion of Christ is transforming and transfiguring my life. My home, my sanctuary, my closet, my farm, are all Bethels.

I was determined my darling wife should go to chapel this morning. She has seldom had an opportunity the last few months. I have undertaken a mother's guardianship.

BINBROOK, TUESDAY EVENING, NOVEMBER 10TH, 1874

Mr. Crombie preached last night about Blind Bartemeous. There were two professed to find peace. We had a prayer meeting at old Rockliffe's in poor row, about 80 years of age. Prayer meeting this afternoon at 6.30 and singing along the street.[42]

We have had splendid weather for thrashing, 4 stacks of corn, 2 of wheat and 2 of barley. Finished the last stack yesterday, yielding 75 qrs., and the one before 64 qrs. The two wheat stacks contained as measured from machine 102 qrs.

Today we have crushed 20 qrs. wheat for beasts.

On Friday last I paid £22 for a cow and calf. The cow turns out to be unsound in her throat and defective in one of her paps. I may call this one of my misfortunes in business.

Yesterday we were dragging with six horses in Binbrook field. The waggoner thinks very little to it. He says he thinks it will require as much working at Spring. A shower of rain prevents us doing the same today.

Mr. Crombie and I had a very pleasant and profitable morning walk and conversation. A great variety of topics were discussed.

The temperature is considerably lower today than on many previous days.

I have commenced paying my labourers 2/9 per day from the 1st November last.[43] Brumpton, Rook, Branwick, old James Wright, Shadlock and James Drew as daily men, and Charles Smith, foreman, Bocock, garthman, Bill Bocock, Bill Smith and Lawton, boys, Holmes, shepherd, and two single waggoners. These with the groom boy constitute the staff of our farm labourers.[44]

BINBROOK, THURSDAY, NOVEMBER 12TH, 1874

Today Mr. Wood of Alford has been over to look at the house. He examined it from floor to roof, from cellar to garrat. He has measured and drawn plans of both exterior and interior. He will give an estimate of cost for bay windows, adding kitchens to back and raising the roof. On Tuesday night we experienced a very sudden change of temperature. The frost was sufficiently severe to glaze our bedroom windows. Last night it commenced snowing for the first time this season while we were in the chapel engaged in Divine service, and this morning the ground was covered over some inches thick.

BINBROOK, NOVEMBER 13TH, 1874. FRIDAY NIGHT 9.30

My dearest wife,

Though you only left home this morning I have several pleasant bits of information to impart. It may appear of trifling moment to an unconcerned observer, but the incidents of today are of great interest and importance to us. Things said and done will make a lasting impression upon our memory. What we have seen has been photographed. For instance I took the train for Alford, which of course you expected I should. I soon found my way to the South Villa.[45] I rang the bell and was ushered into the room and my darling daughter Mabel soon made her appearence and greeted me with her usual smiles. I cannot say which felt most pleasure at meeting nor which felt most reluctance to part.

(Saturday morning, Nov. 14th, 1874.) Not being able to finish my letter last night, I make another attempt this morning, though several hindrances beset me. I had to wait a long time of the kettle boiling for breakfast. I made my own toast and tea. After breakfast and prayer I broke up sticks and abundantly fuelled the drawing room fire. My morning is considerably mortgaged by these domestic engagements. But you are aware what servants are in these days. If they can have their own wants supplied and desires gratified we may fish for ourselves.

Last even [evening] Miss Riggall showed me a photo of herself and school in a very nicely arranged group. My little rosebud of course was in the human bocheuhe [bouquet]. Some of the sweetest beauties the eye can rest upon. How my rough manhood seemed babtised afresh with poetic feeling. Of course, was the warm glow of parental interest. My supreme gratification consisted in Miss Riggall's testimony to Mabel's good conduct. No mistress could possibly be more emphatic in relation to her fidelity to truth. 'I have never found her speak an untruth, and she has never been really naughty or troublesome; of course, I don't affirm that she has always known her lessons perfectly, but she is always so good.' I hear no complaints, discords, irritations, discontents. Would to God my son Denison were as cheerful and enjoyed as much moral sunshine. I am afraid morbid dispositions are brooding in his heart. Every school as well as individual will be gloomy that is not opened to the sun of righteousness.

Yesterday I sold the Partney cow by auction, price £21, also bought reared calf £10/2/6. James Wright, drover. On Wed. last sold Mr. Roberts wheat at 41/6 and barley at 40/-.

BINBROOK, NOVEMBER 14TH, 1874. SATURDAY EVE. SIX O'CLOCK.

My dearest wife,

I received by this morning's post a very kind note from your brother, John, stating that you arrived safely, and with the exception of the missing hamper, which I hope will turn up, all is satisfactory. It appears Frank soon makes himself at home and happy with his Uncles and amid his new surroundings. I trust your health will be improved by the Birstal air and society.[46] I suppose the air is somewhat impregnated with chemicals in consequence of numerous chimneys and effluvias of various kinds emitted from manufacturing warehouses. These smoky and other substances of a finely atomic conformation are diffused through the air you breathe. But I suppose your lungs are sound and will not be injuriously affected by a small amount of defilement and perhaps the air may contain chemicals salutary to other parts of the system. This is mere speculation or even fancy on my part without any basial [basic] facts except the one fact that you came stronger and more vigorous from your last visit. I pray God that the same effect may be produced.

I forgot to name in my last that Miss Riggall expressed her admiration of Frank very strongly. She said, 'He is a handsome boy'. Your brother John says he has very much improved since he saw him last. I am sure diligent attention is being bestowed upon our children. They have been the uppermost thought of minds. We have denied ourselves of much sleep and comfort by night and day. It is very pleasing to find our friends recognising the fruit of our toil. Our children are not imprisoned in a nursery and left to the tender cruelties of servants, but sunned in the constant presence of affectionate parents. Their young natures are evolved by parental smiles. They have many liberties as well as restraints. Parental discipline does not in the least interfere with or check their buoyancy. Playfulness is encouraged. Violent tempers, transgression of household laws, are visited with punishment. Parental authority is upheld and obedience enforced. Penalties have not often to be inflicted upon disobedience.

We have suffered a large amount of anxiety in relation to the physical health of our family. We cannot say that any of them are physically robust, but at the present time enjoy moderately good health. You are considerably better than in former years but still the subject of many pains, weaknesses and much weariness. The toils and struggles and trials and vexations of life often make you sigh. I remarked to you that if you were not possessed of much spirit, self-determination and many other heroic elements in your nature, the late storm of snow and wind would have completely overturned your plans and purpose to visit Birstal. But not the least misgiving ever seem to present itself and, though a December-like day, you braved the journey. We need not come to you in search of effeminacy of character. You are [a] true enterprising tourist. Storms cannot quench your ardour. With a moderate amount of strength you defy obstacles. Accomplishment and endurance are your two watchwords. You love action more than contemplation though you blend judgement with action. Your active preponderates over the reflective power. You believe in business tact and energy carried to the goal of success in life. You believe in the development of capital in holding the expenditure within the income. Will God bless our efforts in the expansion of our property and income, that we have it in our power more amply to supply the gold and silver necessary to carry out His work in the circuit as well as more widely culture our children for his work.

I look at my property in relation to Christ's kingdom. Money is one of the great instrumentalities when rightly applied for the extension and consolidation of Christ's kingdom.

When I think of the low state of our ecclesiastical exchequer in the Market Rasen circuit I am driven to the throne of grace on behalf of my own business. Oh, that He may bless more fully my business enterprise. May He direct me in my loan of money and investment of capital. Knowing that I had taken 20 more shares in Mr. Coatsworth and Sowerby's cake mill, you will not be surprised that the Banker's receipt with the allotment letter came by post yesterday. I may perhaps remind you that Sampson Meanwell has received £300 of our money in loan, though I have not yet received from Fred Sharpley, my solicitor, the proper securities. I must procrastinate no longer. My present belief is that you will succeed in arousing me completely out of my procrastinating spirit. I see so many evils attending it in other persons. It nearly cost our Grimsby trust £5 for arrears of interest. I feel strongly inclined to call £200 in Mr. Hurley holds, as there was an understanding he should only keep it until the Autumn. This also must be looked after next Monday or Wednesday. The season has increased my turnip crop beyond my most sanguine expectations and in consequence I must make another purchase of lambs. I may require three or four hundred pounds for this purpose and if I pay back interest at the rate of, say, 6 per cent and allow Mr. Hurley to keep my money at 5 per cent, I shall lose.

BINBROOK, MONDAY MORN, NOVEMBER 16TH, 1874

My dearest wife,

Yesterday I preached twice at Tealby. In the afternoon from 3rd. ch. I Cor. At night from Luke 23rd ch. first clause of 35v.

I had a powerful time at night. There were three unconverted sinners much affected but would not yield. The congregation was very thin but the Divine glory was manifest. The few disciples present were aroused and sinners convinced. If once we are the means of quickening the church, if once the Gospel chariot begins to move, the circuit will rise. We have rested at low water mark long enough. When the spiritual state of a church is low the funds will be low. Our strength is in our spiritual life. Spiritual life creates unity and unity is the irresistable force. It is the all-conquering power. May I become more than ever a rallying influence.

In praying about institutions I am reminded of the reason, the stern reason, why I am a dissenter.[47] I cannot coincide with anyone of its great parties. There are many things in the Church of England which all intelligent and right minded man must admire. Look at her literature! Look in many quarters at her zeal. How some of her pulpits have risen into eminence and power on a par, we are told, with the best among Nonconformists. But the whole institution is held in bonds by the strong chains of civil legislation. Some of her prayers are model guides for the heart in its deepest devotion, but on the other hand the ambiguity of certain portions of the prayer book is the germ of her ritualism and the creator of the multiplied strife and bitterness. Why should the splendid patronage of Royalty be lavished upon one sect? Even if it were free from error and party strife, or a perfect example of what a sect might be in discipline, in doctrine, or even in moral excellence and spiritual power, then (as long as there were other sects with separate organisations of a somewhat different type) it would be a standing injustice. But what are the facts which glaringly deny such perfection? The contemplation of these arouse the moral horror and disgust of the true dissenter.

But perhaps you will remonstrate with me and shrewdly advise me to look diligently after my farm and remember that I have four dear children and a loving wife to provide for. You remind me that they are growing up and require education, and our expenditure in consequence continues to increase, and you sceptically inquire where the increase of income is to spring from. Now the question is just this. Am I to give to the Lord and to His church a portion of my time or are the world and my family to absorb the whole man. I might be earning money during the hours spent in prayer and study of God's word, but would not that be robbing God. Time must be given as well as money or a curse must rest upon such earnings. One half of this month has expired and though it has brought forth two or three days of keen frost and snow it is still fine, mild and brilliant. This morning resembles October in sunshine and breeze. 'Oh, that men would praise, etc.'

Mr. Marshall has written about the new cart I purchased of him. He asked £15 and would take something off.

I have bought a new rug of Osborne for Charlie.

We sent a cart to Ludbro' Station by William Smith for railway bags but cannot be supplied until tomorrow. Mr. Roberts wants the barley delivering as soon as possible.

Yesterday a very unfavourable report respecting the new cow, the first beast I bought at Taylor's Auction. It has a bad throat and Bocock sent word she had ceased eating.

BINBROOK, THURSDAY, NOVEMBER 19TH, 1874, 9 O'CLOCK, A.M.

My dearest wife,

We are now busy delivering barley and wheat, but do not very rapidly progress on account of bags being difficult to obtain. 1000 are ordered. This appears to be the cause of demurrage charges, as a part of the corn is delivered and detained. It is unjust to charge us for their own delay.

November 19th, 1874

Yesterday a serious trouble met me in Fred Sharpley's office.[48] I called for the purpose of obtaining my security for the £300 lent to Samson Meanwell. The document laid on the table ready. While it was sent down to be enclosed in an envelope Fred began to relate the history of my son, Denison's sudden attack of scarlatina. It appears on Friday last Mrs. J. B. Sharpley of Eastgate invited my son Denison for Sat. eve. and Sunday.[49] At the tea-table on Sat. he was taken with vomiting and on Sunday morning the Dr. pronounced it a decided case of scarlatina.

I called at Mr. Page's and heard his recital, then at Dr. Sharpley's, and from his statements found Mr. Page could exaggerate. Mr. Page said that Denison had eaten a hearty dinner and was playing at football in the yard, when, attempting to kick the ball, missed and fell on his back and hurt his head. Mrs. Page fetched him in to tydy [tidy] him for his visit and observed him look pale and said perhaps he had better remain at home, but he, looking down and unwilling, Mrs. Page did not insist.

The Dr. told me he must not be removed at least of a month, and that if I like he would look out for a suitable nurse, which I agreed to.

I called to see Mrs. Sharpley and was invited to go upstairs; the servant (to whom I gave a two shilling piece) conducted me to the upper room where my dear little son was laying. How quietly and contentedly he lay, in a well-ventilated room, a comfortable fire and bed, the second bottle of medicine on the table. To see him thrown so far out of my own and his dear mother's reach and to have become so complete a burden to his friends shook my manhood. Tears would rush up from the fountain of grief within me. I still feel myself in a fix.

Mr. Page said he was most unfortunate; once or twice when he had a boy about to do some credit to the school and carry off the prize he was taken ill a fortnight before the close of the term. He declared most emphatically that Denison would have taken the prize in his form, but this affliction should not prevent his being promoted next half.

FRIDAY NIGHT, 10 O'CLOCK, NOVEMBER 20TH, 1874

My dearest Lizzie,

You will be gratified to hear that we have for present delivery 136 qr. of barley at Ludbro' Station at 40/- per qr. Four stacks out of the five are now thrashed and delivered, making a total for this season so far of 276 qr.

Yesterday Arthur and I rode with Charlie round by Louth to Grainthorpe. He started a little restively but we managed the journey safely there. I presided over the Wesleyan Missionary Meeting. Mr. French, Markham, Brewin, Barr and Posnett addressed the meeting. We remained at sister Maria's for supper. After which Charlie was harnessed and yoked in the old dogcart, when he began his tricks; he refused altogether as soon as we had passed through the yard gate and sprang into the drain. It appeared a very threatening calamity but the friends came out of the house and helped extract us. A rope was brought by means of which several of us helped to pull the cart out of the drain. It was a considerable time before we could liberate the horse from the harness so that it was able to struggle its way out. At first we were afraid he was seriously injured in his breathing. He was rubbed down with straw while he shook from head to foot and breathed with some difficulty. However, a good walking exercise and a warm drink of boiled beer, ginger and coarse sugar seemed to settle him for the night. We all retired to rest about 1 o'clock in the morning.

When daylight came it revealed to our great surprise that no real injury was done to either horse, trap, or harness or person save the cutting of the halter shank. Everything mercifully preserved in soundness. What a merciful Providence is over us and how vividly manifest in such a deliverence. When plunged into the midst of the most threatening danger, the hand of God is rendered more visible in our rescue.

NOVEMBER 25TH, 1874, WEDNESDAY MORNING, 9 O'CLOCK

My dearest wife,

I am already looking forward to the pleasure of seeing you home again. It will be a fortnight next Friday since you left home. I have told you of the untoward events which have happened during your absence. I sometimes think they have somewhat effected my health. I have experienced a shock to my nervous system. Night before last I felt unusually tremulous while at the tea table, I felt also through the Divine service at chapel, I could scarcely keep still on my seat; this sensation of chilly vibration continued until after 12 at night and until dinner the next day. Your letter made me think I might have taken the fever from my son Denison. Still, it was not agitating fears, for my mind was peaceful and happy. It was not mental alarm but a peculiar physical excitement. As I lay in bed my muscles quivered though my teeth never chattered. It seemed like a restless nervous exhaustion; the system had not power to create a comfortable glowing temperature.

We have had a few nights of sharp rhyme [rime] frosts. I believe three, but this morning is raw and cloudy. I am afraid the weather is too cold for the Birstal air to improve your health as much as heretofore.

It is rather unusual for me to buy lambs at Louth Martimas Fair but I ventured upon 47 of Mr. Ashton at about 41/6, 35 hes and 12 shes. We have delivered 79 qrs. wheat to Ludbro' station at 41/6. Mr. Marshall of Ludford has written about the cart which I bought of him for £15. He offered to give some luck but did not say what. He states in his note that it is finished and would like me to fetch it at once.

Our twitch digging has again commenced, being interrupted by the dressing and weighing up of the corn.

If my cattle thrive as well through the winter as they commence, the 4lbs. for wheat meal each will prove a considerable reduction to my farmyard expenditure. The wheat is only worth about £9/0/0 per ton whilst the cake is £12/10/0 and some £13. Cotton cakes are £8/5/0.

You will perceive by my last that Mr. Vesey came to me in the Mason's Arms yard and said he received the plans from Mr. Wood and quite acquiest [acquiesced] to your desire for a new front. He said it would incur a waste of room by unduly lengthening the entrance hall, and suggested that the front door be placed at one side. He asked me which side I should prefer and I answered without mature thought on the south side as it would be most sunny and pleasant. Afterwards I discovered my future breakfast room and library would necessarily be the present dining room, which will have a northern aspect and have neither morning nor noonday sun. Of the two evils I will choose the least. The front door had better open into the present dining room and that with the southerly aspect will be reserved for every morning use. But to return, we must keep our eye upon the cost. If back and putting out bay windows to the low rooms and raising the roof reduces the expense a hundred pounds, perhaps we had better keep to the original plans. The old family dwelling is doomed under any circumstances to be revolutionised. If we can have it made dry, healthy and comfortable, it will be something for the last half of the century.

The clock strikes 12 and the rain continues to fall, and not having a gig I am more exposed in Esberger's dogcart. The other day Charlie ran away with my dogcart and broke the shaft, split the dashboard, bent some of the irons, and almost destroyed the wings. It is a sad affair that it should have to return to the repair shop having only a few months since come out new; at least the body was new though the wheels were second hand. I told Mr. Esberger that it was useless my spending 35 guineas, as it would just as soon break in case of accident. I find my words come true. £15 suited my pocket much better and when it comes out a second time bearing the burden of renewal it will be little more than half of the original price of the most highly finished carts.

However, it is the exposure to wet which holds me back this morning, as I have no pressing business.

My letters have just arrived and the invoice of a waggon of coals from Mr. Stonehouse of Hull at 20/- per ton. Also a letter from Mr. Wood respecting the plans for enlarging my house.

FRIDAY EVE. 7 O'CLOCK, NOV. 27TH, BINBROOK, 1874

My dearest wife,

I am cheered by the reassurance of your intentions to return home tomorrow, contained in your letter.

Today I sent a waggon and four horses for 1½ tons of linseed and 1 ton of cotton cake from Grimsby. The rest of the horses have been fallowing.

Our dear Denison is still in Mrs. J. B. Sharpley's bed in Eastgate instead of pursuing his studies and carrying off the prize at Christmas as Mr. Page said he would. It is a fortnight tomorrow since he was taken. He had suffered from a cold previously. I wonder whether it caused any predisposition to take the fever. The cold might not be the direct cause, but his power of resistance weakened by it. When the healthy forces in the system are less buoyant disease more easily attacks.

Now, my dearest, let us cheer up. You often seem desponding about our success in life. You think we are very poor and have done comparatively little good. You think the house is unhealthy and the farm unprofitable. Troubles spring up in unexpected quarters. Expensive afflictions, expensive accidents, diseases and losses amongst the flock and herd, breakages amongst middling crops of turnips, short-fall of lambs and 60 of them sold at the low price of 23/0. Now are these misfortunes arising from indolence or want of skills in the manager? Is this non-success to be ascribed to the farmer or the farm? I believe, without self-flattery, you ascribe it mainly to the farm. Now I am willing to admit a considerable portion of your remarks, though the picture you draw is very sombre and dark. You say I am too sanguine about the future and that I am always running my calculations upon eggs that never hatch. Still, I persist in my conviction that God will bless the work of my hands. I will ask you to cheer up once more in hope. I will turn over a new leaf and revolutionise my system of management. If one system does not answer we must persevere in adopting another. If we alter our method of managing our flock of sheep by supplying them with more appropriate food during the critical three months from mid-July to mid-October. We might supplement the sainfoin eddish with summer cabbage. I have commenced cutting for my lambs this Autumn. I really felt ashamed of my hoggets last Spring as I stood by them. They looked inferior to many others. I shall not soon forget my feelings of degration [degradation]. I resolved to give them more attention through both summer and winter. I followed Mr. Riggall's example in not cutting for them until their teeth failed. This has proved a mistake on my farm. I have had some first class hoggets in times past but at present my breeding flock is not remarkable for either size or symmetry.

My dearest I have a firmer conviction than ever that if I use my utmost thought and endeaver the Lord, our Heavenly Father, will not leave us to sink. The responsibilities in connection with His cause are too numerous and weighty for the great Mediatorial

Governor of the world and our affairs to allow us to be crushed. He can hold us up through our faithful perseverance in industry.

He is about to give us a more commodious and brighter home. If in addition to this He enables us to realise more products from the farm, we shall be able to bring up our children in intelligence, industry, and increased Christian influence, as well as our income keep in advance of expenditure. I feel no expansive pride of establishment or equipage. I should like my home to be chastely comfortable. I should [like] an educational degree of taste in the interior finish of the house as well as furniture to correspond. I should like home to be made attractive as far as discretion will allow. We may have beauty without magnificent show. A daisy is attractive and a small home may have treasures placed and hung about it which will please the eye and refine the mind. Domestic happiness may be greatly increased by the right construction of a house and its judicious adornment, providing its chief consist in the presence of Jesus.

We have a right to take a deep interest in and look forward with grateful pleasure to a brightening era in our family history. God is opening up before us a beautiful blue sky prospect of a more airy, spacious, convenient home. We may have some labour, expense, inconvenience in the erection, but, I repeat, if it be God's will, of which I feel no hesitating doubt, He will send us funds from some quarter. Should you like to see my banking book when it returns? I placed it in Mr. Dun's hands on Wednesday last. I feel curiosity as to my position.[50] It is a matter of great thankfulness that my credit is good. Mr. Dun always treats me very politely. It has often been remarked by our friends that all is right at the bank when Mr. Dun says, 'What will you take?' The sweating room is not thought of then. I have written several rather heavy cheques of one kind or another and am afraid they will look awkwardly in the total. Of course, there will be the round sum of £400 I already entered in my diary, placed to my account taken for corn a few days ago from Mr. Roberts, as well as the remaining £20, having put into my purse £13 odd of the cheque received last Wednesday.

In looking out of my bedroom window I see the moon and fancy by the coldness of the air upstairs it must be freezing. The snow has not melted much today though the land and ponds are not scarcely frozen over. The weather seems undecisive, a sort of balance between freeze and thaw. November has brought forth two extremes of summer and winter weather. It is excentric [eccentric] and exceptional. Now I think you must be wearied with a letter occupying more than two hours of my valuable time. I believe it is not wasted. A good stiff balance of gold and silver may possibly accrue from the study. A brighter era may open out of it and our future life [be] sweetened by a larger measure of pecuniary success and intellectual and moral advancement. Let us persevere in imploring God's help.

I took Mrs. J. B. Sharpley a couple of fowls on Monday last.

TUESDAY MORN. 9 O'CLOCK, DECEMBER 1ST, 1874

Lizzie, Frank, Norman, William, my brother-in-law and Hannah, the housemaid, returned from Birstal last Saturday. Frank was delighted to see me.

On the same day we killed 3 pigs for the labourers.[51] Charles Smith's, foreman, weighed 27st. 12lb., Bocock's 31st. 11lb., Holmes 29st. 12lb.

On Sat. night a heavy fall of rain. The sheep were taken off the turnips next morning. December comes in with sudden changes, frosty at night and rainy next morning. Lizzie and I and brother Will drove Pink and phaeton to Louth. We called at Dr. S. to arrange about Denison's coming home, also at Mrs. J. B. Sharpley's, Eastgate, to take a basket containing milk, potted beef, semilina [semolina] mould, etc. for Denison, also a pound of grapes were ordered at Forman's to be sent. Mrs. Riggall came on Sat. to see Denison and sent him some fish, grapes, and went up to see him.

Yesterday Lizzie accompanied Mrs. J. B. upstairs and from her description my heart seemed to yearn over the dear boy. Lizzie said his face looked long and thin, his arms like sticks. She formed an idea that he would require great care to nurse up his strength. Her decided opinion is that considerable time and patience will be required to raise him.

BINBROOK, SATURDAY EVE. 6.30. DEC. 5TH, 1874

Mr. Esberger kindly lent me a close carriage for the purpose of conveying my son Denison home from Louth. I drove Pink over with it this afternoon and called at the Dr.'s, but he would not allow him to come before Monday. I called at Mrs. Sharpley's, Eastgate, and as I climbed their steps Denison was tapping his bedroom window to catch my eye. He looked very pleased to see me. He would like to have returned with me. Praise God! How nicely he appears to be recovering. How kind Mrs. J. B. is to the boy. She and the maids have attended to him, he has required no extra nurse. His parents and friends have provided him with everything he has required. Today every precaution has been taken to prevent infection. The close carriage was lined with thick new sheeting, after being aired with an oil lamp lighted and placed inside, also hot tins and warming pan filled with burning coals.

We are able to fallow again today for two days. Previous Thursday and Friday we had 3 carts on leading gravel from our own pit to boon our road up the shepherd's lodge. We are fallowing the 10 acres which was steam cultivated in 37 acre. Old James Wright left 20/- towards his coals, 2 tons at 25/-, making a total of 50/-. Rook, whom we paid off a week last Wednesday eve., sent up 20/- by Drew. Branwick left 10/- towards coals.

Mr. Wood forwarded plans of my house for our inspection. William, who has been staying a few days with us, took them for

Mama to examine at Dexthorpe. The new front scheme appears the most acceptable.

The old house is destined to undergo a complete transformation. Every part of the house is to be changed except the front kitchen, and it alone remains unaltered. The foreman is now entering the room for the purpose of Martimas settlement.

	£
Machine men for meals	5 - 6 - 6
Tripp's bill for beer[52]	5 - 11 - 0
	0 - 10 - 0
	1 - 10 - 0
	12 - 17 - 6
Harvest present	5 - 0 - 0
	17 - 17 - 6
6 tons of coals to deduct	6 - 0 - 0
	11 - 17 - 6
Fortnight's money minus 4/-	2 - 10 - 0
	14 - 7 - 6

SUNDAY MORNING, DECEMBER 6TH, 1874

Last week we held a day school committee meeting and decided to erect a new staircase from the lower into the upper schoolroom. We thought it would enable us to dispense with the enlargement of low room.

May the blessing of Heaven rest upon us. Grant, oh, most merciful Father, that this school may be conducted in accordance with thy Will and Word. May the mistress have heavenly as well as earthly wisdom.[53] May she have health of body and soundness, clearness and vigour of mind. May she have tact given her to manage and govern.

TUESDAY MORN. 9 O'CLOCK, DEC. 15TH, 1874

Last Tuesday I started by the first train to London. I had to wait at Louth in consequence of the engine breaking down. I arrived in London about 12.30 and found Frank in the Agricultural Hall, Islington, standing by the Lincoln sheep.[54] The Hall is worthy of the exhibition and the exhibition of the Hall. I think largest and heaviest beast was 26cwt. The variety and excellence of the breeds of cattle and sheep was truly astonishing.

When we had completed our survey of this truly magnificant scene we accompanied Mr. Wilkinson, our host, to his residence, 72 East India road. We had a late tea and very cheerful evening's chat. We retired to bed about 11 o'clock. Frank and I slept together in one bed. However, I did not sleep long. It was only like a short doze. I woke in a very fluttered state, my pulse quick, and through many long hours I lay in this restless, sleepless condition. In the morning when Frank arose, I asked him to buy a bandage. I appeared at the breakfast table but could eat nothing, and retired back to my room. I became more agitated and decided to go home. However, I walked with Mr. Wilkinson and Frank to meet Mr. Gray to see the East India Docks and then bid adieu to Frank, Mr. Gray and Mr. Pears and returned with Mr. W. to prepare for my departure. Instead of eating I swallowed a dose of powdered rhubarb and sweet nitre. Mr. Fieldsend of Kirmond[55] and his son Charles entered the same carriage and we had several hours ride together. Mr. Wilkinson accompanied me to King's Cross Station. I felt much relieved after taking the rhubarb.

But I must now return to the recording of Monday's events, 7th December. I took Pink and Mr. Esberger's close carriage to my son Denison, who for three weeks and two days had been confined in Mrs. J. B. Sharpley's (Eastgate, Louth) bedroom by scarlet fever or scarlatina. Monday was the first day that Dr. Sharpley would permit Denison to be removed. I would return God thanks that he still continues to progress as rapidly as we could expect. We have had to take a great many precautions. Several processes of disinfection. Woollen clothes to be exposed to a temperature of 212. They must be placed in an hoven [oven] heated to boiling point.

Tuesday Evening, 8 o'clock
James Drew has succeeded in breaking young LeBonn to plough. Though only three next Spring, he is a pretty good match for old Lofty. He is quiet and good tempered.

Yesterday I attended our circuit quarterly meeting.

On Saturday last I paid Robinson for the four steers bought a few weeks ago, £14 each and 50/- for luck, also ten pigs at 22/6 each.

The weather is winterly, the little snow partially lingers on the ground and for two or three weeks we have frosts more or less sharp almost every night.

Denison said he is stronger than before he had the fever. He seems in good spirits and eats well. He takes six meals a day.

WEDNESDAY MORN. 9 O'CLOCK, DEC. 16TH, 1874

What a great number of deaths at Binbrook and neighbourhood. Poor Barton dropped down dead yesterday while going to his Swinop field in the midst of his business.

We finish fallowing today. Yesterday I ordered Drew to commence bitting three of our young Irish horses and break them into ploughing. They will not be so easily subdued as Le Bonn. The fields are pretty nearly white over this morning. Yesterday we sent two hoggets in the spring cart to Louth to W. Dawson.

The groom brought home from Louth Station a woodcock and pheasant, a present sent by Mrs. F. Riggall to her convalescent grandson, Denison. Today I must see the Dr. to know whether Mabel and Frank may return home, also whether the paper must be torn off Denison's bedroom walls in order to disinfect it effectually.

To restore my nerves to quietude and equilibrium I have

restricted my use of tea and coffee. I think coffee renders me more susceptible to cold. I have suffered much from chilliness and from nervous excitability - occasionally through the whole night season; but with that exception I enjoy remarkably good health. I am wiry and endure almost any amount of exertion without weariness or exhaustion. I feel elastic in step, vigourous in mind. As a rule I sleep refreshingly although the baby Norman has often disturbed us through the night. Perhaps my spirits have not been so buoyant as aforetimes.

However, this morning I feel happy in the love of Jesus. His imperial robes smell of myrhh and alloes and cassia out of the ivory palaces. I still read the Christian Age, Raleigh's 'Quiet Resting Places', Steward's 'Mediatorial Government'.

Last week we carted more gravel to the Lodge road from old 9 acre pit.

I am resolved by the grace of God to pray more earnestly and frequently to my King of Zion. He still wears the royal robes of Heaven and earth.

Charles Shadlock is trimming hedges. Branick assists Bocock to load straw for the cattle. We still cut for our horses with the horse machine. The young horses have cut wheat and barley straw twice per day. The other day I bid Cunningham £35 for a two year old Irish horse. He offered him for £40.

I have ordered a new ministerial publication entitled the 'Expositor', edited by the Rev. Samuel Cox. It is announced to come out on the 21st instant.

Lizzie has just entered the room. My heart is often pained to hear of her many sufferings. Life is often a drag. She is aching this morning with weariness. The servants are tiresome.[56] They waste their time and the work is not properly done. They never think of relieving Lizzie of her burden of nursing. We have had a nursemaid and before her a nurse or footboy, and nothing but disturbance and irritation to the mistress. It is distressing work to govern a household. They want to live in luxury and idleness into the bargain. They want good living and liberal pay for small and scanty service. The old-fashioned system of household economy and method of performing household work is fast becoming obsolete. In regard to time it was formerly the rule 'early morn and early eve', but now late at morn and late at night. The old proverb, 'quick at meat, quick at work, slow at meat, etc.' The time taken over meals and over household work in this dwelling fulfils the proverb in the last clause. Instead of having the annoyance of one wash-day a fortnight or three weeks, we have often three or four days a week. The house is seldom clear of washing or drying or ironing. The different kinds of work are mixed up in never-ending confusion and become a careless kind of drudgery, a gapish, giggling, drawling, reluctant exertion.

Wednesday eve. 8.30
I called upon the Dr. again today. He was very polite and said that I had paid the maid Eliza quite handsomely enough. He was

not aware that I had made her a present. I first gave her a two shilling piece and afterwards, when I brought Denison home I made her a present of 10/- at the carriage door. If any unconcerned person could have peeped into the carriage and seen the precautions taken to prevent the boy from catching cold! The carriage had been well aired for two or three days. Our house colza lamp was burning in it for several hours as well as hot water tins placed on the seats to intensify the heat, and when we entered there were hot tins and hot bricks besides blankets and pillows, almost more than could be utilised. To prevent the carriage from becoming infected the interior was completely covered with sheets.

The Dr. said if we chose to whitewash the paper of Denison's bedroom that would answer the same purpose as tearing off the paper, and he thought that Mabel and Frank might safely return home in a fortnight from today, but he does not advise Denison to go out of doors while the weather continues so winterly.

I called at Mrs. J. B. Sharpley's, Eastgate. She was indeed polite and friendly. Her daughter Jennie said Eliza was pleased with the letter Denison wrote to her. I suppose three of Fred's children have taken the fever. I heard today that Mrs. Williams of Ashby is dying. Death seems to be making serious inroads upon the farmers in this neighbourhood.

My dear Lizzie has just brought her supper. It consists of what a person would expect a mother to take, namely oatmeal gruel and bread. I can endorse what Mrs. J. B. said, that my wife is one of the best mothers. A more self-sacrificing mother cannot be found. If any particular kind of food or luxury prove injurious to the baby she exercises perfect control in her dietary regimen. Many mothers take what appitite [appetite] and desire dictate, but Lizzie can deny herself anything she considers likely to cause pain or uneasiness to the child hanging on her breast. Self-control or self-government is a priceless gem in the character of a mother. It communicates blessings to the next generation. How much of constitution and health may be given to a child by the self-sacrifice of a suckling mother.

THURSDAY EVE. 8.30, DEC. 17TH, 1874

I have spent a quiet and happy day at home with Denison, Mother and our good little babe, Norman. I have assisted in the nursing. A long period intervenes between the invoice from Hull and the arrival of the coals. We have been out of house coals now some days and I and groom have cut a good quantity of wood up to burn. It is difficult to keep up a fire with wood exclusively.

Mr. Rose came and tuned our pianoforte yesterday.[57] I paid him for the year 20/-. The severity of winter has continued and snow has freely fallen at intervals.

The teams are leading manure from crewyard to new seeds in twenty acres.

Lizzie and I have conversed about the new expenditures likely to be incurred by the enlargement of our dwelling. We shall require new carpets for the dining and drawing rooms. The carpets now in use below stairs must be laid in bedrooms. We shall require new dining room chairs. I have spent three sovereigns in [an] Italian marble vase and fountain, also an old painting. I have to give £3 for it but it is to be cleaned and the frame regilded. We must ornament the mantlepieces by degrees as we can afford. The chief ornament of a house is a good library. My books only require rearranging and properly shelving and adjusting to make a room look respectable. If it please God to prosper me in my business, I shall be delighted to obtain more space and convenience for the new editions I may wish to make to my book stores. There is nothing more signally lacking in the house at present than this. In consequence my books are tumbled in confusion in every room and case. I have to send a goodly number of vols. to my brother-in-law, Frank, at Hackthorne.

FRIDAY EVE. 6 O'CLOCK, BINBROOK, DEC. 18TH, 1874

My dearest Annie,[58]

I wonder sometimes whether human ingenuity will ever be exhausted while the world stands. On Wednesday last I brought home a lamp on trial. The price is 1/6. It burns with 6 flames or jets formed into a circle. Lizzie says it is one of my weaknesses to be pleased with new things. Novelties are generally attractive to me when of an inventive character and add to the stock of human improvement.

Today groom and I have chopped and sawn a large heap of wood for the fires. While I was chopping, a Binbrook salver came to ask me whether I would consent to have my sheep salved. He said they were putting 3lb. to the score of ewes and 2 3/4 lb. to hoggets. They salved 35 per day each. They have 3/6 per day and their meat, or 4/- and find themselves. I agreed to pay 4/- per day. I walked into the turnip field to see Holmes, my shepherd. He said the sheep were faggy but not lousy. According to his statement we number

138 she hoggets,
30 feeding drape ewes,
75 he hoggets.

making a total of 243 that we cut for.

Tupping ewes 294
Total 537

It seems a small flock for a hundred acres of turnips. We have already eaten 18 acres in about 6 weeks. The ewes have generally laid on the grass at night. Yesterday the hoggets came into the 16 acre in front of our house. Denison and Mama and I have been playing at a scriptural game. One thinks of a scripture name and the other asks questions about the character etc. and trys [tries] to guess.

Though another winter day, it has been sunny and I think one of the most cheerful days of my life. I have felt physically stronger and more buoyant in spirit. When in good healthy condition, the body is a fine instrument to the mind. I should like to live to accomplish something for Christ.

Today we have carried more manure out of crewyard and spread it on new seeds in far 20 acres.

I am now writing by the light of new lamp. It has commenced flickering. I do not know whether this arises from exhaustion of Benzoline within.

This is the second day of peculiar home life. Lizzie has made special use of me in placing Norman in my arms. He will be nine months old the first of Jan. next.

This morning I scraped up the few coals left and some engine coals amongst the dross. This visit to the coalhouse caused an undercurrent of vexation. However, I bore it silently and patiently. I found the place very dirty, untidy and, of course, unhealthy. However, without any disturbance Betsy took the hint and set to work in earnest in cleaning and removing the impurities.

SATURDAY, DEC. 19TH, 1874

Mr. Cornish, Day school Inspector, came over the other day and made some suggestions respecting little alteration. Last Monday I attended our quarterly meeting. The question of house-taking and furnishing was discussed. It is decided that we take a second married preacher in 1875. I never could see the practicability of this scheme. We can never keep clear of debt under the present system and when seventy pounds per annum is added to our present expenditure, how can we expect to meet all demands, and when we consider further how we are crippled with debts upon our chapels. Binbrook and Normanby are in the most healthy state. The debts on these two chapels are considerably reduced. We have very little more [of] the mortgage, namely £600. I am treasurer for this as well as every fund connected with the society except the day school and Foreign Missions. I am treasurer for the fund raised for the harmonium.[59] There is a debt due to me of £7/0/0. I am treasurer for the Sunday School.

Saturday morn. 11 o'clock, Dec. 19th, 1874
Denison continues to improve. This morning he is dusting and tydying [tidying] my drawer under bookshelves. There is a turn out of papers, periodicals and manuscript books.

Sat. night 8.45, Dec. 19th, 1874, Binbrook
This is the day for paying wages.

I have paid James Drew 33/- for his fortnight, and he returned me 21/- for a sack of wheat bought of me. I paid Branwick 33/- and he returned me 10/- towards coals; this is the second 10/-.

Charles Shadlock returned 17/- out of 33/-, being the remaining sum left upon his coals, namely 2 tons at 25/-.

James Wright returned 10/- towards his coals, being the last sum due.

I am now paying in hard cash £12/15/0 every fortnight. I have been to the village to see Mr. Dixon about a machine coming to thrash on Monday next to commence on Tuesday.

MONDAY EVE. 5.45, DEC. 21ST, 1874. BINBROOK

Today I rode Charlie to Louth and attended the Board. This morning I took the weight of C. Smith's pig. It weighed 33st. 13lb. His first killed, Nov. 29th. Wages £27/12/0.

We sent 5 horses to Binbrook for a part of Mr. Dixon's machine, also a waggon to Ludbro' Station for 2½ tons of steam coals.

We have still gentle falls of snow and the temperature at freezing point, but the roads continue open. Field work has been at a stand now for some days.

I generally contrive to read Talmage's sermons as they appear in the 'Christian Age'.

Old Father Christmas seems to be approaching us arrayed in his white vestments.

I have had some precious thoughts about Christ the last few days.

We have removed the young Irish horses into the grass fields from the 30 acre old seeds where they have mainly grazed since coming on the farm.

Today Betsy Stevenson, cook, has drawn one sovereign towards her wages, Christmas week.

Denison is still a prisoner and amuses himself by turning out several drawers. One drawer contains game cards and other things reminding him of his former amusements before his public school days. In righting out a drawer there is often the pleasure of finding things long lost and sometimes things containing bright memories.

TUESDAY EVE. 5.20, DEC. 22ND, 1874

Today we have been leading gravel from old 9 acre pit to stackyard, 3 carts, 9 horses, 5 loads each, total 15 loads per day. Last night was the most severe frost of the season. The turnips were very hard to cut. I took hold of the handle and assisted the shepherd, as all his strength was taxed to turn the machine. The shepherd and two boys have only about 200 sheep to cut for and if they worked well they might have ample time to spare. Branwick has assisted James Wright to drag for the ewes. James Drew and C. Shadlock filled gravel and C. Smith, foreman, spread and broke. One of our cows cast her calf last night.

Standaloft has been up today and whitewashed the ceiling of our front bedroom where Denison has slept since his return home from Mrs. Sharpley's of the fever. The disinfecting process has progressed very extensively today. The oven has done good service in this matter. Every woollen article must be exposed to high oven temperature. Fevers are not only painful and dangerous but, more than many diseases, very expensive. We are scarcely able to calculate at present the damage done to the woollen clothes, as well as considerable cost of labour, wear and tear, Dr.'s bill, etc. One feather bed and new sheets are very much burnt as well as a woollen mat completely destroyed. I have helped Betsy to wring out half a dozen blankets. The destruction we have to witness from week to week accidentally amongst crockery in breakage, amongst garments and other articles from fire and scortching, is very greivous and trying. My Lizzie is more scrupulous about airing and drying of clothes than many housewives. She will spread undergarments over the fender, and unless there is a constant watch sparks or pieces of live coal are apt to fall out. Many and various are the articles of dress and linen that have been injured.

Last evening I walked to the village to hear Mr. Cope preach. The service was held in the schoolroom. I enjoyed it more than I usually do in the body of the chapel. He preached from, 'Watchman, what of the night, etc'. I felt his sermon less irksome but for the most part interesting, and we had much Divine influence in the prayer meeting.

I had one of the most pleasant walks there and back that ever I have experienced in Christmas week. The moon shone almost vertically down upon the snowy fields which reflected a whiteness most striking and impressive. I think I never felt so much poetry in a winter night. The snow was full of sparkling crystals. I scarcely ever felt such brilliancy. The moon and the snow seemed to banish all darkness and traces of night. I could see to read small type most distinctly. Mr. Cope placed in my hand a leaflet containing an advertisement of the Rev. R. Chew's life of James Everitt [Everett].[60]

WEDNESDAY MORNING, 9 O'CLOCK, DEC. 23RD, 1874, BINBROOK

I received a letter yesterday from Mr. Wood, Builder, Alford, stating that he had seen Mr. Vesey, who has shown Sir Edmond Beckett the plans of my house, and with the exception of one or two minor alterations approves. Mr. Wood also states that he will come over on Monday next and consult with us respecting any further alterations as there is to be no change when the contract is made.

We have commenced thrashing this morning. It is thick and cloudy. The shepherd killed a hogget yesterday and this morning the groom is about to take another to the butcher.

I scarcely remember gazing upon two nights like the last for silvery brilliance. I could walk and read almost as clearly as by day and, oh, the beauty and grandeur of winter has rarely been so displayed. My spirit seemed whelmed [overwhelmed] by the glory of the scene. I never felt the weakness of all artistic representations more impressively. I think it will never glide from memory. Christmas week has brought forth singular natural evolutions and will constitute an era in the developments of my tastes. I felt the goodness of God in transforming winter scenes into the highest of luxuries. My forbodings had been of a gloomy character. I generally feel extreme cold bitterly. Many times my faculties and energies have been frozen with the water. My imagination as a rule has crusted with the earth. Like the grass and wheat plant my imaginative faculties have slept under the snow. I must offer unto God a sacrifice of thanksgiving for the late transformation and glorifying of my winter life. Praise the Lord!

THURSDAY MORN. 9.30, DEC. 24TH, 1874. BINBROOK

Snow has been falling more or less through the night with a drifting wind. Yesterday I purchased a meat saw of Mr. Morton for 5/- which I paid down in cash.

I have just written a letter to Rev. J. Jordan to invite him to preach our Missionary sermons the third Sunday in Jan.

Thursday eve. 7 o'clock
As snow came fast through the day the post arrived late and I have ridden Charlie to Binbrook for our letters. In one envelope were enclosed Mr. Page's bill for Denison's board and school fees. The total is £17/17/6; also a report of conduct, diligence and progress. It appears that he has generally taken the highest marks in his form. In addition to the report, Mr. Page has written a letter of strong commendation and stated that this report would have been much better had he not been laid aside by the fever, and that he most certainly would have taken the prize of his form.

FRIDAY AFTERNOON, 3.45, DEC. 25TH, 1874
BINBROOK, CHRISTMAS DAY

This morning I walked to the village for the purpose of attending the prayer meeting. There were only seven present. Almost everything is covered with snow. I walked over two snow hills which were nearly on a level with the style [stile]. When I reached the brow of the hill my ears were regaled by the sound of a band of music. Though the air was thick the clouds formed a good sounding board to carry and diffuse the Binbrook harmonies far and wide along the surrounding hills. The air was keen and frosty enough to stiffen my beard with rhyme [rime]. I enjoyed the walk and prayer meeting and had the additional pleasure of reading Talmage's sermon on Amos's basket of summer fruit.

We are enjoying a singularly quiet Christmas Day. Lizzie, I, and Denison, and Norman, the baby boy, who has beheld the first Christmas day of his immortal existence. I suppose, in the absence of information, our dear little Frank and Mabel are at Hackthorne,[61] as most likely Dexthorpe blinds are down and the house deserted while the family gathering has taken place and the Christmas lights kindled at Hackthorne. It is a mysterious Providence.

SATURDAY EVE. 5.45, DEC. 26TH, 1874. BINBROOK

It appears in reading the 'English Independent' that the disestablishment question is taking a deeper hold of the public mind. It is an outspoken paper upon public men and events. It never shrinks from exposing any evils or abuses which may exist whether in church or state.

We have had another quiet day at home. We have finished thrashing the stack of oats and the machine is placed between two wheat stacks ready for Monday morning. More labour is required to obtain the sheep sufficient turnips in consequence of being hid in the snow.

Yesterday the groom drove Pink in the dogcart to Ludbro' Station for the Christmas box Mrs. Riggall sent from Dexthorpe. It was composed of turkey, a plum loaf, christmas cake, a seed cake and some sausages. It is decidedly the finest turkey we have had. Lizzie has more work today than she has strength to perform. Hannah, the housemaid, has gone home for her holidays so that it causes a good deal of extra work. I assist a little to nurse baby boy.

We had a sharp frost last night. The window panes were beautifully enamelled. How pulseless the earth seems under the snow.

The Shah's diary of his European tour is published and translated into English. It is a very interesting account of what he saw. My curiosity is somewhat excited by the title of the Congregational Lecture for 1874 by Dr. Reynold's. Subject; 'John the Babtist'.

The 'Expositor' is also announced as ready. Its contents are very attractive and by eminent authors.

Hodson, Fridlington and I each gave an address last evening in Binbrook chapel. Tomorrow night I am planned for North Willingham.

We have had no glimpse of Hackthorne since the family arrival.

Lizzie has been in the room with a piece of cake as a specimen of her handywork. It is a rare event for her to attempt to make bread. However, it is a success. Denison has tasted and he says it is nice. As a rule we have inferior home-made bread. Servants are above being taught and they don't like the labour necessary for the proper working of it. The best comforts of life and even the necessities cannot be had without industry. It is necessary to the mentenance of family health and comfortable existence. It sometimes causes us considerable anxiety when we think of the ignorance of domestic servants. They lack thought, energy, industry. They waste their time and slip over their work. They are extravagant in everything they use. In food and dress, in crockery and other utensils. They are dreadfully independent; it runs out into insult and offensive carriage. Their minds are much absorbed by frivolities of dress and making themselves outwardly attractive and drawing men after them. In going to service they ought to make a house clean, orderly and homely.

MONDAY EVE. 6.30, DEC. 28TH, 1874. BINBROOK

Mr. Wood has been over again today to consider the modifications of plan for improving our house. Sir Edmond has only suggested two alterations, viz. an additional window at the south of the new front room, both upper and lower, and the fixing of fireplaces against an interior wall instead of the outer. It is just what Lizzie and I were intending to ask for.

We have a stack of wheat today.

Our window panes were frosted again this morning and though we have had a fine day the snow has not perceptably wasted. I suppose it is fourteen years since winter has come so severely upon us. I reccollect being at Dexthorpe on my courtship expedition, and on Christmas day Miss Elizabeth Mawer Riggall, my lady love, and myself, went to Aby Grange to hear my brother-in-law, Mr. J. B. Atkinson, preach. It was a sharp snowstorm much like the present. We remember, too, a snowstorm on Christmas day four years ago but it was briefer in duration. I remember walking to Dalby church on Christmas day.

TUESDAY EVE. 7 O'CLOCK, DEC. 29TH, 1874. BINBROOK

Today we have thrashed another stack of wheat, which has yielded 50 qrs. Yesterday also James Drew gave an account of 50 qrs. The oatstack yielded 95 qrs.

I bought a horse of Cunningham this morning for thirty seven pounds ten shillings, aged two years.

Denison is becoming so buoyant and high spirited that it is difficult to hold him within legitimate bounds. He has not sufficient liberty to roam out into the fields or slide or skate on the ponds so as to give full swing to his physical powers. I believe he enjoys a complete restoration to health. His eyes seem more lustrous and his countenance brighter than before his affliction. Through the mercy of God no after disease appears probable. I feel thankful, too, that my own health is much improved during the last few days. The keen air (and this is one of the keenest days of the season) braces up my system. I feel more elastic in my limbs and more vigorous in mind and cheerful in spirits. For some time past I had suffered much from nervous irritation.

The other day I sat at Mr. Plumptree's of Louth for my portrait. He took a vinette and full size likeness. He sent me one of each. I compared them with each other and chose to order one dozen of the vinettes, which have arrived. But what I wish to observe is - I have compared my photo of today with that executed more than twenty years ago and the great change come over my personal appearence is very striking. One of the most striking features in my former youthful appearence is the fine thick head of dark hair depicted. It is not without some feeling of regret that one witnesses such wasting of one of the chief ornaments. A good head of hair is an element in personal [appearance] which cannot be replaced. I remember, too, that my face has become more deeply wrinkled and even furrowed. The eye has lost some of its lustre and my face more developed. I notice by close observation that my gait is more slovenly. I don't straiten [straighten] my back and shoulders as I once did. In fact the entire contour of my face and frame amounts to a kind of contrast as exhibited in the first and last. Several specks have appeared on the curtains of the tabernacle pointing to a dissolution that I need to think more earnestly about a building of God, a house not made with hands, eternal in the Heavens.

My life is verily slipping away without the work being accomplished I had aspired and purposed to perform. I have to ask myself again, am I willing to lay aside every weight, everything that unduly weakens my nerve, that oppresses my spirit, that damps my zeal, that in any degree shades or obscures the Divine light in my soul. Is there any article of diet or any other indulgence of desire or appetite that I am unwilling to renounce which has the least tendency to becloud my intellect or Christian experience or impair my health and so hasten the dissolution of this tabernacle or bring on premature old age?

However, I am trying one or two experiments. To breakfast I drink more than half milk and the rest tea, and the last few mornings a little fat bacon or potted beef and bread of Lizzie's making and cooking, and a batch of delicious bread it is. It is full of good elbow shortening. It requires good labour as well as good yeast and flour to constitute good bread. To dinner I drink tank water filtered, as well as eat every variety of meat. To tea I eat nothing, but take a cup of tea with no addition either sugar or cream. To supper a pint mug of new milk with bread soaked in it.

SATURDAY MORN. 9.30, JAN. 2ND, 1875. BINBROOK

The old year has gone in intense severity.

On Wednesday last I sold Mr. Roberts about 150 qrs. wheat at 42/6 or 43/-.

I brought home with me the first number of 'Expositor'. On Thursday I drove Pink to Ludbro' Station and found Mrs. Riggall and her grandson Frank Riggall Stovin, my second son, who had been spending Christmas at Hackthorne. I think it was the most bitter drive back ever experienced. The snow on the ground, the rhyme [rime] on the trees and hedges and in the air, well nigh perished us. I drove Grandmama back to the station yesterday morning but it was not so severe.

We have had fine thrashing days and finished last night. The wheat is in capital order, dry and bold. The quality is exceptionally good for Binbrook.

There has been a change in the weather through the night. It was raining for a length of time and froze again towards morning. I never witnessed such a row of icicles across my window.

Last night I paid the thrashing [threshing] women 30/-, men £3/12/6.[62]

The report has come in that the roads have drifted up with snow through the night. Up to this time we thought it remarkable that there were no winds to drive the snow into the roads.

Denison is talking about going out after seven weeks confinement in the house. I am going to see if the morning is fine enough for him to venture.

Sat. eve. 6.40
Denison and I have mounted our steeds, Pink and Charlie, and taken a ride towards Ludbro' to inspect the roads. We found them only just passable. Lizzie and her son Frank have called at Mr. Foster's of Ludbro' to see Miss Riggall about Mabel coming home, as she had expressed fears lest she might carry some infection back to school from Denison. It will be a great disappointment to Mabel and to us if [she is] not allowed to come home, though we might forego that if there were any further risk or danger.

Yesterday I saw Mr. Foster about bricks. They are the proper colour and 32/- per thousand.

Last night in reading the 'English Independent' I met with a masterly paper upon the recent theory respecting the non-eternity of future punishment. Rev. Ingram's exposition shows it to be entirely untenable. There is nothing in Scripture or consciousness to uphold it.

MONDAY EVE. 5.50, JAN. 4TH, 1874. BINBROOK

After extreme frosts and rhymes [rimes] the storm generally breaks up. We experience a continuous thaw since Sat. morning. The waggon and four horses bring 2 tons of cake today from Louth. The other labourers clean up [the] stackyard and after today no extra men upon [the] turnip lands.

Having very few pauper cases, I remain at home from Board. Farm, take Frank out on donkey, and read 'Expositor'. Yesterday I entered two new names into my class book. One is Stamp from Fotherby, who has come to Binbrook to manage for Mrs. Barton, whose husband died suddenly in December last while leading his horse and cart up Swinope Hill.

On Wed. last I sent an advertisement for a shepherd, and received an application today from Charles Fletcher of Little Carlton.

The roads were so completely blocked up that Mr. Gledhill could not ride on horseback to Thorganby yesterday afternoon.

TUESDAY MORN. 9 O'CLOCK A.M., JAN. 5TH, 1875

God in his goodness has spared me to see the beginning of 1875. The year 1874 has proved one of great anxiety to farmers. The first strike among farm labourers ever known took place last year. It lasted 9 weeks. It was a very exciting struggle, though the farmers gained the victory and the labourers had to resume work at the old rate of wages, viz. 3/- per day. I trust this year will be one of blessing and peace. Every year brings its troubles as well as blessings.

The snow has disappeared from the fields save where it was drifted into heaps.

The past year has wrought considerable changes in my own habits and character. First one stimulant and then another has been discarded. My nerves are now quiet and my health excellent. Milk, water and tea are my principal beverages. Mr. Gledhill is with us and is talking with Denison about the Lord having taken such care of him during his affliction and raised him while many have died of fever. Glory be to God for what He has done for me and mine.

A register for last half year of subjects of study and conduct of my little daughter, Mabel, now lays before me. The subjects of study pursued by her during the last half year are as follows: Reading, Writing, Spelling, English Grammar, Arithmetic Tables, Geography, Modern History, Poetry. Without seeing other registers from the same school, it is impossible to say how the register compares with the rest, but on the face of it here is an appearence of encouragement.

Tuesday eve. 7 o'clock
The drifted snow continues to waste. One fine sunny day in Jan! What a relief from the severity of the long blast. I enjoyed my breakfast, consisting of a slice of bacon and potted beef, a breakfast cup of new milk with a slight dilution of tea.

After breakfast and family prayer, I walked to the village, a part of journey over the drifted snow, during the morning. I felt strong and well. I found five ploughs in the 16 acre old seeds. It is our first day since the breaking up of the frost.

When I arrived at home the dinner was quite ready, though I did not feel ready for it and only tasted of the good roasted mutton and roasted potatoes. What caused me to cease eating was a very strange sensation of tickling and soreness in my throat, with a small amount of nervous excitement; also suffered from sensations of coldness. My appetite returned a little by [the time] tea was on the table and I partook of an egg, toast and butter, with two cups of tea. Since tea, Denison made me and Frank a plaster for throat and chest consisting of about three teaspoonsful of mustard and the same quantity of linseed. It smarts considerably at present, having strongly drawn and bitten already for about an hour. I have kept the house since dinner and diverted my mind by nursing perambulations alternately in dining room and kitchen. I have been very successful in keeping the children quiet, contented and happy. Frank and Norman have been under my care while Lizzie walked across to see Mrs. Smith. It appears some of Bocock's children were very ill last night. Oh, what a great many diseases are ravedging [ravaging] the village and neighbourhood. Praise God I feel peace of mind often when afflictions threaten and agitate the physical frame. What a multitude of calamities by disease, accident, sudden death, private and public, by land and by sea. What a consoling thought that we are in the hands of a kind and gracious Providence and he can keep us still.

WEDNESDAY MORN. 10.15, JAN. 6TH, 1875

Rent day has come once more. Mr. Vesey has arranged for Sir Edmond's tenants to meet today at Louth at the King's Head Hotel.

I have almost passed a sleepless night through nervous excitement and a quick pulse. I had scarcely any pain, only an interior soreness at my chest. I am thankful for some relief from expectoration while brushing my teeth and rinsing my mouth and throat in cold water. I was tempted to keep my bed today, but my dear Lizzie thought it better for us to rise if possible. Sometimes I think these ever-recurring sleepless nights are owing to my remaining too long in bed, but we are often late in retiring. The snow continues to waste on another damp, mild morning. My Christmas box bills begin to pour in from the post. I have received on Monday last from Geo. Smith seat rents for our chapel: £11/6/5 October quarter.

Wednesday eve. 6.30
Rode Charlie to Louth. Met with J. Iles who bid me £30 for him, or offered to chop. I handed over my rent cheque to Mr. Vesey. I very much enjoyed some oranges in the Market Hall, and the rent dinner came very acceptably. I did not dine like an invalid. My pulse is now about eighty. The conversation at our rent dinner as a rule is not very interesting to me. Shooting, hunting, horses, game, landlords and landed estates, and racing and other incidental topics, constitute the staple subject matter of talk. Of course I feel reserved and can only express assent to certain statements, but very few appeals are made to me personally. I suppose politics are designedly excluded and all other subjects of a controvertial character.

I have enjoyed remarkable strength today considering the night of sleepless purturbation I passed. A measure of relief appears to have come to my chest and throat. Not feeling up to the mark at Louth, I hastened home to tea and found my dear family seated round the table minus our dear daughter, Mabel, who is still excluded from us on account of Denison's affliction. However, I was received with smiling welcomes by the other part of the group and everything is being readily and heartily done to effect my most speedy restoration to health, which lately has caused me more anxiety. I concluded that by a change of diet and beverage I should be able to prevent these repeated attacks. It turns out a mistake and I have not succeeded discovering the panacea. My feelings yesterday at the dinner were not only quite sudden but took me by surprise as I judged the cause had been removed.

Mr. Vesey told me today I might easily venture to lead at least 20,000 bricks.

There were five ploughs again today in 16 acre old seeds. It seems very fortunate that the 16 acre in front of house is now bare so that the sheep can find all the shells formerly hid in the snow before leaving. As far as I am able to judge the turnips have been economised by the snow. The sheep had to live on hard meat.

Mr. Vesey said that his sheep would remain a week longer in the field than they otherwise would have done.

William Norman was 9 months old on the first of Jan. last.

THURSDAY MORN. 10.10, JAN. 7TH, 1875

After a good night's sleep I rose with a very sore throat. It is the most severe attack of throat and chest I have experienced. When I attempt to expectorate the fastness and soreness is something dreadful. I woke in the night nearly melted with persperation by the bread poultice and sponge, which I thought must have performed its office upon me, and removed it and fell into a sound sleep.

My pulse is eighty four.

Five ploughs again this morning.

We are witnessing a series of fine, mild days. The snow has disappeared except the drifts which are rapidly diminishing.

Frank's cold is better and he has eaten a good breakfast of toasted bacon and bread.

Thursday eve. 6.20
This morning I walked to the men ploughing, but felt the air too keen for my throat. I had some conversation with C. Smith about the work. I told him that I had called at Ashley's yesterday about the drill, and he said they had some new ones to make and if ours were sent at once it should be done. He said he could widen it for turnips. At present the rows are too near to admit of sufficient space for the maturing [of] a large bulb. The two-horse scarifier requires a new frame and it can be made to work after the drill. At present it will only fit the water drill rows and last season we were obliged to lay it by in consequence. It is a great advantage to be able to scarify before singling, also again as soon as possible after, and we can only do that with this machine. When the fresh moulds are light and the weeds small they are more easily and effecturally [effectively] destroyed. After hoeing it replaces the soil to the root of the plant removed by the singling. We agreed it would be better to send the two machines together and they could be adapted the one to the other.

I told him what Mr. Roberts said about the order and a horse cart might be sent this afternoon for railway sacks, also that we would bring back a carriage load of bricks, each waggon 1200.

LeBon continues to plough regularly.

I only ate a small quantity of apple bread pudding to dinner, no meat or potatoes. To tea a small piece of toast with a little butter and honey. Lizzie has given me some very effectual Hydropathic treatment,[63] viz. a hot flannel pad to chest, a mustard plaister about my shoulders, a tin of mustard and water for my feet, then a dry sponge to throat and chest, also compress over that. It has promoted expectoration.

FRIDAY MORN. 9.40, JAN. 8TH, 1875

The sound of the gravel rake in the garden indicates the first act and deed in preparation for building. C. Shadlock is removing the loose gravel from the carriage drive that the bricks may be laid in heaps convenient to the bricklayer. The Railway sacks came yesterday afternoon and two loads or two waggons to be filled when they return from plough.

The early morning commenced damp, which to some extent has risen off the earth; still the air is thick and comparatively mild. I coughed more at breakfast time but the complaint has moved from throat into my head which seems more like an ordinary cold, so much so that I think I may venture to run to the village and pay some bills.

Friday eve. 7.45
I paid Mr. Osborne's bill, £16/9/0. On returning home C. Shadlock met me in the yard and paid 21/- for a sack of wheat.

My cold and cough is rather troublesome tonight. I remained in the house since dinner and have undergone my usual treatment.

TUESDAY MORN. 9.30, JAN. 12TH, 1875

Yesterday I attended the Board. I am thankful my health seems much improved. I slept well last night and this morning I feel stronger though my strength has not failed me much through the affliction. Praise God for the hope of again resuming my business, preaching, reading, study, in soundness of body and mind. My cough has not quite gone and the peculiar sensations in the interior of my lungs still continue though not quite so agravated.

Yesterday with two waggons twice to Ludbro' brickyard, and a cart once, we brought 4500 bricks.

Another cloudy morn though the sky was deeply dyed when the sun rose. Whelpton paid me £20 for two fat pigs.

Tuesday afternoon. 3.30
Four waggons and one cart load of bricks, 4500, the same quantity as yesterday.

Today I commence taking codliver oil. I have been digging laurels for replanting. The two pigs sold were weighed this morning, 26st. 5lb. each.

We have had a little rain today and with it a very damp mild air. A singularly small quantity of rain has fallen since the breaking up of the storm and not a single frost. Frank appears much better of his cold. He has enjoyed a romp with his papa excessively. While Denison and Hannah were filling sausages with the machine, we were running and leaping about the kitchen. Lizzie has been fortunate in the cooking of her mincepies. The mince is of a delicious character and the pastry is magnificent and beautifully brown. We had some sausage to dinner and it was precisely to my taste. Oh praise God for such a wife. I wish she had more physical power. Her domestic aptitude is a great comfort to her family. She has doctored me through my affliction and under her skilful treatment my recovery is more rapid that I could possibly have anticipated. At present I have a prospect of becoming more robust than for months past. I am hoping to accomplish 20 more years of hearty service in the cause of Christ in the advancement of His glorious kingdom, while improving my business, making it more profitable, and my house, rendering it more healthy, so that my family may have a good start in life both physically, mentally and spiritually. If it please God I should like to raise them with sound physical constitution, with intellectual development, and spiritual life, also to be able to furnish them with means and capital that they may have full swing to all their powers, either in active business or more retired meditative life. Whether the bent of their talents leads them into a profession or a farm, into the arts or sciences and scholarship, that they may find the congenial sphere where they can best serve God and their own age. If I can give them full scope for the activity of their entire nature that there may be no faculty run to waste or remain dormant, their life will most probably be more enjoyable and happy.

THURSDAY MORN. 9.30, JAN. 14TH, 1875

Yesterday I paid a number of Louth bills:

No.	Name			
1	Ashton		6 -	0
2	Clapham		8 -	0
3	Dimbleby	1 -	0 -	0
4	Coppin		7 -	3
5	Burnett	1 -	4 -	0
6	Shepherd	3 -	3 -	6
7	Ashley	13 -	14 -	0
8	Wells and Johnson, Binbrk.	9 -	14 -	0
9	Stark. do.		8 -	0
10	Geo. Smith. do.		5 -	9
11	Elliot Roper		3 -	0

Thursday eve. 6.30, Jan. 14th, 1875
Yesterday we sold ten couples of fowls at 5/9, total £2/17/6.

I ordered Dr. Reynold's Congregational Lecture on 'John the Babtist' and 'Paraclete' by Dr. Parker.

Yesterday and today we have brought home 9000 bricks. Lizzie bought a penny Almanack. It is a marvellous pennyworth. There are pictures of amusements and pastimes and a very ingenious hieroglyphic for the eventful year of 1875.

I walked to Binbrook this morning and rode Charlie again this afternoon and paid a few bills. How thankful I feel to be able to struggle out of debt. I am afraid some heavier payments still await me. I like to see them stamped and settled very shortly after presentation.

I am under the impression that my cough and lungs are better today. My nervous system is more uniformly quiet and settled. I sleep better and enjoy my food. I feel lively and strong. My interest in business, in books, in Lizzie and the children, in the events of public life, in the Church and nation, in my own public career, is re-awakening. My happiness consists in accomplishing something for all these which will bear retrospection. I am thankful for the measure of health which we experience at present. Frank's cold appears much better. Lizzie still complains of suffering from her head and from the piles.

FRIDAY EVE. 6 O'CLOCK, JAN. 15TH, 1875

Today three ploughs have run in 30 acre old seeds and one waggon has taken 10 qrs. wheat to Ludbro' Station, back carriage 1000 more bricks, making a total of 20250 piled up ready to renovate the old dwelling.

The order has come for the whole of the wheat sold, and we commence on Monday next to quit the remainder.

The weather continues windy, showery, and mild, though the snow still lingers about the hedges.

James Drew is breaking our young Irish horses. I name them according to the following order. The black three year old rising four, Prince; the light bay one, Jerry, two years old rising three; the brown mare, three rising four, Brisk; the dark bay two year old horse rising three bought of Cunningham, Jack. I name him after old favorite Jack, now worn out, that proved one of the most serviceable for running in harness and working on the land. Young Jack has similar strength and as full of promise as the old.

SATURDAY EVE. 8 O'CLOCK, JAN. 16TH, 1875

Five ploughs today until about twelve at noon. In the afternoon the men dressed up two loads of wheat, 30 qrs. James Drew handled the young horses.

I sold Robinson of Binbrook 25 fat ewes at 50/- each, total £62/10/-. My turnips are being very rapidly consumed. The sheep have only been about a week in the 6 acre and they appear about half done. At the present rate we shall run very short of Spring feed.

I have paid the labourers tonight: Bocock, 34/-, C. Smith, foreman, 54/-, Holmes, shepherd, 20/-, James Drew, daily man, 33/-, Branwick, 33/-, C. Shadlock, 33/-. J. Drew paid 20/- towards coals, Thom. Lawton 16/3. Total £11/3/3. The Rev. J. Travis is in the room while I write this record. May Heaven bless him in his Missionary work tomorrow. Denison drove Pink to Louth with phaeton for Mr. Travis.

TUESDAY MORN. 9.30, JAN. 18TH, 1875

We have delivered from three stacks 155 qrs. of wheat to Mr. Roberts at Ludbro' Station. 6 qrs. remain at home for labourers and 6 qrs. of hinderends. It has come out of the barn as it came in from the machine. Yesterday we had a calf taken with a complaint we thought to be spinal. We sent it in a cart to the butcher's to be slaughtered.

We have delivered four loads of wheat the last two days. Our young horses cannot be found this morning.

Yesterday Mr. Paget came to shoot, and dined with us. After dinner he surveyed the plan of our contemplated house and suggested some further additions at the back. He said he would write to Mr. Vesey and Sir Edmond respecting it.

To my surprise Mr. P. gave Denison 5/- to buy a book, any book he likes.

This is a fine bright blowy Jan. morn. My own health appears to be improving almost every day. It is a matter of great thankfulness.

Last night I attended our annual church meeting. The officers and committee were re-elected. Our day school is under the consideration of the education Department for a grant.

FRIDAY MORN. 10 O'CLOCK, JAN. 22ND, 1875

The first fine bright frosty morning since the breaking up of the late snowstorm. My bedroom window beautifully frosted. I write whilst my little son, Frank, is singing and playing with his marbles. He is the only member of my family at home. His mother and brother, Norman, went to Dexthorpe yesterday.

Yesterday we had six ploughs at work, Le Bon and two young horses. They go very nicely. I drove Lizzie and baby to Ludbro' Station with Pink and waggonette.

God is very good to send me two delicious volumes to refresh me in my hours of solitude. Dr. Reynold and Dr. Parker are the two spirits sent to aid me to apprehend Divine truth. They make the Bible appear like a new book. How its power and influence intensifies upon me! Praise God for such prophets raised up in Israel.

Yesterday I lent C. Smith a horse to take his wife to Barnaby.

I am thankful we are able to plough again today notwithstanding a crusty frost.

I thought myself not quite so well yesterday. My cough was more troublesome. I feel a little improvement this morning, but still undecided whether to take my appointment at Owersby on Sunday next. These long distances late at night prove very damaging when the chest and lungs are out of order.

Making a new cribb in the old carthouse forms a very useful stable for our young horses, though they quarrel and kick one another. Brisk has a swelled knee from a kick, also Jack, this morning. We rub them with some oil given to us by Robinson of

Binbrook. It is a matter of great thankfulness that we have so little expense of horse doctoring. I paid Greswell the small sum of 7/- on Wednesday.

Friday eve. 7.45
The two Heaven sent presents are now before me and I read them alternately. Next to my wife and family I enjoy reading and meditation, and these are my most superb home pleasures. My home thank God has become a real centre of happiness.

Not having received my letters until late this afternoon, I have had no opportunity of answering Denison's note in which he informs me that he has written to Hackthorne for Mabel to go to Dexthorpe today, with an urgent request for me to go tomorrow. It is quite evident he is strongly wishful that I should. He gives a pressing invitation from Grandma in addition to his own repeated desire. The question is, what course am I to take with my dear little son and companion, Franky boy. He is a splendid divinely constituted ray of sunshine to brighten my lonely hours. He laughs and sings and chatters and enjoys life as if he were on the borders of Paradise.

I feel a strong desire for a little more rest from preaching, also to see my dear daughter, Mabel. I think it would be prudent to secure a supply if possible for Owersby but if I ride Charlie will Lizzie be too anxious about Frank were I to leave him with Betsy and Hannah, or shall I take him with me by train; if so, he must be a burden to carry from Alford to Dexthorpe.

I continue to take codliver oil twice a day. I gradually increase the dose from a small to a large teaspoonful. I think of increasing further if it aggrees with my stomach. At present I believe it is beneficial in connection with the outward means such as the buckling on afresh of an old electric belt around my loins and lower part of my body, also sponge and compress at my chest. These are good preservatives against our sudden climatic changes. I am praying that God may (if in accordance with His wise and loving purposes) bless these means or suggest others that will restore my health and constitution to their original vigour, that I may be permitted to labour more abundantly in active business thought, that with stronger brain my intellectual faculties may skillfully and wisely grasp both theoretical and practical subjects. Would my physical strength admit a greater strain? Have I overbalanced my labours in spiritual service to the unlawful detriment and injury of my business and carnal profit? Some think that my spiritual service or sanctuary labour has been carried beyond the bounds of discretion.

I gave C. Smith a couple of rabbits this afternoon, also spoke to him about loading the drill boxes for groom to take to Louth tomorrow. I have ordered Mr. Ashley to widen the frame five inches as the five turnip coulters are too strait. He will also construct the frame of the scarifier accordingly. The boxes require to be refitted to the alteration.

We have run 6 ploughs today.

Last eve. I sent poor old Frank Riggall a fowl.

The thought strikes me, if God permit us to enjoy the great gift of a new or restored, enlarged and more commodious dwelling, my Lizzie will find more scope for her tasteful devices. She is fond of a vase and understands the adornment of a home.[64] When there are no flowers in the garden she will import ivy leaves or other sprigs of evergreens to adorn the mantlepiece and table. Generally there are flowers enough to form a wreath or bouquet. I note a great change and ever gracious change towards a loftier and more refined civilization hallowing our dwellings which had not taken place during my childhood.

SATURDAY MORN. 8.50, JAN. 23RD

The landscape is again white. Winter has revisited us. I noticed last night a circle round the moon, which betokens rough weather. It has been a boisterous as well as snowy morning.

I have secured the soap and mercury for bottling the sheep, but the difficulty appears to be to find hands to put it on. Groom has taken Charlie to be shod. The wild winds are rushing from the south [so] that I think it probable the snow will soon go.

I thank God for another comfortable night. I had a fit of coughing while rising, though not while in bed. I think of joining my family at Dexthorpe today.

Saturday eve. 5.30, Jan. 23rd, 1875

I return from my afternoon outing with a devoutly and joyfully thankful heart. I rode Charlie to the Post Office with Lizzie's letter and in coming back who should I meet but Mr. Elliot, the roper, who promised to take my appointment tomorrow. He informed me that if I were willing to contribute half a crown towards the hiring of trap, he would exonerate me altogether, to which I most cordially agreed.

I experienced another pleasure of reading my 'English Independent' as I walked with Charlie's bridle in one hand. In the pages of my paper, by description, there towered up before my imagination the great and grand gothic Independent Memorial Hall which was opened and consecrated on Tuesday and Wednesday last. £72,000 have been well spent. A few memorial portraits and medallions and one or two memorial stained glass windows. One glass window contained a most appropriate subject. A representation of the embarkation of the Pilgrim Fathers.

I shrank from the idea of Lizzie leaving me to myself as I had for some weeks been out of health, but to my great surprise I am lifted out of the trial as the expected consequences have not followed. I have no nervous, sleepless nights. Drooping melancholies come not. God's blessings and comforts have fallen upon me like fruit from the Autumnal tree.

I have to record gradual change from snow to rain and mist, with a lowering of temperature through the day. The snow has well nigh disappeared. In walking through my yard and stables this evening I felt a peculiar pleasure and much gratitude to God in seeing the horses and animals feeding so heartily, enjoying high health after their day's toil. 'To be forewarned is to be forearmed'. In view of future emergencies, I have filled my stables with useful horses ready for the accomplishment of the multiplied tasks. If we intend to secure God's blessing we must drive on the field work. We must bring ourselves into harmony with the laws of God's government. We must honour Him with our implements of husbandry, manual labours and purposes and plans. We must honour Him by obeying the laws of His physical government. We must conform ourselves to His order in the field as well as church and sanctuary. May I venture to hope that by increased diligence, the exercise of a more concentrated and further developed skill, the farm may yield a more abundant and profitable increase. My flock is anything but satisfactory. My corn crop is not superabundant, though the quantity and quality fair, but the price of wheat is low. Considering the minimum character of my flock the turnips are being rapidly consumed. They walk over a large acreage in a short time. The hoggets return, all being well, on Monday next to the Cadeby lane 33 acres, where we hope they will dwell longer than in the last two fields.

Branwick has been partially engaged the last day or two with Augur and cart removing fencing.

The low price of wheat and the small number of sheep for sale next Spring will constitute our agricultural year one of singularly small profit.[65]

D.V. Denison returns to school on Monday next for three o'clock. Let me return thanks to God that his educational prospects have again come round.

SUNDAY EVE. 8.45, JAN. 24TH, 1875

A knock at my door this morning with the evil tidings that the load of straw left yesterday in the barn crew was driven over by a tempestuous wind and smothered to death the best bullock in the yard. A fine red-coloured animal. It is a very mysterious calamity to visit us on the Sabbath.

My reason for penning the record and thus making the month of Jan. 1875 memorable is, I trust, pure and legitimate. I have experienced some pious reflections upon it. As far as we can gather from nature and revelation, the Divine Being exercises His royal control over both the physical and moral worlds and He has a moral end in every dark event. He has a specially beneficent end in all misfortunes which happen to His people. All things work together for good to them that love God. What good can come out of a dead ox? Scepticism might ask. Well, how did the intelligence of the fact affect my moral character? Did it throw me off my guard? Did I in any degree loose my proper Christian balance? Did it disturb my Christian peace? In searching out the facts which had occasioned the death, was I rash in blaming any servants? Did the garthman do it inconsiderately? It appears the load was located differently. The accident could not possibly have happened if the waggon had been placed near the crew fence. An exceptional quantity of straw was placed upon the waggon. However, apart from all details even as to the blame which some might consider attaches to myself, to be candid, I professed to walk round the yard congratulating myself that all was right, but only manifesting my obtuseness in observation not to detect the waggon being in the wrong place, neither the sagacity to perceive the possible or even probable consequences of its exceptional location. However, what are the lessons to be drawn as far as I am responsible for the creation of a better future? Vigilent watching is necessary in both business and spiritual life. May God make me more on the alert.

WEDNESDAY MORN. 9 O'CLOCK, JAN. 27TH, 1875

Yesterday I rode Charlie to a wreck sale. It is somewhat melancholy to witness a vessel that had once ploughed the great deep shivered into a thousand fragments. I commissioned Mr. Ashley's foreman to purchase oak posts providing they sold reasonably.

On my return home I called and took tea with Maria at Grainthorpe. Her son Henry anticipates being called into the ministry next Spring.

Last Monday I received a postcard stating the arrival of the long delayed truck load of coals, and yesterday we sent three waggons for them.

Yesterday was a beautifully mild spring-like day; this morning is thick and murky, November-like.

The bullock dressed on Sabbath morn still hangs in the barn waiting for a customer. Though found dead under the straw, it bled freely and the meat looks very nice and wholesome.

All being well today I must pay my Louth bills. My Lizzie expects me to pay my bills in Jan. and this is the last week. The month expires next Sunday.

My wife remarks that I have been two days without my dinner and it is not right that I should go three days. It will be very injudicious to go a third day.

Wednesday eve. 8.45

Yesterday I paid Maria six pounds for John to give to Mr. Stonehouse next Saturday when he goes to Hull. Today I attended Louth market. Mr. Roberts complained the bulk was not as good as the sample of the last lot of wheat.

I paid Mr. Page for Denison's last half year board and education. I told Mr. P. that he had gone back with his writing during his affliction and holidays. I should like him to be more particular in his person, his dress, pronunciation, manners, neatness and cleanliness. He takes no pride in his personal appearence. He has farming habits of slovenliness in almost everything he does. I told Mr. P. that he requires firm discipline and that I should like him to exercise parental supervision. The boy requires a strong, bracing moral atmosphere.

Mr. Bright gave a long speech on Monday on the disestablishment of the English church.[66]

THURSDAY, 2.30 P.M., JAN. 28TH, 1875

This morning I took Frank for a ride on the donkey. We went to the men ploughing old seeds in the old 9 acre or gravel pit field. We found six ploughs running. There were six yesterday. C. Smith, foreman, gave me the bill for the load of coke I led to the chapel on Monday last, also a settled bill from the station master at North Thoresby for transit of house coals from Mr. Stonehouse, Hull. One waggon, weighing 8 tons 13 cwt, at the rate of 20/- per ton. The charge for carriage being £2/14/0.

This is a fine sunshiny Jan. day. The air felt pure, bracing and balmy. Breezy days are exceedingly refreshing when dry and not too cold. After returning home with Frank, I rode Charlie to the village but made no call except at the Post. It has become daily our centre of attraction. Family diaries are for the most part written in correspondence. Thousands who would never think of writing there autobiography in the form of a diary unconsciously perform the task in the form of epistle.

Mr. Sawyer came this morning with his cart and took one side of the unfortunate bullock. Lizzie and I were talking of having the heart roasted, but I was reminded of our rule (which for years past has been observed), 'never cook anything not actually killed'. If it is found dead, though it may only just have expired and by skill and care be nicely dressed and wholesome, still we exclude it from our larder. We never allow it to come into the house. I will again praise God for the glow of health. Oh, that men would praise Him for His goodness and wonderful work. My Lizzie, too, is better today and has taken Frank with Pink and phaeton to Louth to see Denison and shop a little. Hannah has taken baby in the garden this afternoon.

Branwick has cut the rasberry canes, staked, and tied them up. It is several years since old Tom Smith commenced doing the work. This is the first of a long series that other hands have done it. Poor old Tom has found his mistake of joining the strike last year.[67] I think long on this.

C. Smith will take one load of coals.

The marble fount I bought of Coulam now stands upon the dining table before me. 18/- I believe to be the cost.

I have this morning made searching enquiries of C. Smith respecting the delivery of my last cargo of wheat. He most emphatically declares there is not the slightest delinquency on our part. He said about 70 qrs. of spring or turnip land wheat went in better than sample. Mr. Roberts made a general statement that my bulks had several times been inferior to sample, which I totally reject as true. It must be a harsh and unjust charge because untrue.

I have four young horses alternately running one plough. Brisk mare has the least mettlle and spirit for work. The three colts do their work more easily.

FRIDAY EVE. 7 O'CLOCK, JAN. 29TH, 1875

This morning I walked round the farm. I found six pairs of horses ploughing old seeds in gravelpit field. I had a long conversation with C. Smith about farming business. We decided that all being well we would sow the 16 acre in front of house with white wheat, also far 33 acre running along Cadeby lane. I was expressing some fears about the next crop as the turnips were so thin and light and Smith reminded me that where the turnips were sown twice over there were 7 cwts. of artificial management, and where sown three times half a ton was sown per acre, that even with a middling crop of turnips there would be enough to produce a fair average yield of corn. I told him I thought it necessary to spend £20 in artificial manure for the 6 acres. The weather continues Spring-like. The birds have struck their first notes this morning. The larks have been soaring and warbling in a sort of introductory manner. I said they have begun too early to last, for it often indicates a rough return of winter. The snowdrops, too, are peeping in the garden.

I walked with Holmes through the flock. We have today 210 hoggets. He said he had a fork which had lasted him all the season without breaking until last week. I think the sheep are improving. The hoggets came into the field on Tuesday last and the ewes yesterday morning. A new greenness is being noted as coming over the grassfields.

I am thankful that Lizzie appears better than when she returned from Dexthorpe. This morning Lizzie and I and Frank rode with Pink and phaeton to the village. We transfered the management of chapel sewing basket to Miss Parker and Mrs. Frank Parker. I trust the sewing meetings will commence a new and accellerated movement.

I paid three more Binbrook bills, Mackerill, Mrs. Barton, and Hall.

TUESDAY EVE. 7 O'CLOCK, FEB. 2ND, 1875

On Saturday afternoon last I road [rode] Charlie to Dexthorpe, remained the Sabbath, and returned home yesterday afternoon. My little daughter, Mabel, formed one of our happy group. Having never seen her during the holidays it was great pleasure to have her with me for the Sunday. I heard Mr. Thomas, a Wesleyan preacher, in the morning. After dinner Mr. Riggall, I and Mabel walked to Dalby church in the afternoon. After tea I preached a short sermon in the kitchen. My text was I Cor. 3rd ch. 'Other foundation, etc'. I feel thankful that my chest is sufficiently restored to enable me to preach again. I met Henry Atkinson and Mr. Gledhill at my house last night.

This morning we commenced sowing white wheat in 16 acre front of our house. After hearing Mr. Riggall's statements concerning his experience of white wheat - it requires a congenial soil, a congenial climate. It soon sprouts in a wet season and blights sometimes during the last stage of ripening. The sraw and chaff is inferior to any other kinds as fodder. I have decided not to sow more than this field.

Two of my confined men, viz. C. Smith and Bocock, are hired again at the same rate of wages. Holmes will leave next May. My daily labourers are asking for 3/- per day.

FRIDAY MORN. 9 O'CLOCK, FEB. 5TH, 1875

Another fine frosty morning. We have had two frosty mornings in succession but not to prevent us ploughing and sowing our white wheat. The sparrows are becoming very numerous and they are making a chirping commotion around the house while I am writing.

James Drew has succeeded first rate with the four young horses breaking. A few days ago I was afraid Black Prince was turning lame. We were always zealous of his curby hocks. However, the lameness has passed off again. I hope he may gain strength with age and careful treatment. The other day Mr. Riggall sold his cul hoggets with 6 wethers at 38/- each. If the weather continues sharp I shall be right in not buying many lambs last Autumn. Four months keep is already lost.

It is a great misfortune that young Le Bon has completely failed to get foals with one exception.

On Wednesday last I bought and paid for a box of cartridges, 11/6, also a bottle of magnesia, a box of Liebig's food. Denison came out from school and accompanied me shopping. We spend $2^1/_2$d in bunns and $1^1/_4$d in oranges. We walked up to Mr. Ashley's to see after the drill and ask about a new set of chaff cutting knives. I paid 9d for two brooches repairing at Musson's.

The turnip land ploughs up and works freer than we expected.

SATURDAY EVE. 6.30, FEB. 6TH, 1875

We finished sowing yesterday in 16 acre except headlands. The field has become a powerful attraction to crows and jackdaws. It is only a well-loaded gun that will keep them aloof. They have most keenly watched their opportunities. They have made the tree-tops their watchtowers and I have a fine lesson on natural history spread out before me. The crow's sagacious instinct seems to border on intelligence. They know a gun. They are most sensitive to shot and powder. In the absence of these they are bold and defiant. Many boys have hollored at the top of their voices with very little effect. They are a devouring and destructive bird to a newly sown field when the germ is opening and piercing its way through the soil. The little green spiral indicates where they may dig to advantage. I have engaged in the conflict with them yesterday and today. I perform three feats at once; I tent, read, and study the stirring events of the day.

This noon I experienced a break upon the routine by a visit from Mr. Vesey from Welton. We had more conversations upon our building plans as well as the alterations of garden and drive.

Mr. V. thinks the old orchard must be removed. He wished me to accompany him to the pleasure ground to see if we could not fell enough trees for the next wood sales. We examined the circular plantation and decided to make up the fences for the next summer, and in the next Autumn when the trees are felled the hedges must be stubbed up. A few trees are to remain as ornamentation. Mr. Vesey appears to have altered his tone in relation to tree-cutting down. May I venture to hope that Sir Edmond has not forgotten my letter but given Mr. V. an intimation that an opening had better be made. I trust and pray if it be God's will that next Autumn may prove only the first of a series of sales and a complete transformation may be effected by the clearence of a large amount of wood. It would materially increase my own pleasure and profit if free access were granted to sun and wind that snow and rhyme [rime] might escape as readily and rapidly from this as from other farms. I can never calculate the many acres of corn and other produce destroyed by hedgerows and plantation timber on my farm. May I hope Sir Edmond will give full swing to the axe and cut a large proportion down. It will soon more than meet the interest on building which I may have to pay. It would revolutionise the sanatory [sanitary] condition of the farm, I mean in relation to the flock, and especially to the health of the growing crops. Long shadows created by dense foliage are predjudicial [prejudicial] to the healthy ripening of grain.

TUESDAY MORNING, 9 O'CLOCK, FEB. 9TH, 1875

The weather continues frosty. The turnip land is too crusty to plough, but we can manage to stir the fallows. The ploughs are this morn in Black pond field stirring for cabbages.

Yesterday we bottled the ewes. The men pronounce them very filthy.

Little Frank is fingering the piano while I am writing. I may thank God for three such bright and beautiful boys. They have bright faces, bright intellects. They appear to be sound in limb and constitution. The two youngest have occasional outbursts of fiery temper though the little cloud of anger and wrath soon breaks and the ordinary tenor of their infant existence is a laughing joyfulness. Their life is full of pleasurable activities. A constant change of position and of place, their intelligent eyes observing first one thing in the house and then another and their little tongues telling what they see and what they do. The last few days Norman has felt the idea and desire to step. He is quite springy on his legs. I am going to take Frank on the donkey. Ma and baby will accompany us for a walk.

Tuesday eve. 8.30, Feb. 9th, 1875
Miss Short brought me the Sunday School subscription money and the book to sign. The sum was £1/2/6.

Lizzie has held her sewing meeting and tea this afternoon. About forty persons, young and old, presented themselves. I read one of Dr. Talmage's remarkable sermons. The subject was home life. I had some cheerful conversation with Robinson Fridlington about Talmage as a preacher, and another of his sermons appearing in the 'Christian Globe', a comparatively new penny monthly publication.[68] We live in remarkable times in relation to cheap literature. We have tracts and pamphlets flying though society by thousands. We have periodicals continually multiplying - dailies, weeklys, monthlies and quarterlies. Every department of human thought has its representative expression.

Last evening I occupied the chair on the occasion of the Free Methodist chapel Anniversary, Louth. I gave an address, then followed Rev. Ed. C. Cornish, Rev. Jordan and Griffith. Only a thin attendance at the tea and after meeting, but thank Heaven the interest was well sustained from beginning to close. I was too much excited and discursive. I felt fired up with Divine Power and influence. I spoke some of my views upon the effect of Nonconformity and nonconformist lives upon other times, places and countries, as well as our own. They were the great founders and builders of state. If ever Divine glory and favour shone upon a band of men it was upon the old Puritans and Nonconformists. The tabernacle and the ark of the covenant was with them. The Exodus of the Pilgrim Fathers was the most memorable momentous and fruitful of mighty results of any recorded in history since the Exodus of Israel from Egypt, when History was born. Glory be to God for raising up such a band of men as the Pilgrim Fathers! What an embodiment of the principle of order and the principle of progress. Conservatism and radicalism were the most finely balanced both in their nature, teaching, and action.

WEDNESDAY EVE. 7.30, FEB. 10TH, 1875

On Monday last we sent a waggon and four horses to Captain Nell's mill, Louth, for 1½ tons of linseed cake and 1 ton of cotton. Today we can plough the headlands in 16 acre turnip land, and proceed to the 6 acre. This morning I walked to 6 acre to look at them ploughing, also to the sheep and examined a hogget and a ewe to see the result of bottling. I only suffered the disappointment of seeing about 8 or 10 living fags picked out of the ewe's wool. It is a mortification to incur expense with such result. Of course, one is scarcely a fair specimen.

Today I paid Mr. Esberger's bill. I gave him two ten pound bills and he returned 5/-. Thank God, notwithstanding a shower of Christmas bills, I have been enabled to meet them hitherto. I am still under Providential Mediatorial sway. God in His Goodness is enabling me to throw off the incubus of debt notwithstanding the low price of wheat and the midling crop of turnips and some heavy losses through the year.

THURSDAY MORN. 9 O'CLOCK, FEB. 11TH, 1875

Another keen frosty morning. The sky not so thickly folded with clouds as during the last few days. The clouds hang heavily around but very little rain or snow. Our water barrel was sent the other day to the village for water for the labourers' cottage.[69] It proves the exhaustion of cistern.

I have been firing the gun off at the crows.

Frank has two good crys last night, but I really cannot tell whether caused by pain or temper. We administered Dill water the first time and carminative the second. Yesterday the wheat trade was worse, from 38/- to 39/-. If I were asked to describe our domestic life I must respond that we are a happy family. We have Christ in our home and how many times He has lifted us above our afflictions.

Evil passions have no scope in our house. There is no toleration of quarrel. Every kind of innocent playfulness is encouraged. Last evening when I arrived home from market and entered the nursery my fatherly heart was gladdened to witness the mother bending over and tenderly watching over the little ones. They had the toys and pictures strewed around. Then the effect of my entrance upon Frank was almost magical. He commenced his evening romp. He jumped, ran, shouted, making all sorts of distracting noises and played all manner of mischievous tricks. Whilst Hannah was bathing him there were endless mutual ticklings and violent laughings. We had a splendid development of childlike joyousness. It created a delightful incense through the room. It was a scene worthy of angelic observation. These are fragrant memories for old age to dwell upon in after years.

My Lizzie has entered the room and laid down on the couch. Her strong spirit would not allow this at eleven o'clock in the morning were she not completely exhausted. I take Baby into our bed after his first sleep in bassinette, and Frank in his cot by our bedside, and one or other has disturbed and broke Lizzie's rest now for months past that her strength is very much tested, and this morning she lays in half a faint. There are clouds ever and anon springing out of our horizon.

Here there is one reason that we invite not much company. The family and household is a sufficient tax upon Lizzie's energies. Another reason, our means are not sufficient to provide expensive entertainment.

I want my children to receive a good education. I should like it to be wide, every faculty being developed and made more robust and then stored with all manner of learning. D.V. this is my plan and aim concerning them. I should like to place their fortunes in their heads and characters as well as, or rather than, the pocket.

Thursday eve. 6 o'clock, Feb. 11th, 1875

My dear Lizzie has suffered considerably today from weakness of body. I walked this morning to the six acres and found six ploughs at work. There was some difficulty on account of the frost. The frost having crusted the surface it was not only heavier dragging for the horses but the plough could not lay the furrow over uniformly or tidily. I spoke to C. Smith about my feeling of disappointment in finding undestroyed filth upon the sheep. He said they were very bad, there were thousands upon them. In that case I need not be surprised at a few remaining undestroyed. We used 5lbs of mercury to the hundred and more than an equal quantity of soap.[70] We ran out upon the sheep from the spout of a small tea kettle about one quart of the solution.

I next went to one of the Hall paddocks and made it a promenade for reading and meditation upon the uses of the imagination in every branch of study. It requires a powerful imagination to understand Astronomy. The eye is untruthful and imagination comes in to the aid of the mind in realising the truth. It corrects the deceptions of the eye. This morning while in the field I made an effort not merely to call up a single house, but my own house and farm with its setting. As it stands before me in imagery and I commence to describe its position, a whole panorama of landscape opens out before me. It forms part of the general undulation called the Lincolnshire Wolds. If it be wonderful that I should be able to call up, by the faculty of imagination, a single house after seeing it, how the wonder magnifies a thousandfold when I call up before my mind's eye, for instance, the late Smithfield fat stock show in the Agricultural Hall, spanned by an expanse of arch most striking. I can place myself in one of these remarkable galleries and look over the long rows of immense cattle, or I walk about the building arm in arm with friends in lively conversation upon pleasing topics of various kinds and look at some of the animals singly. I can mark afresh the row of Scots, another of Irish, Welsh, Highlanders, Hereford, Devons, Shorthorns, etc. I can rephoto these peculiarities of colours and forms. A good strong imagination is the finest Art Gallery in the world. It is both a gallery of nature and Art.

FRIDAY MORN. 9.30, FEB. 12TH, 1875

What a change since last night! Most of the snow has disappeared and the temperature lowered several degrees. Could a climate be more changeable than ours? I will praise my Maker and Redeemer that we are permitted to proceed with our turnip land ploughing again today. It is a pleasure to see six ploughs turning over six paralell furrows. I do enjoy to look round a well cultivated farm. In order to do this the work must be pushed forward and kept well in advance. For instance, if the land be ploughed early and becomes well pulverised by frost, it requires less labour to harrow and work at Spring and forms a finer and more natural mould for a seed bed. If we exercise our power to its utmost limit God will co-operate most effectually and a finer and more abundant crop is the outcome and reward. God Himself offers prizes of different degrees and value according to the exercise of skill and industry on our part. Let me then diligently store up in my diary the process of farming experiences and the results thereof.

How much of valuable time and labour may be economised by a constant intelligent observation in the working of implements of husbandry, in the planning of horses and men. Farming is an occupation which affords scope for the continuous exercise of observation and experiment. Farmers must watch the markets, the seasons. He should have some general idea of meteorology. He should know much of science or of Divine government in nature. He should know when to work his land and when to leave it alone. He should know the agricultural signs of the times. He should study the nature and peculiarities of his own farm, yea, moreover, the nature and peculiarities of each field.

When a number of varied experiences are noted down they may be utilised by the next generation or referred to by the writer for the refreshment of memory.

I would again refer to a valuable receipt [recipe] for horses and cattle and sheep. I think it has never failed to cure colic in horses. To make it still more prominent in my record I will copy it out for a second time:

Red oil for general agricultural purposes quantity one gallon.
2 pound of salts.
1 pound of treacle.
½ do. of saltpetre.
2 do. of salt.
8 pints urine or netting.
Boil these substances together, then add when cold:
1 gill of turpentine.
1 do of vinegar.
1 do. of traine oil.
2 ounces laudenum.
1 oz. aether.

Frank has come into the room, and brimful of talk. He struggles out his little germinant ideas. He is trying to master his imperfect articulation. He often talks about Denison and Mabel. He can only think of Mabel as being at Hackthorne. He has run off into the nursery to tell Mama about the little pictures I have explained to him. He seems interested in studying a picture, especially if Papa describes the varied objects. I told him one picture was a number of boys and girls around the table sat for dinner and he made an original observation that they had 'some potted meat for dinner'. He noted a comb in a little girl's hair without my pointing it out to him. I must give him more object lessons so as to enlarge his vocabulary. I call his attention to things in nature.

Friday eve. 7.15, Feb. 12th, 1875
Bocock washed out the iron pot, and I boiled and mixed together the substances named in the receipt and when cold poured the valuable drink into the stone jug and carried it into the old granary.

I have been chopping wood and tenting crows and reading my 'English Independent'. It contains a stirring report of the Liberation Society's addresses delivered at Birmingham.[71] Cannot farming be carried on progressively? Is it not possible to throw on paper a panoramic view of the process as the events unfold? I am reminded that the lambing season is fast approaching and it is time preparations were made. All being well, tomorrow I will go to the village and see for a carpenter to come and repair the turnip trays. They will require cledding with straw to make lamb pens. I am thankful that hitherto we have none cast lamb, which very frequently has come to pass in our flock more or less. Mr. Riggall complained when I was at Dexthorpe a fortnight ago that he had about a score.

I am reminded too that I have some white wheat in the granary which has been there several weeks. We have used a portion of it for seed and the foreman stated that it was in fine condition, but it is time to re-examine it and if necessary turn it over. I wish we had pushed it off when the last lot of red was delivered.

I will praise God of Providence that my health continues good since my last convalescence. I continue to take codliver oil, to wear a sponge and compress at chest, in addition to the skiazza belt round my body.[72] I scarcely reccollect such continued vivacity of mind and body. I enjoy my own sweet home and family, reading, study, and farming, the means of grace, pulpit and platform, society and solitude; neither business, literary nor religious work seems to come amiss. No kind of work that I can name at present feels irksome.

SATURDAY EVE. 6 O'CLOCK, FEB. 13TH, 1875

This is a day of November type; it is a thick, cold, drizzling atmosphere. We have been permitted to go forth with six ploughs into 6 acres turnip land. Comparatively small amount of downfall.

This morning I rode Charlie to the village and settled with Sawyer, butcher. I paid his bill, amounts to £9/9/0, also Grant's do., £5/10/0, also Parker's do., £21/10/0. On Wednesday last Esberger's bill, £19/6/0. Howden for clipping Charlie, 10/6. Yesterday at Binbrook Mrs. Short's bill £13/10/0, Maughan 3/10. My heaviest bills are now paid and tonight posted up or filed.

Mr. Sawyer owed me for 3 sheep, a calf, and the unfortunate bullock smothered under the load of straw, total £21/7/5. The calf made £3/10/0, the bullock £13/10/0. Three hoggets £4/7/0.

Tonight Denison has paid my labourer's wages: James Drew 36/- for a fortnight, Charles Shadlock 36/-, do. Branwick 36/-, do. James Wright 36/-, do. Holmes, shepherd 20/-, Bocock 34/- for himself and boy, C. Smith 54/- for himself and boy, and Tom Lawton, boy, 16/3 for two weeks. Total £13/8/0.

Having noted the finances for the day, I proceed to sketch my dining room. Mama is knelt down by her baby, rocking him to sleep and questioning Denison about the school and about his health and adventures through Hubbard's Hills,[73] leaping over the streams, etc., also about his visit to Dr. Sharpley's house to a party, also about the arrangement of table for tea and supper, also viands, etc. Denison is gumming labels for his books. His

Mother has sewed covers on them. As Denison has come home Mother must hang a proportionate quantity of linen around the fires. On Saturdays every available portion of space is utilised for warming and drying night linen.

SUNDAY MORNING 10.30, FEB. 14TH, 1875

Unable to sleep for half the night, yet thank Heaven able to rise and eat a good breakfast. My first breakfast was a portion of Reynold's 'John the Babtist'. Under his guidance the word seems invested with a charming novelty. It is an altogether new mode of stating and unfolding our everlasting orthodoxy.

Our little pet, Norman, was sorely stormtossed through the night. We had to nurse and dose to relieve his physical troubles. It is by much mutual suffering that our children are raised. It is a wonderful exercise of supernatural power and grace that we are enabled vigourously to pursue the regular round of out and indoor duties. I am afraid (in listening to Norman breathing as he lays asleep in his bassinette) he has taken a serious cold. Lizzie put him to bed yesterday morning in the dining room and by a slip of memory or an accident of non-reccollection left the window open. She has several times grieved and reproached herself for doing it. When I think of my own blunders through life it hushes many a censure when about to issue from my lips.

Lizzie, Denison, Frank, Hannah and Groom have gone in waggonette with Pink to chapel and left me nurse and guardian of the tiny infant. He commenced his immortal carreer as small-featured if not dwarfish in his physical development. Should his physical growth prove tardy and in his prime continue low in stature, I pray that he may be able to quote Isaac Watt's couplets, 'Were I so tall to reach the pole', etc. Mind is still the world's great ruling force.

MONDAY MORNING, 10 O'CLOCK, FEB. 15TH, 1875
Louth Mechanics Reading room - with a large skylight in the roof, a clock over the head of a dark brown bust resting on the mantlepiece. Maps Geographical and Geological, also glass cases containing butterflies, stuffed birds, etc.

This morning I arrived in time with my son Denison. We drove up to King Edward's Grammar School but the school being empty we moved on to meet them. I left Denison's box at the house and walked on to Frank Riggall's for a Winchester of codliver oil; also to Burton's for my 'Christian Age'.

I have just glanced at the comic and illustrated papers which lay upon the table. The political situation appears to assume an old Palmerstonian phase with somewhat of modification. Conservatism is described as partaking of a more liberal spirit and Liberalism is being impregnated with the spirit of Conservatism, the two parties are more closely allied.

Again we have a fine morning for field work; six ploughs in six acres.

Branwick helps Bocock to load straw and works in the gardens.
Yesterday my interest was awakened in the revival carreer of Sankey and Moody.[74] Mr. Cope, our Minister, lent me a paper with a detailed account of their work last Sabbath, a week yesterday at Liverpool. I read the report in walking to my class meeting and back. It is a racy description of the services; building, Sankey and Moody, audiences and whole scene were vividly and courteously described. There are three of Moody's discourses which were specially pleasing to me as I had long felt a desire to read a specimen of his preaching. When they visit London I shall be tempted to occupy my own eye upon the scene.

TUESDAY MORN. 8.30, FEB. 16TH, 1875

Norman requires a good deal of nursing and rocking. I hope his cold is a little better this morning. His mother is washing him from head to foot. I observe his upper gums are swelling for a couple of teeth to cut through. There is suffering connected with the budding of life. Lizzie and I rose before seven and from our window we could see the bright heavens flushed with roseate tints of the rising sun. It formed a splendid contrast to the white rhyme [rime] sheeting the grass. I do not suppose that the frost is severe enough to lock the ploughing. They finished the 6 acre yesterday and completed the day in Cadeby lane 33 acre.

Yesterday I attended the Board.

Miss Johnson called upon Lizzie respecting the club tickets.

Will the florid morn end in a rainy day?

Lizzie took Frank out on the donkey yesterday morn and thinks the fresh air cauzed her to sleep better last night.

The young horses look thin, their appetite has not been good lately. We were a little anxious about Jack, Cunningham's horse, but he has improved a little.

When my wife describes the state of her health, it appears there are three centres of pain and suffering. Her head aches, her eyes smart, etc. I feel thankful that I seldom feel pain in any part of my body or even fatigue from the labours and toils of life.

WEDNESDAY MORN. 9 O'CLOCK, FEB. 17TH, 1875

Glory be to God for what I feel of His goodness. Baby has slept better and we have had a comfortable night. The two little ones have colds. Last eve Mother placed their feet in mustard. Frank no sooner woke than he began to tell me the story of mustard and water. A tallow plaister was applied to baby's chest. It has often been said that prevention is better than cure. Lizzie has a good idea of checking disease in its first symptom and stage.

This is Candlmas Market and the bridal season for the feathered. A short time ago when the weather was fine a gush of melody burst from the woods. Might not these be termed anticipatory songs? Severe weather returning, they were hushed again until yesterday they broke forth in new songs of celebration.

Frank has come into the dining room and is throwing himself into all sorts of postures, climbing up the chair, taking down books from the library, examining the coloured pictures in one entitled 'Basket of Flowers'.[75] The little darling's young ideas shoot and develop while gazing upon pictures. He makes original and spontaneous remarks. I have paid some attention to picture lessons and the more I study them myself my conviction deepens respecting the aid they render the youthful mind in realising history truth. My own conviction is shared by the world at large or we should not have witnessed so large a number of illustrated books. The walls of our homes are being lined with paintings, engravings, water colours; the leaves of our best bound books as well as paper cover periodicals are covered with wood cuts, etc.

Today agricultural labourers will throng Louth and other towns, and no doubt a considerable number will be hired for the ensuing year.[76] A horse and cart has gone to Louth with a number of our own. I have hired two to remain, C. Smith and Bocock.

We think of reserving the lodge for our own use while the building is going on at home.[77] Our house will not be habitable when the roof is off.

It is a damp uncomfortable day.

We have 2 waggons and eight horses fetching 2½ tons of cake, 1½ of linseed and 1 ton of cotton. The waggoners wished to go to the market and said they were willing to take waggons. One waggon will bring 2½ tons of engine coals. We can only raise two ploughs.

It is almost unprecedented for me to absent myself from the market, but Lizzie wishes to meet the ladies at Binbrook this afternoon to consult about the club tickets. Lizzie cannot trust Hannah with baby unless I remain at home.

Binbrook, Wednesday morn. 10.30, Feb. 17th, 1875
Last eve I had the pleasure of meeting Mr. Cope, Boyers, young James Dent, Lingard Wesleyan, on the platform. I was called to the chair.

The speeches were unusually more earnest and intelligent. Both Dent and Cope surprised me. Some heavy showers came about service time and prevented several who might have attended [so] that we had some empty pews. Upon the whole, Ludford never enjoyed a more instructive meeting. They do not contribute much to the Missionary cause. £1/8/0, including collections and boxes. They are a poor people and hampered with debt upon their chapel. In taking down the old gallery and renewing with raised seats, replacing the pulpit with a platform, re-staining and varnishing, and lighting it with new lamps, they have completely transformed the interior, but the debt, old and new together, form a nightmare which I am afraid they will not soon or readily throw off. Their original debt is nearly two hundred pounds. I have one hundred and twenty pounds upon it, and my brother the rest. When I think of the debt upon our chapel and of the general financial state of our circuit I am still of the conviction we are not in a position to take a second married preacher, though it has been decided to do so. I have sometimes almost groaned in spirit before Almighty God that He would send us relief. Why should not we pray for funds as well as souls.

FRIDAY MORN. 8.30, FEB. 19TH, 1875

I rose this morning before seven. The sky looks black and wint-erly. The temperature low and the ground covered with a white sheet. We had a comfortable night with baby. We hope he is some-what improved in his health.

On Tuesday last we shifted the sheep into footroad 20 acres. As I was dressing, I saw 5 pairs of horses march out for another day's ploughing.

Friday eve. 6.30
More snow has fallen through the day with a north-easterly wind. The wind has generally continued south and south-west for some time past. When once it turns round from the land to sea it some-times becomes fixed for several weeks through the Spring, and causes a keen and biting season. I am thankful that the plough is not fastened in the furrow. Parker's man, young Preston, has been two days, yesterday and today, mending old broken trays, sheep troughs, also making a new cribb in middle stable where young Le Bonn is now lodging. We must attend to another item in relation to these cribbs. The caps require to be guarded by a covering of zinc or hooping iron, and the bottoms coated with zinc to preserve the wood from the wet thrown amongst the cutmeat. It has become a habit to steep cake in water and mix it with the horses cutmeat. This is considered the most healthy feed.

The turnip trays we cled with straw for lamb pens. The shep-herd commences tomorrow and Branwick undertakes to cut for the hoggets. I will return thanks to my Heavenly Father that notwith-standing rumours of distemper or foot and mouth amongst sheep and cattle, also of ewes casting lambs, in the neighbourhood, we are mercifully free.

Friday eve. 7.20, Feb. 19th, 1875
Rode Charlie to Binbrook post. Paid Maultby's bill, plumber and glazier, £1/10/0, and on the road read George Dawson's lecture on America.

I often wonder whether in the order of Divine Providence I shall be permitted to see any other country. There are three tours I have a strong desire to make. I should like to see the classic regions of the European Continent, into the East through Egypt and Palestine, and over the gigantic Continent of America.

Before breakfast I read two pages in Reynold's 'John the Babtist'. I have to read and farm as best I can. This afternoon I have braved the storm with my gun and axe alternately. Chopping fire-wood is very healthy exercise but vacant spaces of time were filled by reading 'English Independent'. Last evening I proceeded with Chew's 'Life of Everett'. The interest increases.

SATURDAY MORN. 8.30, FEB. 20TH, 1875

Rose before 7 o'clock, and from my window could see five pairs of horses, geared for ploughing, marching off to the field. The white snow sheet still lays upon the ground. The sky is leaden with clouds and the wind boisterous. Norman was restless through [the] night, at least after the clock struck twelve.

I will again record my gratitude to God for all His abounding goodness to me and mine. It is the Divine Government and purpose concerning us that makes every home and farm event pregnant with interest. There is nothing insignificant when looked at in the light of Heaven and eternity. Every event yields its quota of building power and conserving force to Christ's kingdom. Everything living and inanimate, the stock on the farm, the implements of husbandry, the home panoply and home life are sacred and consecrated. Neither day nor place are regarded secular. We eat and drink to the Lord and give God thanks. With these precious views, feelings, and motions, I take another winterly morning's launch into reading, study, and business.

Saturday eve. 7.30, Feb. 20th, 1875
I have had to shoulder my gun as sharply as a sportsman through the day. The wood pigeons were more hungered by the special wildness of the blast, and left the field reluctantly after one falling a victim to the shot. I had to make a series of promenades from one field to the other. I much dislike banishing crows. They are the farmer's friend as a rule. They pick up many noxious grubs, especially from the newly turned furrow, but they bill up the precious grain if allowed.

However, on one of the wildest winter days, tenting has not absorbed my mental faculties. I have linked myself with the traveller and taken an imaginative tour into other lands, also with the critic and surveyed fields of literature, with the politician and marked the doings and characters of statesmen, with the Divine and considered whether we might form an intelligent theory of the Atonement.

This noon we have felt some anxiety about Norman. He has lost his flesh, one cheek flushed almost crimson, his eyes dull and heavy, the rest part of his face and ears pale and white to transparency, the veins of his forehead being quite visible. He manifested very little animation. His usual cheerful cooing and chattering were hushed. He appears to have taken cold and his breathing somewhat affected. He takes the breast as usual though not quite his ordinary quantum of Liebeg's food. However, he had a nice sleep this afternoon and gained considerable strength and vivacity, which he desired to test on his feet.

MONDAY EVE. 7.30, FEB. 22ND, 1875

A slight frost but not to prevent ploughing.

Attended the Board today. Mr. Benn's foreman had to pay Mary

Wright's daughter her wages up to next May. We had a lengthened discussion upon the case of Elson who could not find his son who had bolted because he had 1/6 laid on to pay towards his father's maintenance. It was decided to give him an order for the house.

Norman is not better but on the contrary. Lizzie thinks he has lost much flesh and lost a great deal of his voice. He cried in a very weak and unnatural tone, the most plaintive and pitiful cry we have ever heard in the house. He does not appear to suffer much pain. He refuses all kinds of food beyond his mother's milk.

Winter seems to settle in upon us again.

TUESDAY EVE. 7 O'CLOCK, FEB. 23RD, 1875

Four ploughs again in Cadeby lane 33 acre. The work difficult in consequence of frost. The distance is only small now between the plough and the sheep.

I will record my gratitude to the Divine Governor of my farm that the men and horses have enjoyed health and strength to accomplish the backward work. This is the end we have aimed at now for weeks past, and though for sometime the severe weather proved obstructive, we feel the more gratified that now the work of the farm is in a tolerably advanced state.

The machine has come into the yeard [yard] for the purpose of commencing thrashing tomorrow morning. We have three stacks of wheat and one of barley and when they are finished the yard will be emptied once more for the season.

While on my tenting expedition I shot another crow. I also started two foxes in Lodge Plot and shot two barrels after them. They appear to make a fox-cover of my farm. They robbed my henroost of about a hundred hens and chickens through the summer. I almost tremble in anticipation of the lambing season coming on account of these theives. Fiddling, from Ludford, came yesterday to catch rabbits. 4 couple was the result of his day's work. I paid him 7/- for himself and youth. They barely earned their meat and wages.

I had an invitation to Dexthorpe tomorrow to hear Mr. Riggall's annual lecture, but in consequence of being out of health from a severe cold and having many things to demand my care and attention [I will not go]. The lambing season is about to begin, or at least preparations are in progress, baby, too, is suffering from weakness and wasting, my cabbages and wheatfield will require vigilant watching, the thrashing should receive a superintending glance. There is a little turnip dragging to be done. The turnips are small and the ewes are eating their own way. James Wright cannot drag sufficient for them without help and I have assisted him a little this afternoon.

These requirements summed up make a goodly quantum of business to fill up the vacant hours. The spare time is devoted to reading and study. These are some of the luxuries of life.

Dr. Higgins has paid us a medical visit today. He made several inquiries about Norman, whom he came to examine and prescribe for. He pronounced lungs free from pulminory disease. He said the bronchial tubes of his right lung were slightly affected. He gave us no account of his wasting, though he was evidently struck with the fact on first looking at him. He said his gums would be better lanced as they felt tough and gristly and retarded injuriously the cutting of his teeth.

WEDNESDAY EVE. 8.45, FEB. 24TH, 1875

I have not done much business at the market. I have paid an old-standing account at Dr. Sharpley, £5/17/0. Just as I was entering the back yard of the Mason's Arms on Charlie, I met Denison, my eldest son. He had come out from school to meet his Father. I gave him a copper or two, an orange, and a few nuts, also a plate of meat at Forman's.

We commenced thrashing this morning, but snow began to fall in the afternoon and again a white mantle rests upon our hills and valleys. I had tea with Mrs. J. B. Sharpley, her two daughters, and Samuel. He complains of asthmatic cough.

I bought 25 qrs. of barley for seed today at 38/-, 16st.

FRIDAY EVE. 6.45, FEB. 26TH, 1875

The thrashing machine stands today on account of the weather. Two waggons have been to Covenham to fetch 25 qrs. of barley (Hollets pedigree). Another waggon has been engaged carrying straw up to the lamb pens and conveying a few trees from the plantation for fencing. The first heavy fall of rain in this month came last night. The snow has disappeared. The wind has come strongly and bitterly from the East today. This stormy weather whets the appetite of the wood pigeons for my turnip tops and cabbages; they keep me busy tenting. The doctor [Higgins] has been over this noon to see Norman. He lanced his gums. He prescribed half a teaspoonful of codliver oil. Dr. Higgins thinks the child is better and reccommended Lizzie to weigh him as the best test whether he wastes. I told Lizzie that I thought there was some improvement. There is more naturalness in his eye and expression, more vivacity and vital force in his general appearence. He has just gone off to sleep in his mother's arms, after being sung to for some time, and is now being laid in his bassinette. Last night I sat by the bedroom fire watching him until one o'clock whilst Lizzie slept. He seems to require periodical rockings to keep him asleep and quiet.

Yesterday young Will Smith went to Louth and brought home from Mr. Ashley's the widened corn and turnip drill and new-framed skarrifier [scarifier].

Yesterday I spent 39/- with a Yorkshire man in nails, false links and traces. Plough traces, two pairs, 10/-, false links at 9d per doz., total 9/-; that leaves a balance of 20/- for nails.

Friday eve. 8.15, Feb. 26th, 1875
Today, whilst tenting and making a promenade from one field to another, I have read and studied Sankey and Moody's career. Their rise from obscurity to notoriety is wonderfully rapid.

This afternoon read my 'English Independent'. Last evening I visited Ludbro' House for tea, the first time I have the pleasure of meeting Rev. Garside, our President of the United Free churches on any social occasion. He and Rev. J. Travis and myself addressed the Missionary meeting at the chapel. I was much interested with Mr. Garside's speech. He compared a missionary amongst the heathen to a fine tree growing out of the middle of a hay stack. I spoke of the universal disposition to pray for the success of Christian Missions. This was the fundamental desire of the Christian churches of all denominations. Many people are earnestly praying for the disestablishment of the English church, whilst many would refuse so to do simply because they have not sound Scriptural views of the nature and constitution of a true Christian church.

SATURDAY EVE. 8 O'CLOCK, FEB. 27TH, 1875

Another wild winterly day. Four ploughs out stirring the fallows in the black pond field. Pink has been colicked very severely for about three hours. Foreman gave her two drinks of our famous Red oil, and a pint of linseed oil, which, we have reason to hope, through the blessing of God has produced the desired effect. Our anxiety increases about Norman. His strength appeared much diminished this morning and through the day. A second bottle of tonic medicine with an half crown bottle of Dr. Jongh's Codliver Oil. The first dose produced sickness and copious vomiting. He looks more faded today. The lustre of his beautiful bright eyes was never so bedimmed and his feebleness never so apparent. A mysterious blight is upon him for the time being. Our Jesus can give the healing touch if He sees best. He can restore him to us. It is evident by the Dr.'s description of his case that there exists a secret known only to Heaven. It is still undisclosed to the Physician or ourselves. Some children die of a wasting disease. We have heard no account of or reason given for the wasting going on in our own darling babe.

I feel the winter very testing to my own constitution and general health. I take codliver oil in its raw and unprepared or unpurified state. Like my little son, Norman, my cold returns upon me.

Today I paid J. Drew 33/-, being one day absent from work. He paid me 21/- towards a qr. of wheat. Branwick 36/- for a fortnight and he paid me 20/-. Shadlock and J. Wright 36/- each. Tom Lawton [and] C. Smith 54/-, Bocock 34/-, Holmes 20/-.

Norman has a body bandage on tonight. I sit watching and rocking him when necessary until about twelve or one o'clock, for Lizzie to have some sleep.

WEDNESDAY MORN. 9 O'CLOCK, MARCH 3RD, 1875

March comes in like a lion. Like Feb. the three days continue in uniform severity. Feb. has not brought with it drenching rains but on the contrary has left our cisterns and drains almost empty. The earth is still wrapt in a thin coverlet of snow and hail.

We could not finish our last stack of wheat yesterday on account of sleet and snow which continued through the afternoon. On Monday we thrashed one stack. Yesterday our lambing ewes were drawn off to the lamb pens, their time having arrived for commencing lambing. We have felt some apprehension on account of a large number having distemper and casting lamb through the district and in the immediate neighbourhood. At Mr. Wilson's sale on Monday last hoggets only made about 45/- and ewes 33/- per head. The prospect for keeping is very dark and distant.

On Monday last I put 10/- in the chapel offering-box as a thanks-offering for the good health of my own flock. I gave, too, to Thomas Pierce a breast of mutton. I called to see him. He has been ill sixteen weeks, and how graphically he and his wife told their tale of suffering. How slight my own winter affliction compared with theirs! The man appears to have two conflicting complaints, rheumatic gout in his limbs and cough and expectoration from his lungs. The medicine which relieves one agravates the other. His affliction began with scarlet fever.

We are thrashing again this morning. C. Standaloft has come this morning to brick up and plaister the new cribb in middle stable where Le Bon lodges, also to zinc the cribb bottom and nail hooping iron on cap to prevent horses from biting.

We have seldom seen the sun the last few weeks. The heavy curtain of cloud has rarely been drawn back, but thickly hung over the face of heaven. The stormy wind for many successive days have fulfilled God's word.

Pink continued very puny and unwell through Sunday. At night we gave her one of Cunningham's balls, and I trust she has improved and [is] out of danger. Her appetite was better yesterday though I heard her cough. It is a severe cold.

Poor old Frank Riggall, once shepherd for my Father, died last Sunday.

Another thanksgiving to Heaven for His goodness in partially restoring my little son, Norman. One of his top teeth has made its appearence and the other is just peeping. The lancing has proved effectual in opening their way into daylight.

FRIDAY EVE. 6 O'CLOCK, MARCH 5TH, 1875

Yesterday we finished thrashing for this season. The three wheat-stacks have yielded 154 qrs. from the machine. I paid off Robinson 20/-, the two Atkinsons 20/- each, and Parker 16/-, the two women 25/-. I presented Foster Blanchard and his comrade Bumper 1/- each.

The lambing has commenced. We have eighty ewes lambed. One

has cast lamb, two have lambed pairs, and five single. The ewes have had no cake, corn, or cutmeat through the winter until yesterday morning we commence giving cotton and linseed cake and oats.

I have now uncorked my Winchester of codliver oil and filled a two shilling bottle.

Four ploughs were stirring fallows in black pond field yesterday and today.

On Wednesday last I bought about 45 thousand early cabbage plants of Croft, the gardener, of Binbrook, also 15 qrs. of seed oats of Coates Sharpley. They are from Calcethorpe, grown by the late Isaac Sharpley.

Today we have rubbed Charlie, Pink and Bonnie with mustard to relieve their coughs.

We experienced a succession of sharp frosts. The turnips are nearly eaten on many farms and the sheep trade is very flat. 50/- each for good hoggets is a low price compared with other things and with fat meat. Mr. Robert Riggall of Ulceby made an observant remark about this season to brother Will. He stated that after the frosts [we have had] the breaking up of the frosts has not been succeeded by the usual rainfall. When the long snow storm passed, its departure was not accompanied by the ordinary rains. This constitutes the exceptional character of this winter.

Mr. R. looks upon this as a sign of another dry summer. I was somewhat taken by surprise. He said that 1825 was a dry summer as well as 1826. It seems to present the present season in a new light to my own mind. We know this fact, that the downfall through this winter was almost exclusively snow. But does this necessarily precede a dry summer? Time will prove.

SATURDAY MORN. 12.30, MARCH 6TH, 1875

A rose-coloured morn often opens into a rainy day. It is the first rainy day we have witnessed for some time.

Another pair of lambs came this morning about six o'clock. The horses have come home from stirring. Will and I have walked to the village and back and held conversation upon novels and novel writers.

The groom has taken Pink and trap to Louth for Denison. The school has a holiday on Monday next on account of one [of] the old scholars having taken a scholarship. Mr. Page said their motive was to give an impetus to the boys to use every endeavour to attain similar distinction.

MONDAY EVE. 7.40, MARCH 8TH, 1875

Today 4 horses and waggon have been to Calcethorpe for 15 qrs. of oats for seed, price 31/-; also another waggon has been to Louth for 1½ tons of linseed and 1 ton cotton cake.

The lambing progresses slowly yet; thank Heaven there are no more cast lambs. My ewes appear quite healthy at present. We have hung one bell round a ewe's neck and tied fresh tarred band round the young lambs' necks to prevent the foxes seizing them. It is the first time we have tried the band experiment as a preventative to foxes. I have taken note of the respective ram marks. The ewes tupped by the two rams I bought of Mr. Clarke of Welton are marked on the near shoulder, Mr. Sharpley's of Kelstern on the far shoulder. Our own old sheep being used the third year on the near hip, Mr. Harwood Mackinder's shealing [shearling] sheep on the far hip.

Four out of the five rams were bought last season and three are shealings [shearlings]. The one bought of Mr. Sharpley is an old sheep but perhaps good for another season of service. Holmes marks off the young lambs like their mothers that we may judge which progeny grow up the best sheep. I hope to improve my flock by choosing good rams, by care and attention to their diet, to keeping them comparatively free from filth and everything having a tendency to engender or promote disease. I think the ewes have had a pretty good supply of turnips through the winter, and recently they have been good in quality. In consequence of being sown a second time they were late grown and full of nuterative [nutritive] juice.

We have a remarkable change in the weather with a change in the moon. Yesterday and today have been fine, genial and balmy days. Today we have enjoyed the cheery sunshine. It has improved my circulation. Another splendid rain came last night.

I enjoyed my service at Torrington. I started off in the morning on Charlie, but was obliged to turn back and take Augur and trap for night. I preached from 3rd. ch. John, 3rd verse. We had a delightful season.

My horses are many of them out of order; they suffer from severe coughs of an influenza type. My waggoner says he has a good receipt [recipe] for horse balls, and approved by Mr. Cresswell.

Will Riggall is still with us, but is far from well.

Annie writes a most meloncholy letter about poor Lizzie Collett. Her histeria [hysteria] borders on insanity. It is a sad calamity indeed.

THURSDAY EVE. 7 O'CLOCK, MARCH 11TH, 1875

I will name this my farm and household diary. I use another vol. for more strictly literary and religious jottings. I often bring them out together and turn from one to the other according to circumstances. As in mistake, I have misplaced my farming notes in the other book, I must refer to page 34 and the five following pages, viz. 35, 36, 37 and 38, extending from March 5th to 8th.

Yesterday and Tuesday were ploughing turnips land in top 18 acres in addition to dragging and working about 4 acres for cabbages.

Croft, gardener, came up yesterday morning and took the chestnut pony rising three years old. He paid me £22/0/0 according to bargain. He and I arranged with the foreman to send a cart and two horses tomorrow morning to fetch the plants.

The last two days the temperature was low; the wind came back into the ungenial quarter, and today the wind blows keen and cutting from the east. Vegetation progresses very slowly, scarcely perceptable, and the prospect of keeping still distant. However, we must bear in mind that March grass is worth little as it is generally treacherous. However, we are not witnessing any unnatural forcing this year, though the last few days have been bright and sunny. Yesterday I purchased four bells to strap around the ewes' necks to excite the suspicions and fears of foxes. We are progressing favourably with lambing. There are strikingly few cast lambs or have dead lambs. The third week ewes appear the most unhealthy; two of them have died and Robinson has taken their carcases today, though not from lambing.

Today we have twicthed [twitched] the cabbage land and commenced ridging and manuring.

Arthur was over my crews yesterday and remarked that our beasts have never been so low in condition as at present. I told him my fodder was never so inferior. There is nothing but wheat straw for them to eat.[78] All being well, I shall have plenty of barley straw next winter, having only sown about 48 acres of wheat.

Yesterday Denison came from school to meet me about one o'clock. I walked down to Plumptree's Photo Establishment and paid 8/- for my doz. Vinettes. Denison ordered half a dozen of each negative taken of William Riggall, his Uncle. I bought him a Scripture text book for a birthday present, price 1/6, also the Little Folks' vol. for 1875, with a beautiful coloured portrait of a young girl, good enough to frame and hang in a nursery, the two price 1/-. I bought of Mr. Birkett 1 bottle rum, 1 of gin and a dozen of bitter beer. I buy it for my friends and not for myself. I never drink anything of an alcoholic nature nor take condiments of a stimulating character such as pepper, vinegar, mustard (not even to beef).

This has been a busy day with me personally. I have used the axe vigourously amongst the firewood. My stick hill is reduced to a very small compass. It was once a high stack of fuel but the axe has brought it low. I have alternately chopped, tented crows off wheat, farmed and nursed and driven my Lizzie, Frank and Norman with Pink and phaeton to post.

Norman's state of health is somewhat puzzling and perplexing. He seems at a standstill in regard to growth and flesh. He takes but little food beside his mother's milk. He will be twelve months old the first of April next. His mother says she is afraid to wean him on account of his poor appetite. He sometimes looks as pale as death, though his eyes are lustrous and he seems more cheerful and lively, yet his original vivacity has not yet returned. He does not realise his former strength and vigour. His mother is often a good deal concerned and anxious about him. However, the weaning day must come, and before long.

FRIDAY EVE. 6.30, MARCH 12TH, 1875

I have to note as a reminder that this is my eldest son, Denison's birthday. He is eleven years old today. Tomorrow he enters upon his 12th year. In referring to my family register I find it recorded; Cornelius Denison Stovin, born March 12th, 1864. He has received one year of classical education in the Louth Grammar school.

On Wednesday afternoon last I took the liberty of walking into the schoolroom during school hours. I saw long rows of boys, grouped according to their ages, engaged in their respective studies. Denison appeared to have a geographical map before him. He gave me a sly glance or two. Mr. Page, the third master, with whom Denison boards, received me very politely and conducted me through the main room into Mr. Hopwood's, the second schoolmaster, where the older and higher class boys are taught. The area of the building appears ample for the boys' health. It is a modern building and ought to be constructed on sanitary principles or in conformity to sanitary law.

But what about its educational furniture and educational machinery? It is entitled King Edward's Grammar School. Then educational forces of a royal character ought to centre here as elsewhere. It is well known that educational forces have greatly multiplied and been diffused over many of the schools in Brittain. The education of these Louth and neighbourhood boys should be of a princely character. As soon as I entered the room a gloomy feeling of disappointment suddenly came over me. I deeply felt the defective character of the boys' surroundings. I begin to question what is there here to enlarge either body or mind to any satisfactory extent. What to quicken the right kind of intelligence? What to fire the boys' enterprize? What to engage their hearts in the work? What to make the acquisition of knowledge their delight? I ask where are all the historic associations of the school? Why are there no grateful memories enshrined on the walls? I saw no memorial portrait. The walls are as bare and blank as when the bricklayer's trowel ceased to ring. All the treasures cased up within them were books, maps, and boys. I know the value of books but their value is enhanced to an indescribable extent by bringing the boys' minds into contact with nature, the Bible, and Art. Let science and the classics go hand in hand. There appears to be no fine open space for sports and amusements. Provision should be made to keep the boys cheerful.

Today we have been manuring cabbage land from barn crew, and splitting ridges.

The man is late home with the plants, not having yet arrived and the clock has struck eight.

Another repetition of black, wild, wintry days, a strong piercing wind with snow and sleet.

The mutton and beef trade were good at Louth Market and sheep trade better. Useful hoggets at Horncastle Mart yesterday from 45/- to 55/-.

Thank Heaven the lambing continues healthy. 5 last night and three today; fine, strong, promising lambs. The poor lambs enter a widely different climate. It has been remarked that the earlier lambs' wool grows more rapidly in consequence of the cold. The weather is more severe generally during the former part of the lambing season and the wool of the lamb is promoted in its growth, thus proving design in the adaptation of the lamb's nature to seasonal circumstance. Where there are keeping and other facilities it is thus more profitable to lamb early. The ewes are generally more healthy and not so inclined to fever and inflamation. Today I have received a written application from Mr. Dunn of the Bank for my ten shilling subscription to the Bible Society. It appears he is unwell and residing for a time at Hastings.

We have received two invitations today; one from Dexthorpe for Lizzie to go tomorrow, and another from Barlings for us all to go on the tenth of April next and for me to preach on Sunday which, if I live, will be my birthday. The weather is almost too bitter for Lizzie to go tomorrow but March keeps up its character for fickleness. We [have] had two or three days of June weather already.

SATURDAY NIGHT, 9.15, MARCH 13TH, 1875

The cabbage plants are from Middle Rasen, and only arrived about eleven o'clock last night. Instead of from 40 to 50 thousands there are seventy two thousands. My waggoner has brought the report that other persons came up and bid from 5/- to 5/6 per thousand. Croft bought them for 4/- per thousand and I agree to give him threepence per thousand profit. Of course we have had to prepare more land and I have endeavoured to glean some men to assist in planting. The land is in splendid condition and I have little doubt through the Divine blessing we shall realise a fine crop. My Foreman begins to be impatient about the Spring sowing. Nearly one half of the month is gone and we have made no commencement. We hope to begin scattering oats on Monday next. Owing to the limited quantity of wheat sown, we have a large breadth waiting for oats and barley.

I feel the rapid flight of time by the quick return of wages night.

James Drew 36/-, and he paid me 21/-, the last instalment of his quarter of wheat. Branwick 39/-, one Sunday in addition, feeding sheep. He paid the last 2/- owing. C. Shadlock 36/-, James Wright 33/-, Lawton 18/4, Bocock 34/-, C. Smith 54/-, Holmes 20/-.

I drove Pink and waggonette with Lizzie, Frank, and Norman, and Miss Alcock to Ludbro' Station. Lizzie has taken her little treasures to Dexthorpe for a few days. I hope and pray that the Lord may take care of them, that no calamity may befall. It will enhance the pleasure of Mabel's visit. It will be a feast to see her little brothers, especially Frank. Norman appears much better today. I thank God that my own strength has marvellously increased. I scarcely reccollect feeling so robust even through the most vivacious period of youth. I can run and work without exhaustion or fatigue.

We have had no gleams of sunshine today, nor does winter relax its stern sway over us. Evaporation is rapid; the roads are dry and clean. Our traps are scarcely soiled by a journey. A solitary song warbles from the thrush and a transcient [transient] one from the lark, as predictions that we are on the eve of a change.

Thank God the ungenial weather brings no reverse to the lambing. Three or four per day, about the same number at night (principally single lambs) come into living, breathing existence.

I trust most of the horses are recovering; the young Irish continue very puny and of course look very thin and spare. I told the Foreman to let them have some creed wheat.

TUESDAY EVE. 7.30, MARCH 16TH, 1875

This is an eventful day. It is full of bright promise. The farm is increasing in young life, animal and vegetable. The horses are improving in health. The farm today has been the scene of varied activity. Croft, the gardener, has planted nearly a peck of potatoes, a new kind of earlys, and sown a bed of carrot and another of onion seed, two rows of peas, two of beans, and up in the lodge garden a quantity of the four pounds of cabbage seed ordered from Carters.

Yesterday George Shaw, Butters, Malan and four boys and Shadlock were planting cabbages, and today the same, in addition to Rockliffe. Yesterday we commenced our new drilling machine. There is no mistake that it is constructed on the most advanced principle of the day. It is a noble machine and performs its work admirably. It scatters the beautiful black oats uniformly from one wheel to the other. Having no heavy coulters to drag, a pair of light horses can pull it with ease. My Foreman can ride and drive them with lines like a coachman. Augur and Coulam were in today. We are sowing sixteen acres and old nine acres now twelve (renominated Gravel pit field) with oats.

C. Smith was hindered yesterday by the sharp frost, also by the difficulty in finding a wheel small enough to sow the proper quantity of seed. We consider about one sack and two pecks the medium for this land.

Last year we found this mode of sowing answered. We had a quarter of barley more per acre than any previous year since this Foreman has been with us. But we must test it through a series of various seasons before we can speak confidently and definitely about results. Should I have an increase for ten years, it will ultimately prove a great boon. Through the kind superintending Providence of God the loss which I sustained through the strike last Spring will then be redeemed manyfold, or to a manifold extent. The strike sharpened my wits to invent some method of sowing with less labour and now one man performs the work of three, and if the corn is more productive by being promiscuously sown than in rows, there may possibly be a clear gain through life.

Let us now review the flock. What a pleasure to walk round with the shepherd this evening. Considering the many discouragements

I have had to contend with, I feel profoundly thankful to the God of all my mercies to witness a lambing season so healthy. It is always an intense enjoyment to see the bloom of health in either man or beast. My ewes and lambs enjoy good health. They lamb with very little difficulty, very few come wrong or dead. Not one single case of fever, mortification, or death, from any cause in lambing. Not many pairs, but fine, brisk, leggy well developed lambs, already beginning to skip like May-day time with their black necklaces on which, with the bells, have proved successful so far in keeping the foxes in abeyance. I look upon this as a remarkable fact, I mean this extraordinary good luck amongst my sheep. It seems so exceptional for me especially as many of my neighbours have experienced a serious taint. Mr. Benn, Burkinshaw, C. Sharpley and others, have had great numbers cast lamb.

The shepherd and I had a conversation upon this subject. He said people might think he was blowing his own trumpet too much but he believed our good luck was in part owing to his quiet manner of treating the ewes during pregnancy. He did not allow the dog to drive or gallop them about. He also turned them into the cow close off the turnips during quickening time. I don't know that it had ever struck me that the time of quickening was so critical yet I see it all very clearly now and wish to impress it upon my mind and memory that in future I may be more than ever upon my guard in relation to this very important circumstance. The seeds of disease are no doubt sown at a critical time like this. I think we have only lost four ewes by death since turning to the rams. It appears we put 395 to the tup and there are 385 left, and six of this deficiency are sold fat with the ten Stamp bought of me the other day at 57/- each.

If a peck of March dust be worth a queen's ransom then it augurs well for a good agricultural year. The roads are clean and dry and continued so for many days past with a low temperature. The wind has fitfully changed through the day, and Holmes thinks we shall have some rain because the peacocks have made such an horrible row. The beauty of their plumage does not harmonise with the frightfully offensive cry sounding through the woods. I was not aware that the cry of a peacock was any signal for us to take our coats and umbrellas.

This morning I walked to the village. I called at Mrs. Barton's. She gave me £20 towards the ten ewes Stamp bought the other day. I ordered $3^1/_4$ lb. mutton for Wm. French, who has been ill. I called upon Maultby, tailor, and ordered a pair of second mourning trousers and wrote out a new note for the sum of £42, having paid two instalments of £5 each, thus reducing the original £52 to £42.

WEDNESDAY NIGHT, 8.45, MARCH 17TH, 1875

A supremely biting wind from the sea has searched through my physical frame in riding to Louth with Pink and trap. The true meaning of a cold March day was fully and newly interpreted.

Today's experience has given me a more vivid realisation of winter cold. But the peacock's cry has only signalised a slight shower and not enough to lay the dust which the wind raised, somewhat to our annoyance. I am thankful to be so well off with turnips and cabbage. Keeping is becoming extremely scarce on most farms and the sheep must inevitably be driven to fairs and markets before the graziers are prepared to take them.

I have taken Hannah to Louth and sent her on to Dexthorpe to assist Lizzie with our two precious babes, Frank and Norman. Lizzie describes Norman as still looking very pale and sickly. It is strange that he does not gather strength or flesh. There is not vital force enough to gain back what he had lost. His assimilating powers are low and weak.

Lizzie writes also to say that I am to send someone over for an Alderney cow which Mr. Riggall has kindly presented to us in consideration of that we bought of him failing and wasting away.

Being alone, perhaps I shall be like Denison and Mabel, begin to count the days when they will all arrive at home to cheer and enliven the dwelling.

Today six extra men have been engaged setting cabbage plants. Will Cousins and father, Rockliffe, Butters, Shaw, Malan and four boys.

C. Smith has fears respecting our new drill because it has cups instead of roller. There is great danger of cup drills throwing out the seed unequally, leaving one breadth thinner than the other alternately. This is a serious evil and one which induces me to change from cup to roller in the preceding one. I feel annoyed that Mr. Ashley did not ask me which I should prefer and given me an opportunity of choosing. Smith holds that the old box would have answered all purposes and another new one was unnecessary. Croft and son have finished sowing the cabbage seed.

THURSDAY EVE. 7.15, MARCH 18TH, 1875

My dearest wife,

I received your interesting note this afternoon. I am sorry you were a little perplexed in reading my letter. The former part and that which referred to meeting you at Louth was written at home before receiving your first letter. The after postscript I wrote at Louth, and in a great hurry. I ought to have crossed out a portion which caused misunderstanding. You speak of remaining until Saturday only. I hope you will not hurry home on my account. I thought you might feel afraid to stay longer as I persisted in saying I would send for you.

Mabel has written a very warm affectionate note asking me to meet her at Ludbro' Station next Tuesday. Miss Riggall wishes her to remain the afternoon for school and come by the six o'clock train but Mabel is particularly anxious to come by the two o'clock train instead.

There is one very bright statement in your communication which greatly delights me. You say Norman is eating better. I wish he would follow his brother Frank's example in that department. There would be some hope of his physical development. I wish he could eat with the same relish that his father has done today. It is many years since I could (if ever) sit down to a hot roasted breast of mutton. In former times invariably my stomach refused the brisket part; but now my appetite is vigourous enough and strong enough for almost any kind of food. If any one has cause to praise God for decided improvement in health it is me. I thank God for the signs of improvement in Norman. The Dexthorpe air and society and treatment may, through the blessing of Divine Providence, form a favourable crisis in his health.

Perhaps you would like to [stay] until Monday next; if so write by return of post. I shall perhaps ride over to Caistor Fair tomorrow for sheep and Sat. for cattle. I am not compelled to send my hoggets to the Fair, having plenty of turnips and cabbage. I hope to be able to keep until Lincoln. The sheep are doing well at present. With the exception of two or three dead lambs we continue healthy at the lamb pens. We have not even a sickly ewe from lambing. It is truly remarkable for us, and exceptional.

I have been variously busy today. My hands engaged in wood-chopping, turnip dragging, crow tenting, riding Charlie to the village, looking at two of Mr. Dixon's rams, buying a one-horse cart built by the late W. Hall for his own especial use, the framework being heart of oak. He was said to be particularly skilled as a wheelwright and carpenter, etc. The price of the cart to me is £10/0/0. It has only been made four months.

Drilling barley in 30 acre. The frost was too severe to commence early in the morning. The duckfeet would not work. We finished cabbage planting today and I paid the men £3 for their time at the rate of 4/- per day. I said it was 10/- per acre but I had forgotten Malan and his boys. We must contrive something in future on a more economical scale.

FRIDAY AFTERNOON, 4.45, MARCH 19TH, 1875

Rode Charlie to Caistor Fair. He is much better of distemper which has prevailed amongst our horses, and not only our own, but through a wide district. I have four young Irish horses look miserably thin and eat very little from its effects.

Today we have finished sowing the sixty acres of old seeds left last Autumn.

The wind is still in the cold quarter, yet plenty of customers turn up to buy the sheep at a slight advance. They make from 42/- to 77/-.

I rose this morning between 5 and 6 o'clock and in starting it looked very much like being a wet journey, but the clouds dispersed and the sun shone brightly. It is exceptional to witness a sunny day this Spring. The heavens have been black with clouds and no rain. The principal part of the moisture through the winter has consisted in snow. If the tardiness of evaporation be any criterion of a dry summer then the signal has hung out visibly for sometime.

I will thank Heaven for His kind Providence in the daily continuance of good health amongst my lambing ewes. I can still note no death or sickness during the last twenty four hours. One ewe has lambed three fine he lambs. Holmes declares he never saw their equal for size and vigour. I observe my lambs are particularly strong. They inhale the bracing air a few times and in a short period are on their legs, capable of running after their mothers. The ewes, too, have a capital spring of milk. Holmes remarks the ewes began to improve from the time of bottling. I have been dragging turnips since tea for the lambing ewes.

My dearest wife,

James Drew has arrived with the Alderney cow. It is a noble present from our dear parents who, like their Heavenly Father, are ever lavishing loving kindnesses upon their beloved children. I think sometimes I feel more esteem and affection for them than for my own parents who are now, I trust, in Heaven. I really don't know that I ever met with a man so sublimely even and uniform in his excellence. There is something violet-like exhales from his very presence. I often feel a kind of indescribable pleasure in his company, perfectly unique. He overflows with real humanity. A Christian fragrance ever evolves from his person and character. In a wise sense he makes the best of both worlds. I am proud to stand towards him in the relationship of step-son. As long as my step-parents live at Dexthorpe it will be the most interesting home (next to my own) in existence. We may not exactly agree ecclesiastically, but we do religiously. In the fundamentals of Christianity practically we are one, if not theoretically. Let my soul burst forth in praise and thanksgiving.

Whatever shall you say to me, my dear Lizzie, for buying a second-hand one-horse cart! It has only been running about four months. I don't suppose such a one ordered new of any of our Binbrook carpenters would cost less than fourteen or fifteen pounds. It is a question whether an ordinary carpenter would build its equal in substance and quality of material, or spend upon [it] the same amount of workmanship. There is not a crevice or slip to be seen in either wheels or body. In one word, it is exceptionally good in construction and material. I think I hear it coming down the road for the first time. It will frequently substitute the heavy carts. You will be reconciled to the purchase when I inform you the cost is ten pounds.

You are perhaps not aware that my flock of sheep is divided and folded in two separate fields. The hoggets in the foot road 20 acres on white turnips, second sown. The lambing ewes in top eighteen acres at a convenient distance from the shepherd's house and lambpens. They walk to their fold and back. They feed on white turnips, too, a late crop and second sowing.

I will preserve two formal legal notices, just received, respecting Frank and Norman's vaccination. As you intend coming home next Monday, I need not send them by post. I am much cheered by your little gleaming note. It contains in a small compass much bright intelligence. I am very happy to hear the Dexthorpe air is bracing up Norman's energies and quickening his vital powers. I trust that his appetite will continue to increase and his digestive organs to strengthen.

SATURDAY EVE. 6.50, MARCH 20TH, 1875

My dearest wife,

I have now lighted my candle and engage my solitary evenings by writing to you. I hope to enjoy the pleasure of seeing our own dear family home next week for the holidays. Mabel will find it hard work to eat her breakfast on Tuesday morning for joy that the very day of departure having arrived.

The Spring quarter comes in tomorrow. Shall we have a change in the weather?

How cold and dry with sharp frosts at night, with complete stagnation throughout vegetation. Winter still perversely holds her iron sway over vegetable life. When will her despotism be broken? Another day of unbroken cloud, storm and sleet.

You anticipated in your note my going to Caistor. I am thankful to inform you that Charlie is so far recovered that I ventured to ride him both days to the Fair. His cough is almost gone. I hope to ride him again tomorrow to my appointment at Ludford.

I feel somewhat disappointed that we progress so slowly with our Spring sowing. The sharp frosts prevent us going out first thing in the morning and the foreman says we only get part of a day's work done. We shall be a long time fetching up our work at this rate. We have about 30 acres or more of turnip land to plough and 114 acres of barley to sow.

Poor Typler has received another kick on his hind leg. The waggoner has rubbed it with Robinson's oil. I have mixed some mustard for the young horses' throats to relieve their cough. Their throats seem sore and consequently eating is painful, at least swallowing.

You will be surprised to hear that notwithstanding the scarcity of grass the better class of cattle of good age sold well, while the younger and poorer were cheaper and more difficult.

Today the waggoner has dragged a part of six acres through the valley and along the beds of twitch. We managed badly in not cleaning the land better in a dry summer like last. We steam cultivated last Spring and again in the Autumn and still we are behind. My wife, your question comes back upon me with renewed force. It is a question you have often repeated, and its reasonableness appears with increased vividness. How is it that with all the extra cost in steam and horseflesh the work of the farm is not more advanced? The principal part of the land ought to be finished sowing in this month.

MONDAY EVE. 7.15, MARCH 29TH, 1875

The last week has continued dry and cold. The farm work has progressed slowly. We have 20 acres or more to plough and eighty still unsown. The lambing is still favourable. We have about forty pairs, and the single ones are very fine and grow rapidly. I scarcely reccollect our lambs looking so well. The cabbages are nearly done as well as the turnips that, if it please God to send us rain and warmer weather, we shall pass through the scarce season without harm.

The Alderney cow which Mr. Riggall kindly gave us the other day has this evening calved two calves.

BINBROOK, SATURDAY EVE. 7.15, APRIL 3RD, 1875

We have anxiously looked for warmer weather and showers. A very slight one came last night and another this evening. Wind south-west and cool. Today I rode Charlie to Caistor and sold Mr.Pale-thorpe sixty hoggets at 54/- and forty he's and she's at 43/-, total £248.

On Thursday last William Norman Stovin arrived to his first year, his birthday being the 1st of April. Lizzie and I drove Pink and phaeton to Louth on that day with him and Frank to Dr. Higgins to be vaccinated.

Yesterday Sir Edmond Beckett came here to look at the house and examined the plans and made further modifications and suggestions. We also changed the front door and lobby to the west instead of north.

Sir Edmond was stiff, formal, precise and cold in his manner. He evidently understands house building to the detail. He is conservative in retaining the present style of window. He made some valuable suggestions respecting the laying of concrete and drainage, etc. He will have it built substantially. I read the specifications to Lizzie last night and, faithfully carried out, it will be one of the best houses for its size in the county.

The work has somewhat progressed this week on the farm, but we still have fifty acres to sow and several acres to plough. Five tons of artificial manure from Robinson's has come to the Station this week. A portion of one load is sown in the six acres where the turnip crop failed.

Yesterday morning Bocock came to the kitchen door to inform me that the foot and mouth disease had visited my cattle. Today the greater portion are taken. It is rather unfortunate that they should have it so near selling time. However, I thank God that the sheep have escaped.

WEDNESDAY EVE. 8.30, APRIL 7TH, 1875

Commenced working the horses two yokes. C. Smith says we can manage to finish sowing all that is ploughed this week. There is enough left unploughed to occupy six ploughs a day.

Yesterday I took train from Louth to Alford to see Mr. Wood about our house. He had pencilled them [the plans] and sent them to Mr. Vesey. He hopes to start building on the first day of May.

THURSDAY EVE. 6.45, APRIL 8TH, 1875

Today I dwell in the bosom of my family. My dear wife and little ones constitute the family circle at home. Our house renovation constitutes an almost inexhaustible topic for conversation. The third set of plans are being drawn and Sir Edmond says they are to be final. Yesterday James Iles seemed to throw confusion into the whole. He suggested that the old house remain pretty nearly as it is, and not pull the chimneys down, which would be a complete revolution of the plans inspected and approved by Sir Edmond. But I said we had no intention to do any such thing. The old house must be thoroughly renovated to remove the miasma which has hung about it for so many years.

George and Pollie came over from Barlings[79] to meet Sir Edmond to see if there were any chance of securing Skallows Hall and turn the house into cottages, but this proved abortive; the landlord was too distant and was unapproachable. However, Pollie made the suggestion that the privies be removed from the kitchen window, which we intend acting upon.

We have finished ploughing turnip land today except the headlands and a small piece of cabbage land. Last night we had a very nice rain though not heavy. In kicking over the clods I find they are not wet through. This is a foggy day and there is still a rawness in the atmosphere. The pastures are very short. It is unfavourable weather for my cattle just at the present juncture. Yesterday they seemed like recovering but this cold damp day retards them. The white cow formerly from Snitterly is suffering most. The two young calves from the Dexthorpe Alderney have taken the disease and Bocock thinks one of them will have difficulty in recovering. He is afraid it will die. I believe this disease has visited us three times in four years.

Today C. Shadlock has sown some of Robinson's corn manure on wheat stubble 20 acres. Some is sown on a portion of 6 acre turnip land and on part of foot road 20 acre. We aim to sow it where the turnips miss or are very light. I am thankful the horses are considerably improved in health. The four young Irish work again.

We have a very strong and tall thorn hedge on two sides of our cow close, which I have let to Harness to plash at 5/- per chain. It is a very high price but it requires a good deal of banking to be done and a considerable amount of coarse wood will be cut out.

The lambing season is nearly expired, only about half a score being left to lamb. There appear to be fifteen barren. According to Holmes' account we shall raise 305 lambs from 295 ewes. This is moderately fair luck when we consider how our neighbours have fared. I have often thanked God that my flock has escaped the distemper which has visited many so fatally this Spring. We have very little loss amongst the lambs since going into the pastures.

Holmes was obliged to kill one of the she hoggets today and was doubtful whether it will dress good meat as its blood was so black.

Yesterday Denison came out to meet me as usual. He is fond of having an hour with me in the town. It is a change in the routine of his recreations. He has considerable preference to business and active life. School work is dry and somewhat distasteful to him at present.

FRIDAY EVE. 7 O'CLOCK, BINBROOK, APRIL 9TH

3 new bedroom grates 17/- each.
4 new mantlepieces 30/- each.
1 new low room do. 60/-.
2 new grates, dining and drawing room. 60/- each.
2 cupboards with bookcases with glass doors.
2 new iron bedsteads. £5 each.
1 new washhand stand and dressing table. £5 each.
1 new washhand do. 20/-.
2 new carpets for dining and drawing rooms, and new furniture for dining room, about £60.
Hangings for best bed. £15.
Stairs and landing carpet. £5.
Summer and winter curtains. £15.
Window blinds. 20/-.
According to our present calculations the cost of refurnishing the renovated and enlarged dwelling will amount to at least £120/0/0.

Another strong, cold, northern breeze with drizzling rain. We have finished ploughing the Spring corn land this afternoon, and as soon as the weather permits the course is open for scattering the remaining portion of seed.

The ten quarters of sainfoin has arrived, which we purpose drilling in the wheat stubble 20 acre.

I am afraid the cold and damp winds are searching disastrously through the afflicted cattle's constitution. Two out of the three crewyards have sheds to shelter them. They raise their backs and look very miserable. They present a most meloncholy aspect. I am led to fear lest the permanent effects prove calamitous. I can only pray, if it be God's will, we may soon witness a more favourable change. There is this consolation, that we have an all-wise and loving [Father].

SATURDAY EVE. 6.45, BINBROOK, APRIL 10TH, 1875

Tomorrow being my birthday we have had some commemorative plum cake for tea this evening instead. My wife is very skilful in many kinds of confectionary. She is gifted in plain and fancy cooking and in general housekeeping. She is a cheerful, loving wife, a good housekeeper, a faithful friend, a tender, watchful and wise mother. Her offspring will ever have reason to bless her memory. She lavishes attention and labour upon her children. She sacrifices many an hour of needful rest for their safety and comfort.

Oh, the pain and weariness she has endured for their sakes! I sometimes wonder what the result of the large combination of diligence and perseverance will be. I can only say that whenever my own thoughts recur to my dear mother's memory I feel a general impression of gratitude for the treatment I received at her judicious hands. Many a wise and holy lesson were inculcated.

Today four horses and waggon have carried home two more tons of linseed and one of cotton cakes. I am thankful that the cattle are gradually recovering, at least those in the shed crew which were taken first.

As the day became a little dryer after more rain through the night we ventured to finish drilling the footroad twenty acres. It is the strongest and most tenacious bit of land on the farm. The drill went from foot road to top eighteen acres this afternoon. We have now a little more than two days' work sowing. Most of the land is working down in fine condition. The beautiful rain has saved considerable labour in harrowing and rolling.

James Drew is unwell at home, off two days this week. Paid him 30/-. Branwick 39/-, one Sunday. C. Shadlock 36/-, James Wright 36/-, C. Smith and Bocock £4/8/0. Lawton, boy, 17/6, two Sundays. Holmes, shepherd, 20/-.

I have given Holmes orders about the placing of the sheep troughs on the hills and poorer parts of the fields, also to search over the sheep nets, throwing together those which require re-tarring and those which only require mending, and leaving the rest aside to be sold amongst waste material. I have bought 12 new nets, 50 yards, 15/- each. Elliot says the hemp does not absorb sufficient tar when new but after being in use one year they will re-tar to great advantage and extend the wear a much greater length of time.

In walking through my cowstable the other day I observed Bocock cleaning out the cows' water troughs. He says they poke cutmeat and other refuse into them with their horns, which soon begins to ferment, causing an offensive smell. He performs this work about once a fortnight. He has not had the pipes stopped once this season.

It reminds me of Coney's ignorance and mismanagement in cutting the pipes through into holes by pushing down an iron rod every time they became obstructed. This caused serious labour and expense. It required a plumber and bricklayer to rectify it.

The clouds have broken very nicely this afternoon and the sun seemed quite cheery after a long absence. Tonight the moon and stars are very beautiful and pleasing. I have just taken a romp in the garden, and, while meditating and praying, various thoughts have crossed my mind. Some of my habits of long standing have already made a mark upon my physical form. My habit of reading while walking has bent my head and neck forward. I must endeavour to draw up my person into its more natural shape.

SUNDAY MORN. 9.15, APRIL 11TH, 1875

This is the great red-letter day of my life. My immediate career commenced forty five years ago today. It is an appropriate season for retrospection. How have I conducted myself during these momentous years of my biography? What will be the eternal issues? I feel it has been a broken and imperfect tissue. I have come short of my ideal. I have not reached the standard raised for attainment. Yet, thank God, aspiration and ambition still glow, and the struggle continues. I am still hopeful of myself and society at large. Few lives have been more blessed, at least since I gave myself to Christ.

TUESDAY EVE. 8 O'CLOCK, APRIL 13TH, 1875

Horsework has been done in four separate fields today. We were rolling in foot road twenty acre, Cambridge rolling in top eighteen acres. In consequence of James Drew being unwell at home, C. Shadlock was sowing small seeds with donkey, and Branwick harrowing with Jet. She goes very infirm. Her legs and feet are nearly done. C. Smith and James Wright sen. were drilling barley in middle 20 acres wheat stubble with Coulam and Augur. Wright junior followed the three horses duckfoot, and Will Bocock two young horses and harrow.

Mr. Robinson's artificial manure laid out very visibly on the hills. The soil pulverises freely and forms a promising seedbed. We dug the twitch out in the Autumn and again this Spring. A considerable quantity of Red Robin has already made its appearence, which is, I have no doubt, fatally disturbed. The land must be thoroughly well cleaned for a crop and for laying down with sainfoin.

After dinner Mr. J. Iles called for the tythe, £5/18/3. Invariably give him a cheque as it is tantamount to a receipt.

I am thankful to find in going over the stables the horses' health and appetite returned. C. Smith remarked today they eat as much in one day now as during a whole week. Another matter of thankfulness is that the cattle are improving, with the exception of one of the twin Alderney calves which appeared to be recovering until 11 o'clock this morning, when it was suddenly taken worse and died, to Bocock's surprise.

THURSDAY EVE. 8.45, BINBROOK, APRIL 15TH, 1875

Yesterday I sold Mr. Roberts about 60 qrs. of red wheat at 41/6 and 50 qrs. white at 47/6. We also finished sowing barley, and today we are drilling sainfoin, 4 bushels per acre in middle 20 acre; wheat stubble also sown with barley.

Yesterday morn was a white rhyme [rime] frost. No frost this morning, but the air continues chill. We are enjoying two or three fine sunny days. The sun went down deep in colour and ominously for more dry weather. We are sowing small seeds in six acres today.

James Drew is somewhat better and returned yesterday to his work. He feels better at work.

The Spring corn is all sown and the main part of the land is in a finely pulverised state. The small seeds over seventy acres and C. Smith said that two more fine days will nearly complete the process. The sheep are costing a good deal in cake in consequence of the shortness of the pastures. The troughs are out in every field, both grass and clover. Most are having half a pound of linseed and cotton cake in equal quantities. The shepherd carries them water from the black pond.

The cattle appear to have recovered from the foot and mouth attack without much injury.

SATURDAY EVE. 7 O'CLOCK, BINBROOK, APRIL 24TH, 1875

The weather has somewhat disastrously changed from Spring to winter. Holmes reports a white rhyme [rime] this morning, and ice as thick as a halfpenny piece. He was able to take off a panshion [panchion] of water the whole sheet of ice without breaking. Of course the pastures have wasted. Through this week we have had one or two very slight showers, scarcely sufficient to quell the dust.

The sudden death of James Drew has shaken my nerve, for I have felt a little jealous of my own state of health. The harassment of Lincoln Fair and this event have upset me to some extent. My feelings are very peculiar and desponding.

Dearest Lizzie, yesterday eve I arrived safely home and was thrown into a serious fit of agitation in receiving the intelligence of the unexpected death of James Drew. Having left you behind, and returning to an almost deserted house, I fell into a state of nervous excitement and depression of spirits. However, I must fall back upon the consolation that I am in the Lord's hands and He will do what is best.

We are engaged delivering red and white wheat and bringing coals for labourers.

I paid Whelpton for half his time in repairing plantation fences, 19/3, also my constant labourers, James Wright, 36/-, Branwick, 36/-, C. Shadlock 36/-, C. Smith 54/-, Bocock 34/-, Holmes 20/-, Lawton, boy, 15/-.

BINBROOK, WEDNESDAY MORN, 8.30, APRIL 28TH, 1875

Glory be to God for a few drops yesterday morning and again this. Having received very little dew the last few nights, a few drops are very precious, though only as much as a slight dew, for this is about what our rains amount to.

My dear wife and two infants returned from Hackthorne yesterday afternoon. I was delighted to see them. I seem to have become so thoroughly domesticated that my happiness is diminished in their absence. May God help me to provide for their comfort and efficiency in life.

I thank God that the weather is milder, but the ground looks parched and vegitation makes slow progress. The pastures continue extremely bare. The clouds gather and disperse without refreshing the earth. For many days past the Heavens appear to promise but very small fulfilment.

I paid Croft the remainder of his bill for cabbage plants and gardening, £17. He had received £12 of this sum on account. I can perceive them grown the last few days but they thirst. We are dragging with six horses instead of stirring with ploughs. We are burning the first coat of twitch in Binbrook field and 20 acre, in small heaps. This is unique on my farm in April.

We have delivered 83 qrs. of red and 45 qrs. of white wheat to Mr. Roberts at 41/6 red and 47/6 white.

Servants hired.

THURSDAY EVE. 7.45, MAY 20TH, 1875

Yesterday I hired two Waggoners;

John Dawson, Louth, first waggoner.

Wages, £24/0/0.

Samuel Gant Harrington, second do.

Wages, £19/0/0.

Betsy Stevenson, Ulceby, cook and all, for the summer.

Wages, £11/0/0.

I may exclaim with the poet, 'Oh, for a heart to praise my God,' for a beautiful rain commencing on Tuesday last about half past four o'clock in the morning. The land was unprecedently dry and thirsty. We have experienced the dryest Spring within the reccollection of the oldest living persons. We have had very little difficulty in cleaning land.

In consequence of the long drought, I felt almost that my Spring corn was in jeapardy. I had forty or fifty acres later sown than my neighbours, and having an unusual breadth of Spring corn sown I was considerably anxious about my venture. My pastures have not recovered from the early stocking. They are exceedingly bare.

BURTON'S SHOP, LOUTH, JUNE 7TH, 1875, EIGHT O'CLOCK

Conveyed Denison with Pink and dogcart back to King Edward's Grammar School.

The dry season continues with unprecedented severity for Spring, being the dryest ever known. The pastures are barer than ever witnessed so early, grass even as scarce as in ordinary dry seasons the latter part of summer. The showers that come often end in a few drops. The thunder showers fall very partially.

The last few days we have led about 20,000 more bricks from Ludbro' Station, made at Falsthorpe brickyard, of a superior class. On Saturday last we fetched a waggon load of lime from Mrs. Clapham's kilns. We found also a vein of splendid sand in the old 9 acres gravel pit field. This morning we send a cart down to Ludbro'

Station for bricklayers and tools to commence the work of house enlargement and restoration.

I am thankful to record that my corn mentains its colour remarkably well considering the few and scanty showers that have fallen. I have seen no cabbages look so forward as well as my own in this neighbourhood. At present my farm looks fairly, perhaps not quite so forward compared with nearest neighbours, still the Spring corn presents a rank appearence. I like to see a dark green hue. It is the luxuriant colour in June. My land does not scarp and dry out so soon as Frank's at Hackthorne. He makes bitter complaints about his corn. He describes it as fading and wasting every day, and more threatening than last year. Mrs. Riggall wrote last week that they had a beautiful shower last Friday afternoon. They were more favoured than we. We had not so much as would amount to a good dew. A few drops have fallen again this morning.

Cattle is lower in price than for many years passed. Frank has sold his wool at 45/- per todd, 400 hoggets and 600 ewes. There seems a good demand for the new clip, which is not likely to be very heavy as last summer, and this Spring being ex [tremely dry] the sheep and lambs are pressed into the market prematurely and consequently the flocks are considerably reduced. The new clip must necessarily be smaller.

The Almighty has a design in sending these droughts; we may not be permitted to see the precise purpose but we know that all nature is arranged and in full action to serve the great Mediatorial monarch, the risen Redeemer.

NOTES

1 Grandson of J. B. Sharpley of Louth who, with Denison, was a weekly boarder at Louth Grammar School.
2 By Victorian times, endowments for grammar schools, stated in sums relating to money values of the sixteenth and seventeenth centuries, had become very small. The Head and other masters had to supplement their income by taking boarders, and charging fees. The law only allowed grammar schools to apply their endowments to the teaching of classics. Any other subject had to be paid for out of fees. White's Lincolnshire Directory (1872) states that the Louth school 'is free for Latin and Greek to all boys admitted by the Trustees; but for all other branches of education each pupil pays from 10s. to 25s. per quarter according to age, under the name of "head money"'.
3 White's Directory (1872) gives a more encouraging picture of the exterior. 'The school [rebuilt in 1852] with other requisite buildings... form a pretty and compact structure and are of brick and stone dressings, in the Tudor style. Cost of whole about £3000.'
4 See First Journal, note 24, p. 120.
5 Harvest suppers were less common in the latter part of the nineteenth century (although some wealthier farmers later

revived them), but this reference to the tradition of riding with the last load still remained on farms.

One youth would shout out (with others blowing horns),
'I've rent my clothes and torn my skin
To get my master's harvest in.
We have not thrown over, nor yet stuck fast,
And the load we are on is the last... the last...
Hurrah.'

(Winn Diary, September 11th, 1844, mentioned by James Obelkevich, 'Religion and Rural Society, South Lindsey, 1825-1875', Clarendon Press, 1976, p. 58.)

6 Obelkevich comments that Methodist services in South Lindsey were often scheduled so as to avoid direct conflict with those in the parish church, and members often attended both church and chapel on the same day ('Religion and Rural Society', p. 214). In some parishes, however, the parish clergy were hostile to Methodists, and C.S. commented on such a situation in his last journal in 1893, when he had moved from Binbrook to Hogsthorpe in the marsh district.

7 Louth Union Board of Guardians. See First Journal, note 77, p. 125, and Introduction, p. 14.

8 Tennyson, who was a pupil of the school in 1816, testified that his Headmaster was 'a tempestuous flogging master of the old stamp', and there seemed to have been little change some 60 years later. Mr. Page, who was in charge of the boarding house, was first assistant to the Warden. In 1875 his salary was raised from £100 to £110 (Minutes of Louth Grammar School Governors, Lincoln Archives).

9 The Denison family were absentee landlords, residing in Yorkshire, so that the tenants might not have expected to attend the funeral, as would the tenants of a resident landlord (see Appendix IV). C.S.'s own relationship with his first landlord, however, was, as he described it, closer than was customary between absentee landlords and their tenants.

10 The foreman's and shepherd's cottages, built in 1856, were the only cottages other than the lodge which then existed on the farm.

11 See First Journal, note 74, p. 125.

12 The Second Journal starts in September 1874, and the labour troubles to which he refers (also on p. 146) took place between February and May of that year. (See Rex Russell, 'The Revolt of the Field in Lincolnshire', section IV, for contemporary accounts.) The labourers were striking for an increase of wages from 18s. to 21s. per week, and more cottages to house them on the farms. A lock-out by local farmers in the Binbrook district followed the strike, and C.S. was one of the 46 farmers who signed a public notice on Wednesday, March 11th, 1874 initiating the lock-out. Deadlock was followed by a compromise, but after this there was an increased drive by the unions for emigration.

13 See Introduction, p. 10.
14 First Journal, p. 51.
15 Both died in 1855. His eldest sister was only aged 27. See Appendix III.
16 One of the chief grievances of tenant farmers was the preservation by the landlords of plantations and hedgerows, as cover for game, to the detriment of the farmers' crops. See Introduction, p. 12.
17 The new landlord's son-in-law, who spent more time at Binbrook than his father-in-law, and regularly had shooting parties over the farm. See also First Journal, note 161, p. 132.
18 See also First Journal, note 92, p. 127. The Second Journal gradually reveals the increasing difficulties of the Free Methodists to maintain the circuit and village chapels without increasing the burden of debt. Movement to the towns and emigration were beginning to depopulate these rural areas, and prosperity was declining. Many villages still had three Methodist chapels - Wesleyan, Free and Primitive Methodists.
19 His third son, born May 1st, 1874.
20 A mill where cattle cake was made. Linseed was being imported in considerable quantities.
21 Dr. F. W. Farrar, Dean of Canterbury (2nd edn., London, 1874).
22 At the Free Methodist chapel, Binbrook.
23 'The Mediatorial Sovereignty, the mystery of Christ, and the revelation of the Old and New Testaments', 1863. George Steward was an Independent minister.
24 The influence of his dominant mother-in-law, Mrs. Francis Riggall of Dexthorpe is clearly evident. The Dexthorpe family seemed determined that the new home of their eldest daughter should have all the attributes considered suitable for the household of one of the 'new' farmers of the later nineteenth century.
25 His brother-in-law, who lived at Hackthorne.
26 Binbrook Hall was 3 miles from the village.
27 In both journals there are a number of instances of confined labourers drawing on their annual wage for specific purposes. Day outings to nearby Lincolnshire seaside resorts took place every summer. Farm labourers with their families would go in gaily decorated hay waggons to Cleethorpes or Mablethorpe.
28 A nursemaid had been added to the domestic staff of cook and housemaid to look after the two young children, Frank, aged two, and the baby, William Norman.
29 Mr. J. Iles was tenant of the adjoining Binbrook Hill Farm, also a part of the Denison estate.
30 The farm was first tenanted by his grandfather, George Stovin in 1810. See Introduction, p. 3.
31 See note 10 above. Many farm workers had to travel long distances to work each day from the rented accommodation in Binbrook and other 'open' villages. Binbrook Hall Farm at this date had cottages for the foreman and shepherd only, and one

large bedroom in the foreman's cottage where the single waggoners slept.

32 The Aggregate was an annual circuit event combining special Sunday services at which the President was usually asked to preach, and a tea and meetings on the following Monday.

33 Steam ploughs were first used in cornfields in 1857. From the mid-1850s also, stationary steam engines were employed to move the plough to and fro across the field on an endless wire rope. From 1860, Fowler developed the use of 2 engines on opposite ends of a field, each end having a winding drum (Michael Partridge, 'Farm Tools Through the Ages', Osprey (1973).

34 It was not until 1891 that two more cottages were built.

35 The carte-de-visite, a small photograph, $2^1/_4$ x 4 in., came into vogue in England during the 1850s, and was the first popular form of portrait photograph that appealed to all classes. The backs of the cartes were used by photographers to advertise their studios (B. E. C. Howarth Loomes, 'Victorian Photography', St. Martin's Press, New York (1974).

36 In 1862 twenty Methodist Day Schools existed in Lincs. It was a rare expansion, outside market towns, from the very successful establishment and maintenance of Sunday Schools. The greater provision was made before 1870, and they existed only for a few years. Numbers varied from 250 to 350. (Rex Russell, ' A History of Schools and Education in Lindsey, Lincolnshire, 1800-1902', part 4, Lindsey County Council Education Committee, 1967). Advertisements in the 'Lincoln, Rutland and Stamford Mercury' in 1872 and 1874 for a schoolmistress for the Binbrook School were signed by C.S., showing his prominence in the management of the school. The 1874 advertisement stated that a 'certified Female Teacher' was desired for the school 'which will be under Government Inspection'. Her other duty was to play the harmonium in the chapel. The salary in 1872 was £45. In 1874 applicants were asked to 'state salary'.

37 Mr. Dixon was the contractor mentioned in the First Journal, p. 49.

38 Skallows Hall: see First Journal, note 148, p. 131 and Appendix VIII.

39 Prayer meetings and class meetings during the week were central to the practice of members of the chapels.

40 'Quiet Resting Places and Other Sermons', 1863. Dr. Raleigh was a leading Congregationalist, Chairman of the Congregational Union in 1868.

41 First Journal, note 150, p. 132.

42 Special prayer meetings and a public display of evangelism were part of the missions aimed to convert the unbelievers.

43 After the strike and lock-out earlier in the year, farmers in the district took a tougher line on reducing wages. Rex Russell quotes extracts from contemporary issues of local papers in 'Revolt of the Field': '18th September, Boston. "The farm-

ers in one of the villages east of Boston have reduced the wages of the labourers to 2s. 6d. a day." 13th November, Alford. "Many on the Wolds have returned to work at 2s. 6d. per day, but those on the marsh still hold out" ' (p. 75).

44 I.e. 6 daily men, 5 confined men (foreman, garthman, shepherd and 2 waggoners), 3 farm boys and a groomboy: total 15.

45 The private school in Alford, then attended by Mabel, aged 9. It was run by Miss Riggall, a relation of the writer's wife. The school, as advertised in White's Lincolnshire Directory (1872), shows that on its staff were teachers unusually qualified for a small girls' school. The Assistant Head was 'G. Gregory, M.B. Oxon', and one of its 'efficient and accomplished governesses' held 'First Class University Certificates (Honours) for Latin, French, English and Mathematics and a South Kensington Certificate for Continental French, German and Drawing'. Pupils were 'successfully prepared for the Cambridge College of Preceptors Examinations', and 'the Laws of Hygiene were carefully observed'.

46 First Journal, note 16, p. 119.

47 See Introduction, p. 15.

48 Another Sharpley cousin, and his solicitor.

49 Wife of his mother's cousin, J. B. Sharpley, see Introduction, p. 4.

50 Until the last quarter of the nineteenth century many farmers kept no accounts beside their pass book at the bank. 'Not one in ten had the foggiest idea of whether the corn or the cattle or the poultry were each paying their way' (J. G. Cornish, 'Reminscences of Country Life', 1939, pp. 62-3). Sales, purchases, wages, etc. are recorded in the Journals of C.S. When there were gaps in the Journals, presumably no record was made.

51 A pig was part of the annual wage 'in kind' of the 'confined' labourers. At Binbrook Hall Farm this included the foreman, garthman and shepherd.

52 It was customary for free beer to be provided for the harvesters.

53 See note 36 above.

54 His wife's brother, Frank Riggall of Hackthorne.

55 Charles R. Fieldsend, whose farm adjoined Binbrook Hall Farm.

56 First Journal, note 155, p. 132.

57 New style farmers and their families allowed themselves what was not merely a rising standard of living but one which also expressed their social ambitions. The farmhouse itself took on a new role: 'Farmers' wives abandoned the dairy for the parlour, now adorned by a piano' (Obelkevich, 'Religion and Rural Society', p. 53). See comparison between farms in the writer's mother's day and 1874, First Journal, note 72, p. 125.

58 His wife's younger sister, who in later life became the second wife of Rev. Henry Lunn, Rector of West Ashby and father of Sir Henry Lunn.

59 This entry gives some idea of the responsibilities borne by the

one or two leading Free Methodists in each village chapel, and also the financial burdens attached, of which his wife bitterly complained.

60 James Everett (1784-1872), Wesleyan minister expelled from the Methodist conference, 1859. (See First Journal, note 45, p. 121.) Accumulated a unique collection of Methodist treasures. Author of satirical pen portraits, and known as the 'literary Hogarth of Methodism' (W. J. Townsend (ed.), 'A New History of Methodism', Hodder & Stoughton, 1909).

61 Farm tenanted by Frank Riggall.

62 Women and children all helped with the threshing. At Binbrook Hall the women and children would very likely be members of families of the farm labourers. On some farms they were part of gangs organised by a grand master and going from farm to farm. The Rector of Binbrook in 1867 wrote a paper strongly criticising this practice (Lincoln Archives). The practice was dropped in the latter part of the century.

63 First Journal, note 64, p. 124.

64 First Journal, note 72, p. 125.

65 45s. 2d. per quarter. In 1874 it had been 55s. 9d., see Appendix VII.

66 John Bright (1811-89). Liberal statesman, born at Rochdale, the son of a Quaker mill owner. With Cobden initiated the Anti-Corn Law League. Together they led the struggle for free trade. Largely instrumental in securing the passing of the Reform Bill of 1867.

67 See note 12 above.

68 Another of the many religious periodicals for which he seemed to have an inexhaustible appetite.

69 Water for drinking was drawn from one of the two pumps in Binbrook village.

70 Throughout the journals he mentions a number of different methods he tried for salving sheep, none very successful. See First Journal, note 49, p. 122.

71 One of the most active of the early Liberal Associations arose in Birmingham under Mr. J. Chamberlain.

72 Seemingly the 'electric' belt mentioned in the First Journal, p. 89. One of the numerous advertised remedies for rheumatism, colds, etc. He was constantly fascinated by new remedies and new inventions.

73 A noted beauty spot on the outskirts of Louth.

74 Dwight L. Moody (1837-99), a prominent American evangelist who gave up business for missionary work. In 1870 he met Ira D. Sankey, a hymn writer, and with him became noted for contributions to the growth of the 'gospel hymn'. They made extensive evangelical tours in Great Britain between 1873 and 1875. Moody preached the old fashioned gospel, colourfully emphasising the literal interpretation of the Bible.

75 One of the very popular moral children's tales, published by Ward, Lock & Co. See First Journal, note 123, p. 130.

76 Candlemas market was one of the Louth Hiring Fairs.

77 The Lodge was a very small cottage, used sometimes by members of the shooting parties who came to the farm. It would be quite inadequate to house the Stovin family. The lack of journal entries from June 1875 to May 1876 would certainly be caused by the total upheaval during these months, and his wife and children most probably lived for long periods at the home of her parents at Dexthorpe.

78 Unlike barley straw, wheat straw is largely indigestible for cattle.

79 The writer's elder brother, George and his wife Polly, did not stay long at one farm. They had moved from Sotby to Barlings between 1872 and 1875. In 1873 they applied for a farm on the Duke of Portland's estate near Mansfield, but decided not to accept it. His application was referred to in correspondence by the agent: 'Mr. Stovin, the other applicant, I have since heard, joins to his other avocations that of Methodist parson so we are as well without him'. (Papers in Manuscripts Department, Nottingham University. Information given by Mr. A. C. Pickersgill.) In 1895 they moved back to Binbrook Hall Farm when Cornelius's eldest son, Denison, left to take over a farm near Alford, Aby Grange. George and his family lived at Binbrook Hall until 1907, when the farm was sold.

POSTSCRIPT

Almost a year after the last journal entry in June 1875, Cornelius made two brief journal entries in May 1876 recording the completion of the rebuilding of Binbrook Hall, and the birth of his youngest son, Walter, on May 10th. There is no further record until late August when Lizzie, again weak and ill after childbirth, went on prolonged visits to her brother at Hackthorne and her parents at Dexthorpe. Cornelius had the companionship of his friend, Mr. Bond, who had recently been appointed as minister in the Market Rasen Circuit, and the conflict between his intellectual interests and practical concerns is sadly evident in a journal entry of September 12th: 'He seemed to wake up within me my old love of books and reading. However am I to extricate myself from the dilemma caused by bad times?'

In spite of an abundant harvest, a favourable seed-time and 'a large purchase of wethers' in November, in the hope of prices advancing in the Spring, the journal entries cease with a disastrous entry on January 1st, 1877: 'In examining my banking account, I find it overdrawn to the amount of sixteen hundred and thirty five pounds. Dr. to Garfitt & Clayton. £1635.'

It was fourteen years later, in 1891, that he turned to the Log Book in which he had written his First Journal and brought his family record up to date:

> It is a long time since I have written anything in my diary. In the meantime many important events have happened, events in connection with our family life. Denison took a farm last Spring at Hogsthorpe with a good proportion of grass land. Mabel is keeping house for Mr. Biggott. Frank is learning the business of market gardening at Ealing with Mr. Steele. Norman is helping me to carry on the business of Binbrook Farm. Walter is living at Dexthorpe and rides on his pony to Alford Grammar School. Margaret Annie is under Miss Belamy's tuition, Uncle Frank's and Aunt Mary's governess.[1] Ida Ruth Riggall is still at home.[2]

In 1892 he exchanged farms with Denison, and with his younger son, Norman, to help him on the smaller farm he could give more time once again to reading and preaching. He found his reception at Hogsthorpe 'cordial and hearty', and his village congregations were large. The formation of the Hogsthorpe Mutual Improvement Society, which he helped to initiate and in which he took a leading part, became well patronised and was a welcome forum for debate and discussion. He became reconciled, too, to the flat marsh countryside:

> I have now been here twelve months... I have a sublime compensation for the rolling hills and dense gigantic groves in the magnificent sea on the other side of Chapel bank. I can walk for miles without fatigue. I have been able to study more deeply and preach with more vivacity. Life feels more youthful and buoyant, and sometimes brimful of enjoyment.[3]

He now had energy, opportunity and time to resume his personal writing; but in the journals written after 1892 the preacher dominated the farmer, the spectator of events, the participant in them. His withdrawal from Binbrook Hall Farm, the centre of his life and thought for over sixty years, so that his eldest son could take over the larger farm, meant for Cornelius Stovin a less actively challenging life style. Reconciliation to the move was achieved with serenity and grace, but not without loss to a man whose vigour of mind and body was still unimpaired.

NOTES

1 Born in 1878: see Appendix III.
2 Born in 1883: see Appendix III.
3 Journal, May 6th, 1893.

APPENDIX I
Chronology

CORNELIUS STOVIN

1830 Born on April 11th at Binbrook Hall Farm
1855 Death of his mother, Elizabeth Sarah Stovin (née Sharpley)
1861 Marriage to Elizabeth Mawer Riggall of Dexthorpe, Spilsby
1864 Birth of eldest son, Cornelius Denison
1865 Birth of daughter, Mabel
1872 Birth of Frank Riggall
1874 Birth of William Norman
1876 Birth of Walter
1878 Birth of Margaret Annie
1883 Birth of Ida Ruth Riggall
1892 Left Binbrook Hall Farm for smaller farm at Hogsthorpe
1895 Farmed at Conisholme
1898 Farmed at Normanby
1913 Farmed at Firsby
1918 Retired to Louth
1921 Died on January 16th at George Street, Louth

APPENDIX II
List of Journals and Other Extant Material

1849–52	Sermon notes and drafts.
1868	Journal of Farm Tour in Ireland .
1870	Journal of visit to Oxford and edited version in form of lecture.
1871–77	Journals written at Binbrook Hall Farm.
1890–91	Journal entries written at Binbrook.
1892–95	Journal entries, sermon notes, farm receipts, notes of family and national events. Written at Hogsthorpe.
1895–97	Journal entries, sermon notes, animal receipts, etc. Written at Conisholme.
1910–13	Short entries made while at Normanby, ending with note of move to Firsby.

APPENDIX III
Stovin Family Tree

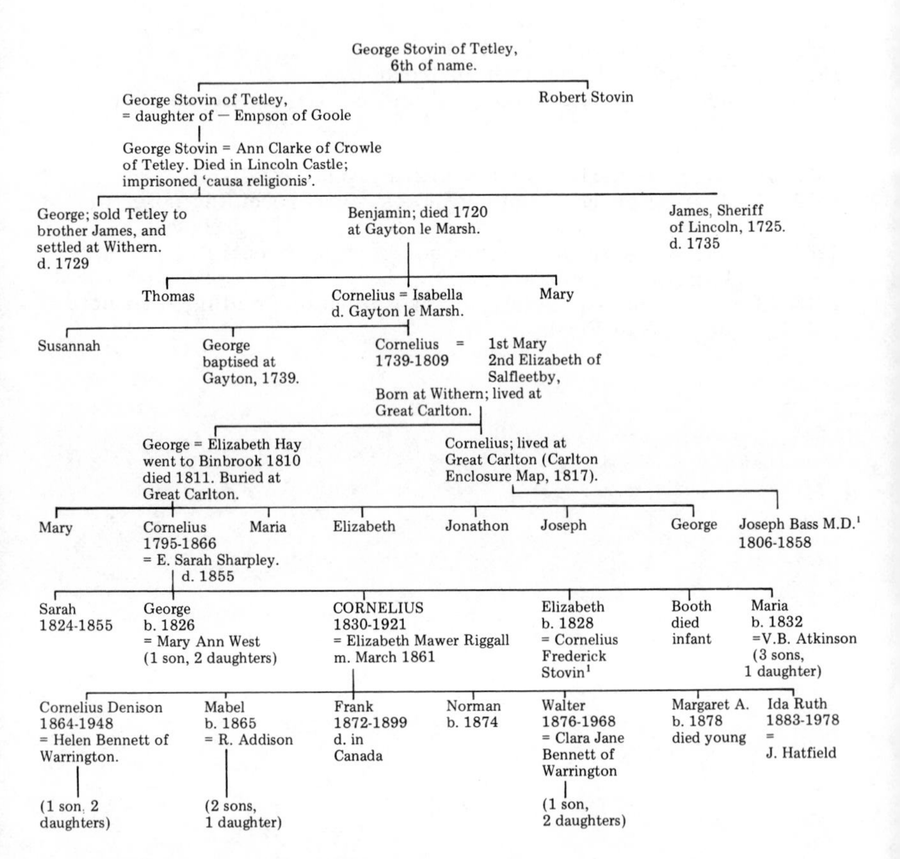

[1] Joseph Bass Stovin, father of Cornelius Frederick Stovin, M.D. (1 son, 1 daughter).

APPENDIX IV

Landlords of Binbrook Hall Farm, 1820-1907

The Denison family acquired two neighbouring farms, Binbrook Hill and Binbrook Hall, about 1820. The member of the family who owned the estate during Cornelius Stovin's father's life, and his own life up to 1874, was Edmund Beckett Denison, afterwards Sir Edmund Beckett, 4th Baronet.[1] His wife was the great-grandniece of Lady Denison (widow of Sir Thomas Denison, Justice of the King's Bench, 1741-65, under whose will he by Royal licence, 8th September, 1816, took the name of Denison, but resumed that of Beckett by another Royal licence, 9th December, 1872).

His son, Sir Edmund Beckett, succeeded his father as 5th Baronet in 1874, when he resumed the patronymic of Beckett (only) in lieu of that of Beckett-Denison. He was Chancellor and Vicar of York, 1877-1900. In 1886 he was created Baron Grimthorpe of Grimthorpe in the East Riding. He married Fanny Catherine, 2nd daughter of John Lonsdale, Bishop of Lichfield in 1845. They had no children. He died in 1905 and was succeeded by his nephew.

The Family Estates in 1883 consisted of 1,663 acres in the County of Lincoln, 1,459 acres in East and West Ridings of York, and 274 acres in Hertfordshire. In total, worth £7,517 a year. His principal residence in later life was near St. Albans, although during the period of the earlier diaries he wrote from Doncaster.

After his will was proved in 1907, the Lincolnshire farms Binbrook Hill and Binbrook Hall are known to have been sold.

Cornelius Stovin found Sir Edmund Beckett (in contrast to his father) cold and unapproachable, but an able business man. The comment in 'The Complete Peerage' bears out this estimate of his character and ability:

> He was possessed of considerable mechanical and scientific attainment, endowed with a tenacious memory and the power of incisive speech, and ably led to the Parliamentary Bar. He was a Conservative and a Protestant. His writings, although showing capacity and generally common sense and uncommon knowledge, are marred by vituperation and egotism.

NOTE

1 The Complete Peerage.

APPENDIX V

Plan of Binbrook Parish, Including Farms

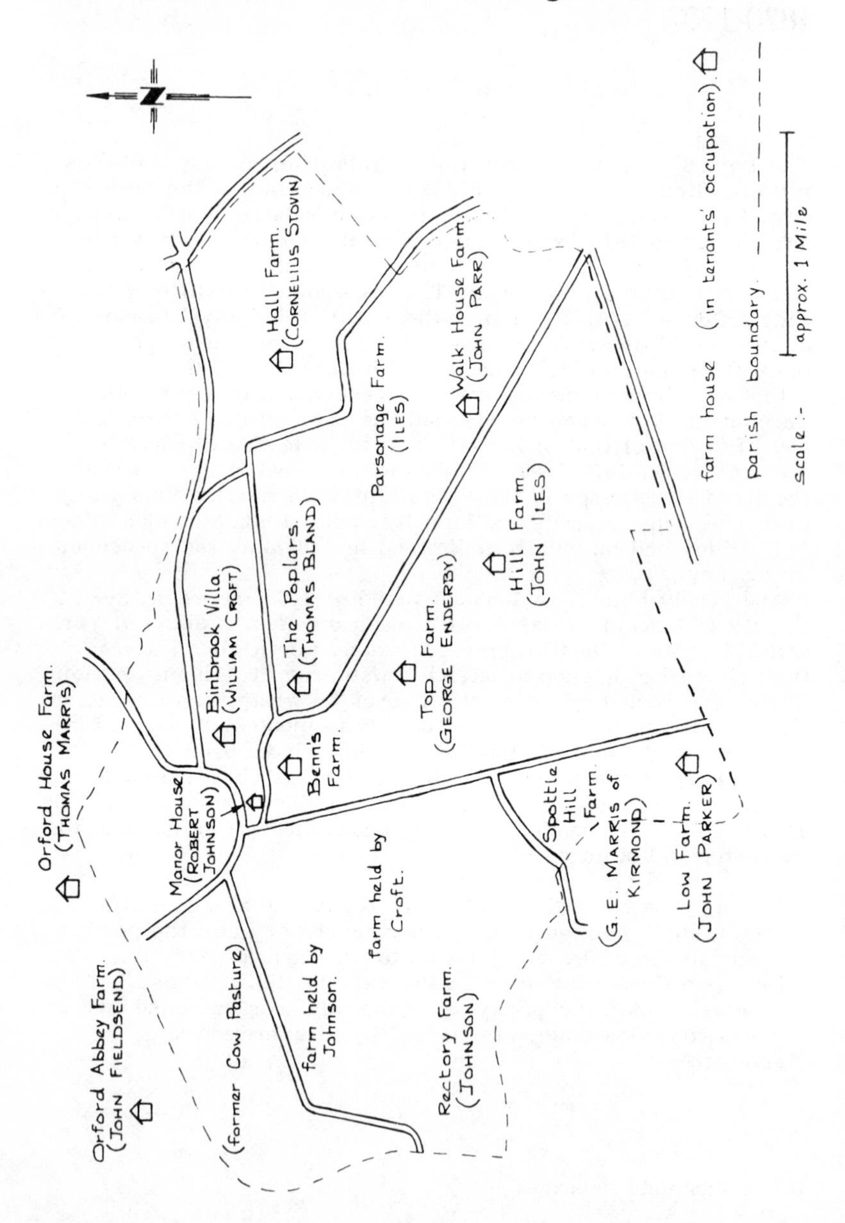

Source: R. J. Olney (ed.), 'Labouring Life on the Lincolnshire Wolds. A Study of Binbrook in the Mid-nineteenth Century'.

APPENDIX VI

Sketch Map of N.E. Lincolnshire (including towns, villages and farms mentioned in the Journals)

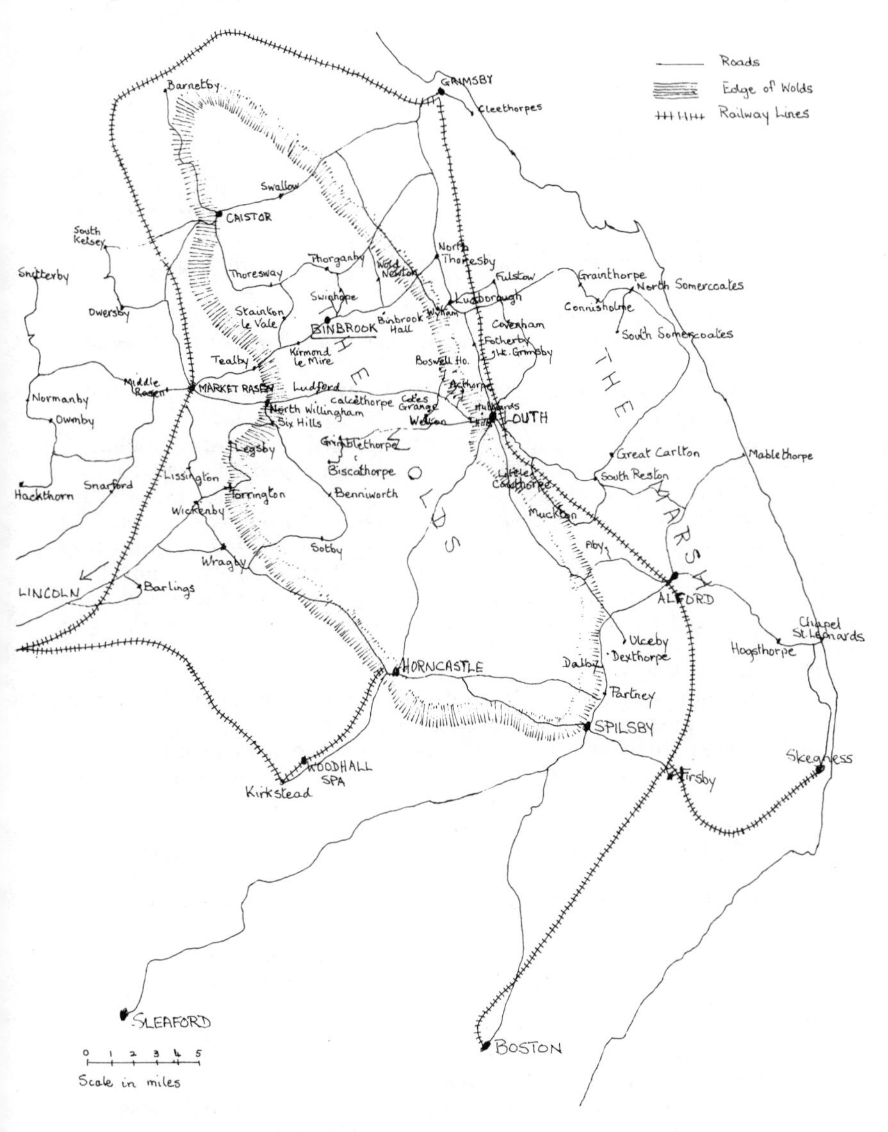

APPENDIX VII
Extracts from Agricultural Records, 1870-1879

Taken from Records of the Seasons, Prices of Agricultural Produce and Phenomena observed in the British Isles, 1883, later updated.

1870 Wheat 46s. 11d. per quarter.
A rather dry year with excellent crops.
A rather cold spring with little rain. Keep became short. Summer hot and dry with regional violent thunder storms. Harvest weather good and autumn fine and mild, but Nov. and Dec. became unusually cold. Crop results very variable, according to distribution of storms.
Another severe epidemic of foot and mouth disease.

1871 Wheat 56s. 8d. per quarter.
A rather wet year with crops above average but somewhat damaged.
The ten years from 1871 to 1880 were unusually wet, the average rainfall being about 20% above normal.
A wet spring on the whole, though with some dry spells. May dry and cold, but June very unsettled, as was July. August provided a good harvest month and the fine weather continued into September. October and November were cold and dry. District variations, many districts much rain in late September. Early hay good, but later crops much damaged by rain. Wheat yields average but badly laid and much affected by mildew.

1872 Wheat 57s. per quarter.
Wet and fine spells alternated in spring but much barley not sown until May. May cold and wet, the wettest May for many years. Snow fell on April 21st in southern England, and a hard frost occurred on May 12th. June and July more than average rainfall, but mostly in heavy storms, and there were fine intervals for hay-making. August and September relatively fine, but autumn was excessively wet. Many districts made good hay. Wheat harvest gathered during fine weather in August but it had been much damaged by July storms.
Pleuro-pneumonia of cattle caused high mortality.
Formation of National Agricultural Labourers' Union.

1873 Wheat 58s. 8d. per quarter.
A showery summer with a poor harvest.
Crops much affected by poor seedtime (spring cold and backward lasting well into summer), and by frosts when plants were in bloom. Low yields of wheat.

1874 Wheat 55s. 9d. per quarter.
A year of good harvests.
Jan. and Feb. wet and mild. March dry, a good sowing month. April showery. May dry and cold. June, July and August fairly dry. Some heavy thunderstorms about mid-summer. Rain set in during September, and rest of year wet, October unusually so. Wheat excellent, barley rather light but of good quality, except some damaged by rain. Oats very poor, hay good but light.
First shipment to Britain of refrigerated meat from U.S.A.

1875 Wheat 45s. 2d. per quarter.
Very wet summer, particularly in July, crops suffered accordingly. Wet in January, followed by fairly heavy spring. Much rain in June, even more in July. Harvest weather reasonably good in August and September. Autumn wet. Hay very poor. Wheat yields well below average. Barley poor, with much laid corn.
First shipment of grain from U.S.A. to England, also chilled beef.

1876 Wheat 46s. 2d. per quarter.
Good weather in harvest, but crops suffered from bad weather at sowing time (in spring and previous autumn). Baker records: 'This was a rough wet month, and but little sowing done. Ewes and lambs do very bad owing to the inclement weather, and the hay having been made so bad in 1875 sheep were very poor and weak this spring, many lambs died; in some flocks not more than 50% reared. Half the barley not sown by the middle of April. Finished barley sowing May 9th.'
Summer hot and dry. Heavy rain followed in September, and in December gales and heavy rain.
Wheat low yields, tho' excellent grain. Barley poor. Turnips likewise poor, tho' swedes good.

1877 Wheat 56s. 9d. per quarter.
Another wet summer with poor yields.

1878 Wheat 46s. 5d. per quarter.
A warm wet summer with crops about average. Wheat crops above average, but damaged by rain in July and August (thunderstorms).
Poor sowing season in Autumn.
Epidemic of swine fever.

1879 Wheat 43s. 10d. per quarter.
An unusually wet summer with very bad harvests. Quality of corn so poor Baker reports: 'No corn to sell worth naming, and nobody cares to buy English produce, the quality is so bad. Farmers ruined in every direction.'

NOTES

1 Extracted from J. M. Stratton and Jack Houghton Brown, 'Agricultural Records A.D. 220-1977', ed. Ralph Witlock, John Baker, 1969.

APPENDIX VIII

Villi Plan of Farm and Schedule of Fields

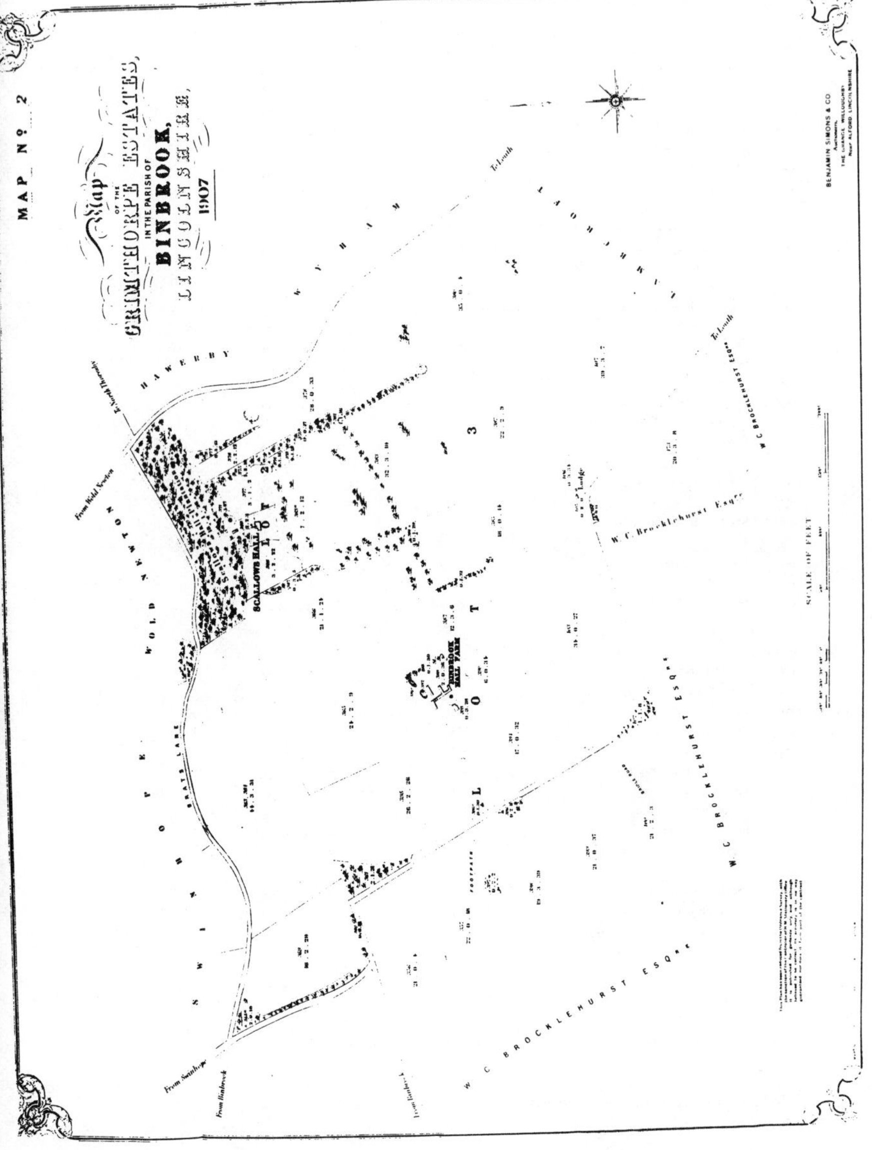

Source: From Sale Catalogue deposited in the Lincoln Archives Office.

SCHEDULE of LOT 3.

IN BINBROOK.

BINBROOK HALL FARM.

Mr. George Stovin, *Tenant.*

Nos. on Ordnance Map.	DESCRIPTION	CULTIVATION	QUANTITY A.	R.	P.	TOTAL QUANTITY A.	R.	P.
173	Little Limber Hill	Arable	20	3	8			
356	The Twenty Acres	Do.	21	0	4			
357	Foot Path Twenty Acres	Do.	22	0	18			
359	The Seventeen Acres	Do.	16	2	29			
363, 364	Brats Field	Do.	44	3	31			
365	Black Dike Close	Do.	24	2	9			
366	The Six Acres	Do.	21	1	24			
378	Low Lane Close	Do.	28	0	33			
380	Far Low Lane Close	Do.	35	0	4			
382	The Eleven Acres	Do.	22	2	9			
383	Part of Pleasure Ground	Pasture	32	3	19			
385	Lodge Platts	Arable	18	0	14			
387	The Twelve Acres	Pasture	12	3	6			
389	Farm Building and Stack Yard, with Double Cottage and Garden	..	2	0	36			
390	Paddock	Pasture	6	0	34			
391	Pond	..	0	0	16			
392	Do.	..	0	0	18			
393	The Hall Farm House and Garden	..	0	3	28			
394	The Sixteen Acres	Arable	17	0	32			
395	Home Close	Do.	26	2	26			
395a	Double Cottage and Garden	..	0	1	30			
398	Middle Twenty Acres	Arable	19	3	39			
399	The Twenty Acres	Do.	21	0	37			
400	Bridle Road Twenty Acres	Do.	21	2	3			
403	The Thirty-three Acres	Do.	34	0	27			
405	Lodge and Garden	..	0	2	0			
406	Paddock	Pasture	0	3	34			
407	Big Tinkers Hill	Arable	39	3	7			
						513	0	15
	IN HAND.							
355	Screed Plantation	Wood	2	0	10			
360	Beech Screed	Do.	0	0	31			
361	Beech Plantation	Do.	2	1	31			
367	Beverley Plantation	Do.	0	3	5			
375a	Pt. Plantation	Do.	0	0	17			
381	Pleasure Ground Plantation	Do.	1	1	16			
384	Pit Plantation	Do.	0	1	29			
386	Lodge Platt Plantation	Do.	0	1	32			
388	Stack Yard Plantation	Do.	0	1	30			
396	Clump Plantation	Do.	0	2	11			
397	Do.	Do.	0	2	2			
402	Three-Cornered Plantation	Do.	1	1	8			
404	Lodge Plantation	Do.	0	0	14			
146a	Triangular Plantation (in Swinhope)	Do.	0	0	5			
						10	3	1
	TOTAL OF HALL FARM					A. 523	3	16

Let to Mr. Geo. Stovin on a yearly tenancy, which terminates on the 6th April, 1908.

Tithe free.

No Land Tax has been paid for the last 20 years. It is therefore believed to be Land Tax free.

The Tenant pays the ordinary Rates.

Source: Lincoln Archives Office.

GLOSSARY

Blistering. Various contemporary recipes for 'blistering' exist, e.g. applying 'spanish fly', ammonia, mustard, to strains or sores.

Bottling. Applying a liquid mixture to sheeps' backs to kill lice.

Bulls (on corn-drill). Coulters.

Cattle plague. Rinderpest.

Cledding (with straw). Usual spelling cladding. The turnip trays - flexible, temporary fencing moved to different parts of a field to keep the sheep in one area at a time which was lined with bales of straw to protect and keep in the lambs.

Cull rams. Rams too old for breeding.

Drape ewes. Old ewes, no longer fit for breeding.

Fallowing. Leaving land 'resting' or bare, and ploughing or cultivating it in some way at intervals to rid it of weeds.

Fold (v). To fence off a small piece of a field to give sheep sufficient food for one day.

Hinderends. Shrivelled grain sorted out from the best and used for animal food.

Hoggets. Sheep from one year old.

Keeping (n). Grazing for livestock.

Locks. The dirty wool from around the sheep's tail, sold separately from the fleece.

Luck. 'Luck Money!' An old custom whereby the seller gave a small extra sum in cash to the buyer at the time of sale. Still in use in some areas.

Marling. Spreading clay on light soil to prevent loss of moisture.

Poll evil. An ulcerous sore on the nape of a horse's neck.

Prick firing. 'Firing' was applying a red hot iron to the legs of a horse to strengthen the tendons. 'Prick firing' replaced the thin piece of metal used for firing with a pointed object.

Sainfoin. A legume, like lucerne.

Salving. Rubbing into the sheep a specially prepared ointment to kill 'fags' or lice.

Scarifier. Horse-drawn implement to cultivate land and kill weeds between the turnip rows.

Shearling rams. Young rams which have been shorn once.

Skit (in lambs). Scour or diarrhoea.

Stedding (n). Crewyard.

Tedding. Turning the hay in the field to dry.

Tenting (crows). Scaring crows with gun, clapper or tin with stones in it.

Todd. A weight of 28 lb.

Tumbrells. Feed troughs for cattle.
Tupping. Putting the rams in the field with the ewes.
Twitching. Clearing the fields of 'twitch' or couch grass.
Wethers. Castrated male sheep.

FARM MACHINES

Many of the implements and machines mentioned in the Journals (and listed in the index) were manufactured by R. Hornsby, Agricultural Machine Manufacturer & Iron and Brass Founder, Grantham, Lincolnshire, e.g. 'Hornsby's old horse works' (First Journal, p. 23), 'Hornsby's reaper' (First Journal, p. 26). The influence of Richard Hornsby & Son in foreseeing the needs of the changing agricultural industry, and producing what was needed, is illustrated by C.S.'s enthusiastic references to new developments during his lifetime, from the Hornsby plough 'whose execution will astonish the world' to the steam harrow and the 'portable' steam engine (capable of towing a threshing machine). Details of the firm's achievements during the nineteenth century, and illustrations of some of the machines mentioned by C.S., are given in 'Hornsby's of Grantham, 1815-1918', Bygone Grantham (1976).

One of the original Lincolnshire waggons used on Binbrook Hall Farm is still in the possession of Mr N.M. Stovin of Glaythorpe Manor, Cornelius Stovin's great-grandson.

BIBLIOGRAPHY

Altick, Richard D. 'The English Common Reader: A Social History of the Mass Reading Public, 1800-1900', University of Chicago Press, 1957

— 'Victorian People and Ideas', printed in U.S.A. for J. M. Dent and Sons Ltd., 1974

Beastall, T. H. 'The Agricultural Revolution in Lincolnshire', Lincolnshire Local History Society (History of Lincolnshire Committee), 1979

Best, Geoffrey 'Mid-Victorian Britain, 1851-75', Weidenfeld & Nicolson, 1971

Briggs, Asa 'The Age of Improvement, 1783-1867', Oxford History, Longman, 1979

Clapham, J. H. 'Economic History of Modern Britain, 1850-1886', C.U.P., 1930

Cornish, J.G. 'Reminiscences of Country Life' (1939)

Court, W. H. B. 'A Concise Economic History of Britain from 1750 to Recent Times', C.U.P.

Cruse, Amy 'The Victorians and their Books', 1935

Dunbabin, J. P. D. 'The Incidence and Organisation of Agricultural Trade Unions'

Graves, Algernon 'A Dictionary of Artists Who Have Exhibited Works in Principal London Exhibitions, 1760-1893', Kingsmead Reprints, 1969

Horn, Pamela 'Victorian Country Child', Roundwood Press, 1974

Howarth-Loomes, B.E.C. 'Victorian Photography', St. Martin's Press, New York (1974)

Kitson Clark, G. 'The Making of Victorian England', Methuen, 1962

Laslett, T. P. R. 'The World We Have Lost', Methuen, 1971

Legouis, Emile and Cazamian, Louis 'History of English Literature', J. M. Dent and Sons Ltd. 1951

Mingay, G. E. 'Rural Life in Victorian England', Heinemann, 1977

Obelkevich, James 'Religion and Rural Society, South Lindsey, 1825-1875', Clarendon Press, 1976

Olney, R. J. (ed), 'Labouring Life on the Lincolnshire Wolds: Study of Binbrook in the Mid-nineteenth Century', Occasional Papers in Lincolnshire History and Archaeology, The Society for Lincolnshire History & Archaeology, 1975

— 'Lincolnshire Politics, 1832-85', O.U.P., 1973

Partridge, Michael 'Farm Tools Through the Ages', Osprey, 1973

Reader, W. J. 'Life in Victorian England', Batsford, 1964

Robinson, David N. 'The Book of Louth', Barracuda Books Ltd, 1979
Rogers, Alan 'A History of Lincolnshire', 1970
Russell, Rex C. 'The Revolt of the Field in Lincolnshire: The Origins and Early History of Farm Workers' Trade Unions', The Lincolnshire Nat. Union of Agricultural Workers, 1957
— 'A History of Schools and Education in Lindsey, Lincolnshire, 1800-1902', part 4, Lindsey County Council Education Committee, 1967
Stratton, J. M. 'Agricultural Records', John Baker, 1969
Thirsk, Joan 'English Peasant Farming', London, 1957
Thompson, F. M. L. 'English Landed Society in the Nineteenth Century', Routledge, 1963
Townsend, W. J. (ed.) 'A New History of Methodism' (also H. B. Workman and George Eayrs eds.), Hodder & Stoughton, 1909
Turner, E. S. 'Taking the Cure', Michael Joseph, London, 1967
Vidler, Alec R. 'The Church in an Age of Revolution', vol. 5 of the Pelican History of the Church, Penguin Books, 1971
Watney, Marylian 'The Elegant Carriage: Illustrated Record of Horse-drawn Vehicles', J. A. Allen & Co. Ltd, London, 1961
Young, G. M. 'Victorian England: Portrait of an Age', O.U.P., 1936

ARCHIVAL AND LOCAL SOURCES

ARCHIVAL

Births, Marriages and Deaths Registers, St. Catherine's House
Census Returns for 1851, 1871 and 1881, Lincoln Archives Office.
Records deposited at Lincoln Archives Office:
  Binbrook Vestry Minutes
  Free Methodist Baptismal Registers
  Louth Free Methodist Circuit Preaching Plans
  Minutes of Louth Grammar School Governors
  Minutes of Louth Union Board of Guardians
  Paper by John Huntley, Rector of Binbrook on Agricultural Gangs, 1867
Sale Catalogue of Grimthorpe (Binbrook) Estates

LOCAL

Details from Sharpley Genealogical Table, members of the Sharpley family
Details from Stovin Genealogical Table, Dr. Peter Stovin, Cambridge
Details of history of Binbrook Hall Farm, Mr. Michael Sleight
Details of Riggall family, Miss Winifred Riggall
Robinson, Peter, Louth and the Rise of the Free Methodist, unpublished paper
Rogers, Alan, The Emergence of the Town as a Focus for Religious Activity in the nineteenth century, unpublished paper
Russell, Rex, Friendly Societies in the Caister, Binbrook and Brigg Area in the nineteenth century, unpublished paper

GENERAL INDEX

PLACE NAME INDEX

NAME INDEX

PROFESSIONAL MEN AND PUBLIC OFFICIALS

RELATIVES AND SOCIAL ACQUAINTANCES

VILLAGERS (LOCAL)